W9-BGD-590

THE WAITE GROUP'S®

Master C++

LET THE PC TEACH YOU OBJECT-ORIENTED PROGRAMMING

Rex Woollard, Robert Lafore, Harry Henderson

WAITE GROUP PRESS™
Corte Madera, California

Conceptual Development: Mitchell Waite, Rex Woollard
Development Editor: Scott Calamar
Software Programming: Rex Woollard
Software Technical Reviewers: David Calhoun, Jake Kirk
Book Author: Harry Henderson
Book Exercises: Robert Lafore
Book Content Editor: Heidi Brumbaugh
Cover Illustration: Alan Okamoto
Production Manager: Julianne Ososke
Design and Production: Barbara Gelfand

© 1991 by The Waite Group, Inc.

Published by Waite Group Press™, A Division of The Waite Group, Inc.
200 Tamal Plaza, Corte Madera, CA 94925

Waite Group Press™ is distributed to bookstores and book wholesalers by Publishers Group West, Box 8843, Emeryville, CA 94662, 1-800-788-3123 (in California 510-658-3453).

All rights reserved. No part of this manual shall be reproduced, stored in a retrieval system, or transmitted by any means, electronic, mechanical, photocopying, desktop publishing, recording, or otherwise, without written permission from the publisher. No patent liability is assumed with respect to the use of the information contained herein. While every precaution has been taken in the preparation of this book, the publisher and author assume no responsibility for errors or omissions. Neither is any liability assumed for damages resulting from the use of the information contained herein.

All terms mentioned in this book that are known to be trademarks or service marks are listed below. In addition, terms suspected of being trademarks or service marks have been appropriately capitalized. Waite Group Press™ cannot attest to the accuracy of this information. Use of a term in this book should not be regarded as affecting the validity of any trademark or service mark.

Turbo C++ and Borland C++ are registered trademarks of Borland International, Inc.
AT&T is a registered trademark of American Telephone and Telegraph.
IBM PC, AT, PS/2, and OS/2 are registered trademarks of International Business Machines Corporation.
MS-DOS and Microsoft Windows are registered trademarks of Microsoft Corporation.
UNIX is a registered trademark of AT&T Bell Laboratories.
The Waite Group® is a registered trademark of The Waite Group, Inc.
WordStar is a registered trademark of MicroPro International Corporation.
Zortech C++ is a trademark of Zortech, Inc.
Excerpt of review of Master C: Let the PC Teach You C. *Reprint from* PC Magazine, *June 1, 1991,*
    © 1991 Ziff Communication Company.

Printed in the United States of America

93 94 • 10 9 8 7 6 5 4 3 2

Woollard, Rex.
    The Waite Group's® Master C++ : let the PC teach you object-oriented programming / Rex Woollard, Robert Lafore, Harry Henderson.
        p. cm.
    Includes index
    ISBN 1-878739-07-7 : $39.95
        1. Object-oriented programming (Computer science) 2. C++ (Computer program language) 3. Master C++.
I. Lafore, Robert (Robert W.) II. Henderson, Harry. III. Waite Group. IV. Title. QA76.63.W67 1991
005.13'3--dc20   91-43336
                                                                                        CIP

INTRODUCTION TO THIS BOOK

This book is designed to get you up and running with Master C++, a CBT (computer-based training) product that turns an IBM PC or compatible into a friendly and intelligent C++ instructor.

The book is divided into two parts. The first part, consisting of chapters 1-6, is the user's manual for Master C++. Chapter 1 explains what Master C++ is and specifies the hardware required to run it. Chapter 2 covers the simple process of installing Master C++ on your PC. Chapter 3 surveys the main features of Master C++ and explains its menus and screen layout. Chapter 4 suggests a number of ways that Master C++'s features can best be used to help you learn C++ in a systematic but enjoyable way. Chapter 5 provides an overview and outline of each chapter of the Master C++ CBT, listing topics and subtopics. An estimated completion time is given for each chapter as an aid in scheduling and curriculum planning. Finally, Chapter 6, organized in a question-and-answer format, is designed to help you identify and solve any problem you may encounter in installing or using Master C++.

The second part of this book provides supplemental and reference materials that you will be able to use as you develop your own C++ programs. Chapter 7 gives an overview of the process of developing C++ programs and introduces and illustrates some of the important programming tools provided with many C++ compilers. Chapter 8 provides extensive supplemental exercises to test and reinforce the concepts studied in Master C++.

Chapter 9 provides an overview of the many standard ANSI C library functions and C++ stream input/output classes that are provided with most C++ compilers. The overview includes alphabetical lists of keywords, operators, and functions organized according to topic, as well as lists that can help you identify which functions your program needs in a given situation.

Chapter 10 is a detailed reference to the C++ and ANSI C keywords, operators, preprocessor directives, standard values, functions, and streams classes. Each reference entry gives a definition, syntax description, example call, and other details of using the language element or library function. You can use the alphabetical reference when you need to quickly look up a C++ function you can't remember, or when you are away from the computer and wish to study or review the C++ "vocabulary."

Two appendices are also provided: Appendix A is a summary of the Master C++ option bar commands. Appendix B is a brief guide to further reading about the C++ language and Borland/Turbo C++.

We recommend that you read Chapter 2 completely before installing the Master C++ software so you will understand what is involved in the process. Then install Master C++ on your PC, and look at Chapters 3 and 4 to familiarize yourself with the program's features and various strategies for using them. (We also recommend that you work through the online tutorial, which takes only a few minutes, to familiarize you with use of the menus and screens.) You're then ready to begin learning C++.

PREFACE

The Waite Group is well-known for bringing tutorial and reference materials to C programmers and making the C language accessible to everyone. While the success of books such as Stephen Prata's *C Primer Plus* and Robert Lafore's *Microsoft C Programming for the IBM* was very gratifying to us and to our authors, we knew that we could not rest on our laurels.

A printed book, no matter how well organized and lucidly written, cannot provide the kind of interactive learning that a student experiences in a classroom with a real live teacher. So back in 1987 The Waite Group began thinking about what a "computer book of the future" would be like. We decided that it would be as much as possible "a teacher on a disk." The software would be smart enough to teach you and test you, to probe for your weaknesses and offer remedial work when necessary. The software would tolerate a variety of answer phrasing, so you wouldn't have to guess the exact wording that would be acceptable. To help provide variety and reinforcement in learning, questions would be presented in a variety of forms such as fill-in, multiple choice, and true/false. Perhaps most importantly, you would write real program code, solving problems step by step.

Our teaching software would also take advantage of the organizational flexibility of the computer medium. Students could choose chapters from a menu. Within a chapter, sub-menus would offer major topics. But we would also provide a way to "jump" to any topic of interest so that advanced students could skip material they already knew, and students who had already completed the course could review material selectively.

The first fruit of this effort was *Master C*, and it has met with widespread enthusiastic acceptance. It also prompted a great demand for a similar product that would teach, from the ground up, the increasingly popular descendant of the C language, C++, along with the principles of object-oriented programming.

It was a natural next step to take Robert Lafore's new book *Object-Oriented Programming in Turbo C++*, and build a new interactive training package, Master C++. We sincerely believe that *Master C++* provides one of the most effective ways to master the new technology of object-oriented programming in general, and C++ in particular. Because the concepts to be used by a new generation of programmers are rich but unfamiliar, we think it is more important than ever to provide a course that can adapt itself to students from a wide variety of backgrounds. As always, we welcome your feedback and suggestions about *Master C++* and all other Waite Group Press products.

DEDICATION

To Maharishi
>—Rex Woollard

To Bjarne Stroustrup, who made it all possible
>—Robert Lafore

To my brother Bruce
>—Harry Henderson

ACKNOWLEDGEMENTS

The Waite Group would like to thank Rex Woollard for his relentless effort of programming and testing the software, and coping with questions of installation and configuration. Harry Henderson wrote the extensive user and reference manual that accompanies the software, and we deeply appreciate his perpetual good-natured responsiveness to the winds of change that sometimes buffet "the cutting edge."

Robert Lafore provided the source material for this computer-based training system, and re-immersed himself in the subject matter to come up with the additional exercises to keep students of C++ stimulated.

We gratefully acknowledge David Calhoun for so thoroughly scutinizing every word, comma, and nuance of the CBT's text to acheieve perfection and Jake Kirk for his invaluable and careful review of the *Master C++* program from day one. We also thank Mark Peterson for his skilled advice on the newest C++ additions.

Thanks to Heidi Brumbaugh for going above and beyond the call of editing, and thanks to Julianne Ososke and Barbara Gelfand for making the production process for this book swift, painless, and elegant.

Rex Woollard would, first and foremost, like to thank his wife Laurie for her support throughout the months of development effort, and Robyn, his 12-month old daughter whose innocent delight lifted his spirits when they were particularly overwhelmed. His thanks also go to his parents, who were always there to help when pressures began to mount.

In addition, he would like to thank many colleagues at Sir Sandford Fleming College whose interest has contributed to a polished final product. In particular, Charles Pascal and Derek Scott provided the administrative support which made all this work possible. Finally, Rex would like to thank both Scott and Mitch of Waite Group Press who displayed remarkable patience as the deadlines slipped by.

ABOUT THE AUTHORS

Rex Woollard is a co-author of *The Waite Group's Master C*, the Waite Group Press' first computer-based tutorial, on the C language. He is a professor of Information Systems at Sir Sandford Fleming College in Peterborough, Ontario, Canada, and is currently researching the application of expert systems with statistical process control. When not working with students and computers, you can often find him plying the white waters of the Canadian wilderness.

Robert Lafore has been writing books about computer programming since 1982. His best-selling titles include *Assembly Language Programming for the IBM PC and XT, C Programming Using Turbo C++, Microsoft C Programming for the PC,* and most recently *Object-Oriented Programming in Turbo C++*. Mr. Lafore holds degrees in mathematics and electrical engineering, and has been active in programming since the days of the PDP-5, when 4K of main memory was considered luxurious. His interests include hiking, windsurfing, and recreational mathematics.

Harry Henderson has written or edited numerous books on computer languages and operating systems for The Waite Group, Waite Group Press, SAMS, and other publishers. Some of the books he has co-authored include *Unix Communications, Unix Papers, Tricks of the MS-DOS Master, second edition, Microsoft QuickC Programming, The Waite Group's QuickBASIC Bible,* and *Discovering MS-DOS, second edition*. He also works with his wife, Lisa Yount, writing school textbooks and trying to avoid tripping over cats.

CONTENTS

Using Master C++

I

CHAPTER 1
➤ WHAT IS MASTER C++?

The C programming language has proven to be powerful, versatile, and popular, and it will no doubt be with us for many years to come. However, recent years have seen the coming of age of what many programmers feel will be its successor, C++. C++ provides the conceptual and organizational benefits of object-oriented programming while preserving the considerable investment the industry has in trained C programmers and working C code. C++ is thus a natural migration path for many thousands of C programmers. Not only that—with Master C++, this exciting new language also becomes an easily accessible first language for students and beginners.

MASTER C++ BOOK AND SOFTWARE

Master C++ is a package consisting of a book and software on disk. The software is a menu-driven program that takes you through a systematic course on the C++ language. This course uses the techniques of computer-based training (CBT) to present C++ topics *interactively*. When you work with Master C++, you don't just *read* about programming in C++. Master C++ tests your understanding of each topic and has you write real C++ code. The variety of testing techniques used by Master C++ helps reinforce key concepts while avoiding a boring sameness and repetition. Master C++ ensures that you truly understand each lesson by evaluating your progress and offering reviews when necessary.

The book you are now reading serves as both a guide to using Master C++ and as a detailed reference to the C++ language. The first four chapters help you get started with Master C++ by taking you through the installation and use of all the features of the software. Chapter 5 presents the "course map"—an outline and overview of the topics covered by Master C++, chapter by chapter. (Because an estimated completion time is given for each chapter, students and teachers can use the course map as an aid in devising a study plan.) Chapter 6 is designed to get you back on track in the rare cases that something goes wrong when you install or try to use Master C++.

The remainder of the book is designed to aid your transition from student to working C++ programmer. Chapter 7 gives an overview of the process of developing a C++ program, and can help you approach the use of the compiler, linker, libraries, and other tools found in a modern C++ program development environment. Chapter 8 provides an extensive set of supplemental exercises to help you practice your coding skills. Chapter 9 gives an overview of the elements of C++—keywords and operators. There is also a summary (by name and task category) of the libraries of ANSI C functions commonly available to the C++ programmer, as well as the C++ streams class library used for console and disk I/O. Finally, Chapter 10 is an alphabetical reference that includes every C++ keyword and operator as well as the ANSI C library and a selection of C++ streams functions. The book concludes with two appendices covering further reading on C++ and a summary of Master C++ features.

Taken as a whole, Master C++ explains everything from the broad concepts of object-oriented programming to the actual steps and techniques used in the design and development of C++ programs. When you complete the lessons in Master C++ you will have covered all the topics fundamental to being a proficient C++ programmer.

Nearly all the examples in Master C++, with the exception of some graphics and file operations, are "generic" C++; that is, they're meant to run on any standard C++ implementation, including all those that compile for the IBM PC and Apple Macintosh, as well as those that compile for minicomputers and mainframe computers. Occasionally, Master C++ discusses implementation-dependent matters, such as differences in the ways files are stored and in the use of graphics library functions.

FEATURES OF MASTER C

Master C++ has evolved over a period of several years. Master C++ is based on our best-selling book, *Object-Oriented Programming in Turbo C++* by Robert Lafore (Waite Group Press, 1991).

The underlying software engine was developed during seven years of research at three educational institutions. The first product of this research was Master C, a book and software package that teaches the C language using the techniques discussed above. The content of Master C++ was developed with the aid of feedback from Master C users as well as by noting important trends in C++ programming. By blending this powerful software engine with the excellent writing of a proven book, The Waite Group has created an effective learning tool.

Master C++ is organized into 14 tutorial chapters, each covering a broad topic such as "loops and decisions" or "objects and classes." Each chapter is presented as a sequence of text screens. After you have read each screen or series of screens, Master C++ asks questions and finds out if you understand the topic. The questions may be true/false, multiple choice, or fill-in-the-blank. Often the questions are repeated in different ways. One time a question might require a complete word to be typed in, another time it may be presented in true/false format. Varying the type of question helps keep the learning experience from falling into a rut. One of the beauties of Master C++ is that it can change its questions to make sure you are really thinking.

Master C++ is designed to present concepts in the sequence found to be easiest by most students. If you have trouble answering particular questions, however, Master C++ goes into the *Recall* mode, and "sends" you to the point in the tutorial where your knowledge is weak. After you successfully complete the recalled lesson you return to where you stumbled and then proceed with additional material. This means that Master C++ won't let you become "stuck" or confused. Master C++ tailors the instruction to your particular strengths and weaknesses—something no book can do.

STRATEGIES FOR USING MASTER C++

There are several strategies for using Master C++, accommodating students with varying backgrounds and interests. It is likely that you will want to experiment with more than one of them.

Using Master C++ Like a Book

The most obvious way to use Master C++ is to approach it like a regular book, starting at the beginning and moving through its material in a linear manner, from Chapter 1 to Chapter 14. Since Master C++ and our book *Object-Oriented Programming in Turbo C++* have these chapters in the same order, you can buy that book and read the corresponding chapters when you are away from the computer to reinforce your learning.

Jumping Directly to Tutorials

A real strength of Master C++ is that it is possible to jump directly to those C++ topics that are of interest to you. You can skip the preliminary sections of instruction and move right into the areas you want to understand. This can be particularly helpful if you are an experienced C programmer and don't, for example, need to learn about loops and decisions. (We should note, however, that C++ adds features to many areas of C programming. Experienced C programmers may wish to examine the course map in Chapter 5 of this book and check for concepts that are new to them.)

Master C++ will analyze your work in the review lessons, and if your answers to recent questions indicate that you may be confused, it will send you to the proper lesson, so you can't leave the course confused. Once inside a Master C++ lesson, you have control over moving forward and backward through the screens of material. At any time you can branch off to use related Master C++ features—you will always be returned to your original position when done.

Studying a Single Concept via the Master C++ Glossary

Master C++'s built-in Glossary provides a third way to use this powerful learning tool. After looking up a related C++ keyword in Master C++'s Glossary, you can request a lesson on the defined word. This can provide a special training path that is finely tuned to what you want to learn.

Using Master C++'s Review Sections

If you already have some familiarity with C++ and just want to check your knowledge for weaknesses, you can use the review sections of each chapter. These reviews present a condensed summary of the content of the chapter, along with quizzes to test your understanding. Since taking the entire course can consume several days of work, the reviews provide a quick way to avoid the need for studying certain chapters.

HOW MASTER C++ ENCOURAGES LEARNING

Master C++ has several features that customize your course in the same way a good personal teacher would. You will come to appreciate these features as you work with Master C++, but here is an overview of them.

Sophisticated Answer Judging

Master C++'s skills are most apparent in the way it assesses your responses. Master C++ is designed to accept a wide range of possible user responses. You can misspell the answer, abbreviate it, and even give the answer in a poorly structured sentence, and Master C++ will still recognize if the answer is correct. Some questions are open-ended—there are many ways to phrase a correct response. Master C++ is able to figure out what you mean if you are close. This is unlike most computer-based training systems, which require you to type the exact answer in order to move forward.

Retains Student Progress Information

As you complete various lessons, Master C++ retains information about your progress. When you ask for a list of your achievements, Master C++ tells you which lessons have been completed and what your "score" is. The score is the percentage of correct answers, with 80% being considered "mastery." Master C++ will also tell you what lessons you have finished, and which you still need to work on.

Digital Bookmarks

You can quit Master C++ at almost any point in its tutorials. When you return later, Master C++ will take you back to the exact point in the lesson in which you were last working.

Meaningful Feedback on Wrong Answers

There are wrong answers and there are wrong answers. Master C++'s feedback to answers varies depending on the nature of the questions. With particularly easy questions, a wrong answer causes the system to respond immediately.

With more demanding questions, Master C++ brings more of its expertise to bear. For example, if you answer a question incorrectly, the answer is analyzed and checked against anticipated problem areas. The system then responds with relevant hints designed to help you clarify your understanding. You will then be given an opportunity to try the question again.

In some cases, if you are still having difficulty with a particular question, Master C++ will present the same question in a multiple choice format. If you still you have trouble with the question, Master C++ will switch into the Recall mode.

Recall Mode

Master C++'s Recall mode is one of its most powerful learning elements. Following the presentation of a question and the subsequent answer analysis and helpful hints, you might still be having difficulty with a particular topic. Here, Master C++ will automatically return to a tutorial lesson covering that topic. You will then have a chance to review this related material before trying to answer the question again.

Online Glossary

Because you may encounter unfamiliar terms or keywords, Master C++ includes an online Glossary. At any point in the course, you can look up related C++ terms for additional information. Master C++ will even attempt to match close spellings when you are unsure of the exact term. With many of the terms, the Glossary will offer to link you to related instructional material. If you choose to work with the related material, afterward you will be able to return to your jumping off point—the place where you first invoked the Glossary.

This feature provides an alternate and powerful learning path. Ordinarily, you are likely to access learning material by choosing lesson items from a menu. Using the Glossary, you can jump directly to instructional material by entering the desired term or keyword. There is no need to walk back and forth through menus. This feature is useful in a variety of circumstances. In one case, you may already be familiar with the C++ language, but need to reference the learning material on some specific topic. Using the Glossary, you can jump directly to the appropriate subsection from anywhere in the course. You don't have to use the menus at all.

Even if you are using the menus as your primary path to learning material, you can make good use of the Glossary path. Imagine that you are working through a lesson dealing with control loops, and you encounter references to the ++ operator. Without leaving the lesson on loops, you can use the Glossary to explore other lessons covering the ++ operator. When finished with the ++ operator, you will automatically be brought back to your jumping off point—the lesson on loops. You can pick up where you left off.

Master C++'s "Personality"

You can choose whether Master C++ will respond to your answers in a re-laxed, "friendly" way or in a more businesslike, concise way. The friendly "personality" may be helpful for working with students who may be anxious about their performance. The more terse personality can save a little time for experienced students who are reviewing previously mastered material.

Calculator

An online 9-digit, scientific calculator is also included. It supports standard trig functions and constants such as *pi*. It does not do pointer arithmetic nor allow you to do segment math for the Intel family of microprocessors. Nev-ertheless, it can be a useful tool for your programming work.

Let's Get Started

Now that you've been introduced to ways of using the features of Master C++ it's time to get started. Please turn to Chapter 2 to learn how to install the software on your PC.

CHAPTER 2
➤ INSTALLING MASTER C++

Installing Master C++ has been tested with common PC configurations, and the installation software is designed to work automatically with a minimum of work on your part.

PRELIMINARIES

Before you begin installing Master C++, you should review the system requirements and note any special circumstances that may apply to you. The README file on your Master C++ disk and the following discussion provide the necessary information.

Using the README Files

Take a few minutes to read the README file on Disk One of your Master C++ package. This file may contain information that was obtained after this book was printed, and may include notes on the use of Master C++ with particular hardware or software environments. You can display the contents of the README file by putting Disk One from your Master C++ package in a floppy disk drive and entering the MORE command at the DOS prompt:

```
C:\>MORE < A:README <Enter>
```

This will let you read the file a screen at a time. (Note that we show DOS commands in all capital letters for clarity, but you can type any command in lowercase if you wish. The (ENTER) symbol means to press the (ENTER) key to send the command to DOS.)

Alternatively, you can turn on your printer and use the command

```
C:\>PRINT A:README <Enter>
```

to get hard copy. You should also consult the README file for help with installation problems or if Master C++ does not run properly after installation. (Also see Chapter 6, *In Case of Trouble*, for answers to common questions and problems.)

System Requirements

Master C++ can be installed on virtually any MS-DOS based machine. The minimum system configuration is an IBM PC, XT, AT, or compatible, with 384K of RAM, a floppy drive, a hard drive, and a monochrome screen that supports highlighting. Though a monochrome monitor is supported, Master C++ takes best advantage of a color monitor, on which highlighted and regular text is much easier to read. Master C++ requires approximately 2.2 megabytes of storage space when installed on your hard disk.

Overview of Installation

The core programs for Master C++ and their associated data files are supplied on 360K IBM PC floppy disks in a compressed format. Because we have used a compressed format, you must use the INSTALL program on Master C++ Disk One to get Master C++ up and running—simply copying the files will not work. You can, however, make a backup copy of each of your Master C++ disks using the DOS DISKCOPY command, and install Master C++ from the backup disks. You can also use the DOS COPY command to copy the contents of each 5.25" disk to a 3.5" disk for installation on a system that has only 3.5" disk drives. In this case, be sure to copy files disk for disk; you'll need three 3.5" disks even though Master C++ will fit on two (720K) disks. If you don't have access to a 5.25" disk drive, see the coupon in the back of this book for our 3.5" disk exchange offer.

The first time you install Master C++ you will be asked to enter your name and the serial number printed on Disk One. Your copy of Master C++ will then be updated to include this registration information. Later, if you choose to install Master C++ on another computer system, the registration information will already be recorded; you will not be asked to enter your name and serial number again. *Master C++ can legally be used only on one computer system at a time.* Be sure to fill out and mail in the enclosed registration card. That way we can inform you about possible updates and related products that might be of interest to you.

ANSI.SYS and NANSI.SYS

Master C++ requires that a device driver be installed in your PC in order for it to be able to control the screen properly. A driver called ANSI.SYS comes with all versions of PC DOS and MS-DOS. However, many people may not have ANSI.SYS installed on their PC. Don't worry if you don't have ANSI.SYS installed. The Master C++ installation process automatically loads an ANSI.SYS compatible driver, called NANSI.SYS, to your root directory, and creates a copy of your CONFIG.SYS file that contains the additional line DEVICE = NANSI.SYS. (Your old CONFIG.SYS is saved as CONFIG.OLD.) Once you restart the computer, NANSI.SYS will be activated and Master C++ will be able to work properly. (By the way, NANSI.SYS is actually faster than ANSI.SYS when writing to the screen, so you may prefer it to ANSI.SYS for general use.)

If you have ANSI.SYS already installed, or prefer to use it instead of Master C++'s NANSI.SYS, you can restore your old CONFIG.SYS file with the DOS command

```
C:\>COPY CONFIG.OLD CONFIG.SYS <Enter>
```

You can then eliminate the NANSI.SYS file with

```
C:\>DEL NANSI.SYS <Enter>
```

If you want to use ANSI.SYS, make sure that it resides on the hard disk and that the command DEVICE = ANSI.SYS is in your CONFIG.SYS file. If ANSI.SYS is in a directory, such as DRIVERS, make sure the device name statement in CONFIG.SYS is DEVICE = C:\DRIVERS\ANSI.SYS.

INSTALLING MASTER C++

Before starting this installation make sure you have at least 2.2 megabytes of free space on your hard disk to hold the Master C++ files. Take a moment to record the serial number of Master C++ Disk One in this guide. You will be asked to enter this number during the first installation.

Steps for the First Installation

Follow these steps to install Master C++ for the first time:

1. Start your computer.
2. Place Disk Two in the A: drive (you can also use drive B:).

3. Select drive A: by typing: **A:** (ENTER) (or type **B:** if using drive B:).

4. Start the INSTALL program by typing: **INSTALL** (ENTER).

5. The first screen, shown in Figure 2-1, will display the Master C++ logo screen, overlaid with a dialog box that requests you to enter your first and last names, and the serial number on Master C++ Disk One. Following this step, your copy of Master C++ will be permanently registered in your name. Note that you must enter a name and a valid serial number or Master C++ will not be installed.

6. As the installation program proceeds, explanations will appear and you will be asked to insert each of the subsequent Master C++ disks. You will also be able to choose the drive letter of the hard disk on which you wish to install Master C++.

Figure 2-1. The opening screen for the INSTALL program. You must enter a name and a valid serial number

Note: During the installation process, status messages will be displayed to detail the system's progress. These can be ignored unless you encounter problems.

As noted earlier, during installation Master C++ will install a "device driver."

Steps for a Subsequent Installation

Should you choose to install Master C++ again, you will follow the same steps which are outlined above, except step 5. Since you will have already registered your copy of Master C++, you will not be asked to enter your name and disk serial number a second time. (If you are installing Master C++ on a new machine, you should remove any previous installations of the same copy on other machines.)

Master C++ should now be properly installed. Restart your machine (you can do this by pressing the (CTRL), (ALT), and (DEL) keys together) and turn to Chapter 3 to begin learning how to use Master C++.

CHAPTER 3
➤ EXPLORING MASTER C++

Before you continue, make sure you have followed the installation steps given in Chapter 2. If you had not been using the NANSI.SYS (or ANSI.SYS) device driver before you installed Master C++, restart your PC to load the device driver. (You can do this by pressing (CTRL)-(ALT)-(DEL).)

GETTING STARTED

To start Master C++, first switch to the \MCPP directory that the installation program created. (If you specified during installation that a different directory be used, use the name of that directory instead.)

```
C:\>CD \MCPP <Enter>
```

Now type:

```
C:\>MCPP <Enter>
```

The first thing you'll see will be the logo screen shown in Figure 3-1. It is displayed while several additional program and data files are loaded into your computer.

After the logo screen is displayed, you will see a welcome message inviting you to explore the online introductory tutorial. We recommend that you try this tutorial now by pressing **T**. The tutorial will guide you through the simple procedures you will use in working with Master C++.

If Your Text Doesn't Display Properly

Before proceeding to explore Master C++, make sure that the characters on the screen are clear and easy to read. If they aren't and you're not sure what to do, see the section of Chapter 6 titled "I can't read the screen very well."

When you see the first screen of the tutorial, the word *highlighted* should be brighter than the surrounding text. Master C++ uses highlighted text to emphasize important words and program code. Descriptions and explana-

Figure 3-1. The opening screen for Master C++ appears immediately after you start the program

tions contain highlighted text to identify essential concepts or keywords of the C++ language. In other cases a large section of program code may be displayed. Here, one or more parts of the code will be highlighted—parts that are the current focus of discussion. As you progress through the explanation of the program, the highlighting will shift to different sections of code to reflect the changing focus of attention. If you need to adjust the highlighting, see the section titled "The text isn't highlighted" in Chapter 6.

The Main Table of Contents Screen

Following the welcome (or when you complete the tutorial) you will see the Table of Contents screen for Master C++, as shown in Figure 3-2. This is the main screen or "menu" and is used for accessing the 14 chapters of Master C++.

From the main lesson menu you may go to the beginning of the lesson for a given chapter by typing its number. Each lesson begins with a submenu

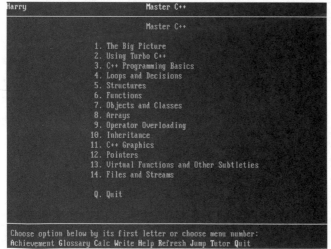

Figure 3-2. The main table of contents screen: you can access any chapter from the menu or choose a command from the command bar

similar to the Table of Contents menu, offering a series of topics within the lesson. Just press the number for the topic you wish to explore. (Generally, it is best to tackle the topics in the order presented, since some topics may require knowledge of preceding ones.)

Each numbered item on the Table of Contents menu represents the corresponding chapter in the book *Object-Oriented Programming in Turbo C++*. (Note that the last few chapters in the book are not included in Master C++ due to their specialized nature.) Likewise, the topics offered in the sub-menu for each chapter correspond to the main headings in the book.

In Chapter 5 of this manual you will find a course map outlining and summarizing the main points covered in each lesson. You can use the course map to help you find particular topics of interest without having to examine all the menus.

Parts of the Screen

Master C++ presents a consistent screen layout to make "navigation" of the learning system easier. Every screen has three general areas as shown in Figure 3-3.

➤ **Main Instructional Area**

➤ **Top Line**

➤ **Option Bar**

Each of these areas serves several different functions.

The Main Instructional Area

The large center part of the screen is used to present all instructional material. This material includes explanations, notes, and examples, as well as questions and feedback.

The Top Line

As Figure 3-3 shows, the area above the top horizontal line, called the Top Line, indicates three things. The left corner displays your first name, which appears on every screen. This is the name that was typed into the "first name" field dialog box when the software was first installed. The name is useful in a classroom environment where it allows a teacher to identify which students are working specifically on Master C++.

The particular lesson on which you are working is identified in the center portion of the Top Line. In the case of the tutorial it shows only a title for the lesson. On a typical screen, the title will contain the

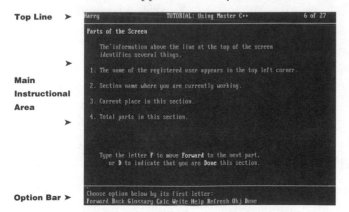

Top Line ➤

Main Instructional Area ➤

Option Bar ➤

Figure 3-3. Three parts of the Master C++ screen

chapter number (between 1 and 14), the section number within the lesson, and the name of the section. So, for example, *7.3 Constructors and Destructors* means we are looking at the screen for Chapter 7 (Objects and Classes), Section 3 (Constructors and Destructors).

The top right corner of the Top Line always tells you the screen number you are currently viewing and the total number of screens that make up the lesson. Thus *1 of 26* means you are viewing the first screen of a total of 26 screens.

How Master C++ Numbers Screens

Obviously, the total number of screens per lesson varies. That's pretty well expected. But because of the way Master C++ is designed, the total number of screens may vary even for a given lesson, depending on when and how that lesson is entered. Thus a complete lesson as entered from the main menu may have 26 screens, so the first screen you see will be numbered *1 of 26*. If in the course of the lesson you answer a question incorrectly and seem to be confused, Master C++ will guide you through a review of the relevant material. This review "mini-lesson" might have only 4 screens, the first of which will be numbered *1 of 4*.

Another way the total number of screens for a lesson can change is when you quit after partially completing a lesson. For example, if you quit Master C++ while on screen 4 of a 20-screen lesson, when you return to the lesson by restarting Master C++ you will see *1 of 16* in the top right corner. Since you have already successfully completed the first four screens, you will not be presented with them when you return, and only 16 screens will remain. This shows Master C++'s ability to remember where you left off and give you the most recent statistics. Whenever you reenter a lesson directly from the menu, however, you will always be presented with the full collection of screens, even if you have worked on the lesson before.

The remaining discussion in this chapter is devoted to the Option Bar, since it is there that you control Master C++ and access its many special features.

THE OPTION BAR AND ITS FUNCTIONS

The Option Bar appears at the bottom of the screen. It consists of a number of keywords which identify specific functions available as you use Master C++.

These functions let you navigate your way through Master C++. You can select chapters and topics to study, move forward and backward through the lesson screens, explore the Glossary, review your achievements (scores), and use other features of Master C++.

An option is invoked by typing the first letter of its name. For example, to invoke the Help option, you would type **H**, to move Forward you would type **F**, and so on. (You don't need to type capitals; lowercase will do.)

The actual options appearing in the Option Bar vary slightly as you use Master C++. When a Note or Example option is available, it flashes in the Option Bar area to call your attention to the fact that more material is available. (The standard options do not flash.)

Forward and Back

The first two options are invoked by typing **F** for Forward and **B** for Back, the two most common ways of moving through lessons. When you choose to move forward, Master C++ moves to the next element in the lesson. Sometimes this involves adding more information to the material already shown in the Main Instructional Area. In other cases, a completely new screen is generated. The Back option takes you one step at a time to each preceding screen, allowing you to review material as desired. Note that if you choose to move back while at the first screen, you will be taken back to the point where you entered the lesson. Usually, this will take you back to a menu, since menu access is the most common path into lessons. If you entered review lesson material after answering a question incorrectly, or entered through the glossary, then you would be taken back to that starting point.

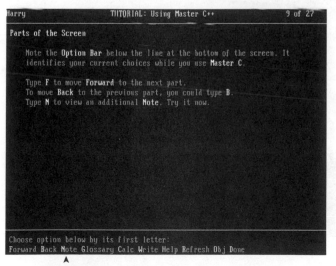

Note is flashing

Figure 3-4. The note option flashing on the option bar

Note and Example

When the options *Note* or *Example* appear flashing in the Option Bar area it means you can access an additional window containing related information about the current concept. (See Figures 3-4, 3-5, and 3-6.)

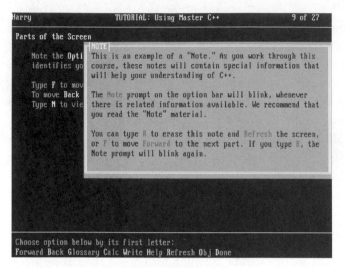

Figure 3-5. The *Note* window opened

A *Note* window may contain additional information that further clarifies a point, it might contain the output of a program, or it might be an alternate approach to coding some operation. Alternately, a *Note* window may address the issue of machine dependency (for example, the differences between UNIX and MS-DOS implementations), it may amplify the details of some underlying organization and structure, or it may just be an interesting aside. We recommend that you read all available notes and examples the first time you go through a lesson. (You may wish to skip them when reviewing the highlights of a lesson.)

When Note is flashing, its window is displayed by typing **N** for *Note*. Once you have read the note you can erase its window with the **R** (Refresh) key, or move to the next screen (with the **F** (Forward) key and also remove the window. Once you have left a screen that contains a note or example, the flashing option disappears.

An *Example* window usually contains a specific C++ example, which extends the idea displayed in the main instructional area. This additional information can be viewed by typing **E** when Example is flashing as an option in the Option Bar.

In both *Note* and *Example* windows only a portion of the original main screen information will still be visible behind the windows. To view all of the original main screen information again, you can choose the Refresh option by typing **R**.

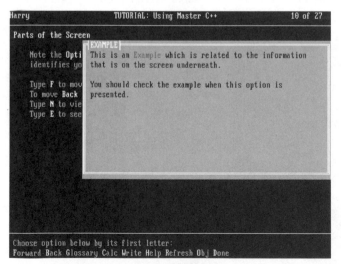

Figure 3-6. The *Example* window opened

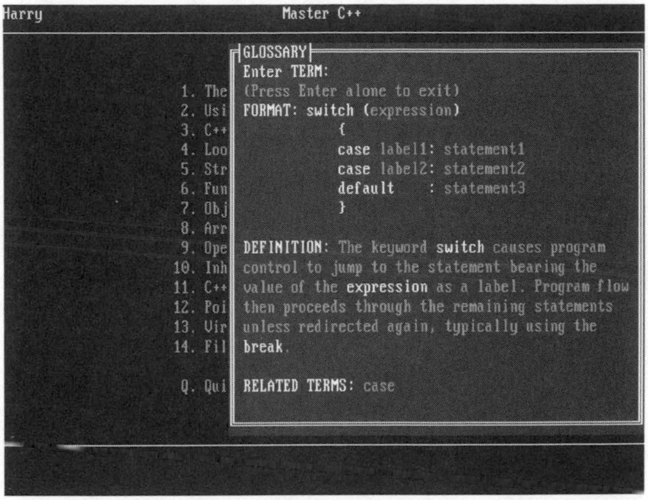

```
 Harry                    Master C++
                 ┌GLOSSARY┐
                 │ Enter TERM:
      1. The     │ (Press Enter alone to exit)
      2. Usi     │ FORMAT: switch (expression)
      3. C++     │              {
      4. Loo     │          case label1: statement1
      5. Str     │          case label2: statement2
      6. Fun     │          default    : statement3
      7. Obj     │              }
      8. Arr     │
      9. Ope     │ DEFINITION: The keyword switch causes program
     10. Inh     │ control to jump to the statement bearing the
     11. C++     │ value of the expression as a label. Program flow
     12. Poi     │ then proceeds through the remaining statements
     13. Vir     │ unless redirected again, typically using the
     14. Fil     │ break.
                 │
      Q. Qui     │ RELATED TERMS: case
```

Figure 3-7. The *Glossary* window opened

Glossary

The Master C++ *Glossary* provides online access to a collection of terms and concepts related to the C++ language. When you invoke the Glossary by pressing **G**, you are asked to enter a term and Master C++ searches for it—trying to match close spellings when an exact match is not found. In Figure 3-7, we look up the term *switch*.

After displaying the related information in the Glossary, you are given the opportunity to enter another Glossary term. Or you can leave the Glossary mode by pressing the **E** key without entering any term. The Glossary information remains on the screen, but you have access to all the items on the Option Bar again. You can choose to move Forward or Back, or access any other available option. More uses of the Glossary option are discussed in Chapter 4, *Using Master C++ to Learn C++*.

Calc

The online calculator is called *Calc*. It provides access to trigonometric functions, the constant *pi*, and standard arithmetic operators. In addition, Calc supports parentheses and adheres to the rules regarding order of operations. Arithmetic expressions can span more than one line. To enable the Calc option type C; to exit Calc press the **E** key without entering an expression.

Write

The *Write* option, accessed by pressing **W**, presently displays the address and phone number of The Waite Group, the publishers of Master C++. A future version of Master C++ may use the Write option to allow sending electronic mail to an instructor.

Help

When working inside a lesson, if you activate *Help* by pressing **H**, you are presented with a window giving a small menu of help items and your name and serial number. One help menu item gives a brief description of the function of each of the active options in the Option Bar area. Another allows you to change the display from color to monochrome.

Objective

Activating the *Objective* option by typing **O** brings up a window containing the objective for the current lesson or the menu. The objective is useful in determining the goals of the chapter, and for determining how long the chapter would normally take to complete. As you move from lesson to lesson, you can invoke the *Objective* window to list the essential elements of the active lesson. The information in this window identifies the main topics to be covered, an estimate of the time required to complete the material, and the "mastery" level.

Mastery consists of passing 80% of the questions asked in a chapter. We chose this value because we felt it was the best compromise between just passing knowledge of C++ (70% Mastery) and a complete understanding of the language (90% to 100% Mastery).

A few lessons contain no questions because the lessons are introductory in nature. When a lesson has questions, the mastery level will be displayed in the *Objective* window; when there are no questions in a lesson, no mastery level is set or displayed.

Done and Quit

You may exit from the current lesson—either instructional material or a submenu—by typing **D** to invoke the *Done* option. This will return you to the section of Master C++ where you entered the current lesson or menu. The Done option will *not* save any achievement information, and you will be asked for a confirmation. You use Done when you are reviewing material and don't need to complete all the screens. This may be during a Recall mode or when using the Glossary.

The normal way to complete a lesson is to use the *Quit* option. When you type **Q** to Quit and then confirm your choice, you will end your current tutorial session and your achievement information will be saved. When you come back to the tutorials for another session, Master C++ will return you to the point where you previously exited, using its *bookmark* feature.

You can't quit Master C++ from certain screens because Quit is not available on the Option Bar. For example, if you are in the middle of a question,

Q won't be available. In such cases you can still abort Master C++ by typing (CTRL)-C, (ENTER), (ENTER), which will take you back to the DOS command line, or to the shell interface that was running when you started Master C++. You will not get credit for the section you were in if you abort with (CTRL)-C.

Now that you understand how to navigate in Master C++, turn to the next chapter to find out how the program works, and how to best use it to learn C++.

CHAPTER 4
➤ USING MASTER C++ TO LEARN C++

You have seen that the Master C++ menu screens are easy to understand and that navigation using the commands on the Option Bar is simple. In this chapter we will look at what is going on "behind the scenes" when you interact with Master C++. By understanding how Master C++ asks questions and responds to your answers, you will be better able to use it as an effective learning tool. We will also explain how Master C++ keeps track of your progress. Finally, we will suggest some alternative approaches to studying and reviewing material with Master C++.

HOW MASTER C++ ASKS QUESTIONS

Master C++ uses an age-old method of teaching; it presents facts then it presents questions to see if you really understand the facts. Questions that Master C++ presents may be fill-in-the-blank, where you must complete a sentence or type in a specific word or phase; multiple choice, where there are three or four possible answers; or true/false. Most teaching software stops here. What is special about Master C++ is that if you are having difficulty, it will intelligently alter the question and ask it again.

Presenting Alternative Questions

Let's say the first time you take a lesson you get the question, *What is the name of the computer part which can store large amounts of information even when the computer is turned off?* The correct answer in this case is "disk" (however, Master C++ also accepts "floppy," and several other related answers). The next time you get to this question it might be rephrased as, *In a computer, RAM can store large amounts of your information, even when the computer is turned off. True or false?* This question requires a true or false response, yet it essentially deals with the same material as the original question. This technique of question alteration does two things: it makes the test less repetitive, and it aids understanding by presenting the same material in different ways.

Use Abbreviated and Shortened Answers

Master C++ asks many open-ended questions. In these cases there may be many ways to phrase the correct response. This is particularly true with questions presented in a fill-in-the-blank format. Master C++ allows you to approximate the complete answer much as a real teacher would; if your response consists of shortened words or partial phrases that still contain the basic meaning of the answer, it will be judged to be correct. This allows Master C++ to consider the widest possible range of correct answers and not penalize a user because the answer wasn't typed exactly as the computer expected it.

In the previous example the complete answer is considered to be "floppy or hard disk," but the user can answer "disk," "hard drive," "floppy," and variations of these terms. So when questions deal with definitions and concepts, feel free to use shortened answers. When you respond with a correct but partial answer, Master C++ will also give you the complete answer for reference. However, when questions deal with the details of C++ programming code, be sure to include all the required elements. As you probably know, computer languages are less forgiving than English when it comes to specifying something. Also remember that when Master C++ asks you to enter lines of C++ code you must be careful about the case; C++ *is* case sensitive.

For true/false questions you can also simply type **T** for true and **F** for false; there is no need to spell out the entire word.

Questions that Get Progressively Easier

In some cases, a question may be structured so that it becomes progressively easier if you enter an incorrect answer. If you answer the question incorrectly, as a first step, Master C++ will usually offer some helpful hint that relates to your particular incorrect answer. For example, suppose you are working in lesson 3.2 *Preprocessor Directives and Comments.* Master C++ asks you:

What is the purpose of the #include directive?

and you type the answer:

to let you edit the program

Master C++ responds:

No. The name of the directive implies its purpose.
Your answer: to let you edit your program Please try again.

Thus Master C++ gave you a hint (look at the name *#include* itself for a clue to the directive's purpose).

Another way Master C++ simplifies a question is to accompany it with a series of possible answers (essentially a multiple choice question). For example, Master C++ asks you the question:

Suppose you are developing a program. What statement would you use to include the contents of the header file FSTREAM.H in your program?

If you answer this question by typing:

include fstream.h

which is wrong, because it lacks a necessary element, Master C++ will present a "hint" and give you another chance:

You forgot the # symbol
Your answer: include fstream.h
Please try again

Notice that for a wrong answer the *Feedback* window always displays what you typed so you can review it and compare it with what Master C++ says. Next suppose you tried again and typed this answer:

#include fstream.h

This is still wrong, because in this case there needs to be angle brackets around the file name fstream.h. This time Master C++ recognizes that you are having problems, and like a wise teacher it will still not say you are wrong. Instead Master C++ may present a multiple choice question that includes the actual answer:

#include <fstream.h>
#include <fstream.h>;
#include <fstream>
include <fstream.h>

Multiple choice questions are easier than equivalent fill-in-the-blank questions. With a fill-in-the-blank question, you must recall the answer without any cuing. With a similar multiple choice question, you can survey the four choices and select the best answer (the first answer is correct here.). In the first case, skills of recall were required; in the second, skills of recognition.

Finally, if you still haven't answered correctly after several tries, Master C++ will give you the following message:

You are having difficulty and can review some related material. Use Forward to start the review or Back to avoid the review and repeat this question.

By pressing **F**, you can then go to a review lesson that will cover the previous material. After you finish the review lesson you will be returned to the question that gave you trouble, and you should be able to answer it correctly and continue with the lesson. Alternatively, you can type **B** to skip the review to return to the question and answer it again.

Recognizing Incomplete Answers

Master C++ employs an interesting technique to accept incomplete answers and prompt you for the remaining parts. For example, suppose Master C++ asks

All C++ programs begin execution with a function that is always called. The full answer is:

and you type

main

Master C++ will present this text in its *Feedback* window:

Your are correct so far. Continue.

Master C++ is telling you that you have typed an almost complete answer, but something more is still needed. If you follow this by typing the () needed to complete the header of the *main* function, Master C++ will say you are correct and move to the next question. Otherwise, Master C++ will judge the answer as incorrect.

Blackboards: Accumulating Answers Windows

The *Accumulating Answers* window provides a way to let you respond to questions that build a complete C++ program or program fragment (see Figure 4-1.) In these cases Master C++ has you write the program step by step. After each question is answered the resulting code appears in a specialized window called the Accumulated Answers window. This window allows you

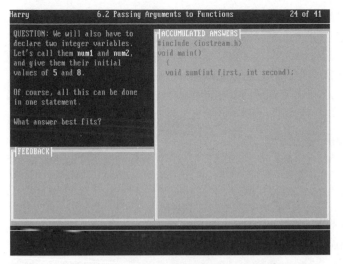

```
Harry               6.2 Passing Arguments to Functions        24 of 41

QUESTION: We will also have to    ┤ACCUMULATED ANSWERS├
declare two integer variables.    #include <iostream.h>
Let's call them num1 and num2,    void main()
and give them their initial       {
values of 5 and 8.                   void sum(int first, int second);

Of course, all this can be done
in one statement.

What answer best fits?

┤FEEDBACK├
```

Figure 4-1. TheAccumulated Answers type of question

to see the program grow as you move through subsequent questions.

With the *Accumulated Answers* window on the screen, the area allocated for a user's answer is only about half a screen width. However, long answers continue on the next line automatically.

Note that Master C++ does not record your achievement in answering an accumulating question until you have answered the complete question. So, be sure to answer all parts of the question if you wish to get credit.

Some accumulation-type questions do not use an *Accumulating Answers* window. Also, if an accumulating question doesn't have an *Accumulating Answers* window, you cannot insert a bookmark until you have gone through all of the screens for the question and have entered your answers.

RECORDING YOUR ACHIEVEMENT

Just as with most schools, Master C++ provides you with a record of your achievement—a "grade" that measures your mastery of the material presented. Since everyone has trouble one time or another, Master C++ also makes it easy to review material and take the test again.

Approaching Mastery

Each time a question is presented in Master C++, your attempt at an answer is recorded by the software. If you get it right you are given credit for that question. However, if you get it wrong or use the Review option to repeat it, you don't get credit. Master C++'s approach is that you must go completely through a lesson and answer at least 80% of the questions correctly. Therefore, if at the end of a Master C++ lesson more than 20% of the questions were answered wrong or have been reviewed, you will need to repeat those questions to pass.

Using the Achievement Option

Master C++ saves a record of your progress in a subdirectory called REGIS-TER. When you select A , the Achievement option, Master C++ searches the two files containing information about your progress. It then displays a short highlighted word or graphic symbol in front of each section, as follows:

80%-100%	A number between 80 and 100% indicates that you have successfully completed the lesson. Any score of less than 80% displays the word REPEAT in front of the section.
BEGUN	BEGUN indicates that you used the Done or Quit option to exit from a lesson before its end. BEGUN lets you know that the lesson was started but is not complete.
DONE	DONE is displayed in front of those sections that were completed but did not have any questions, and hence had no scores.
REPEAT	REPEAT is displayed in front of those sections that were completed with a score of less than 80%.
REVIEWED	REVIEWED is displayed in front of those main menu items (chapters) that were examined via the Review menu heading. The individual chapter menu will have a score posted for the Review section.
■	A square graphic character is displayed in front of sections that have not been started.

Posting of Achievement

When you successfully complete an entire lesson set (that is, all the lesson items in a chapter) a record of that success will be posted to the originating menu, *but only if you choose the Achievement option on the lower level or the just completed menu.* For example, suppose you complete all lessons in the lesson, 2: *Using Turbo C++.* In order for this information to be posted to the top-level of Master C++ you must choose the Achievement option before you leave the menu for lesson set 2. This approach is used to speed the processing of Master C++. Without it, your movement from menu to menu would be uncomfortably slow.

Resetting Achievement

If you wish to remove all your achievement information (scores) so that you can start Master C++ over, you must delete the two files in the C:\MCPP\REGISTER directory. One of these files is named LIST, the other is named whatever you typed into the first name field of the dialog box at installation. You can use this DOS command:

```
C:\>DEL C:\MCPP\REGISTER\*.* <Enter>
```

(Note that you do not remove the directory itself, only its contents.) You can then start Master C++ and work "from scratch." Note that all records of previous achievement are lost. Please note, however, that Master C++ is licensed only to one user.

OTHER WAYS TO LEARN WITH MASTER C++

Computer-based training systems are often criticized for being too linear. With some programs there is only one set order for learning—it doesn't matter that you already know some of the material, you just want to review something, or perhaps you want to explore a particular concept in more depth. But Mater C++ is different. While the Master C++ menu system provides fixed sequences of topics, there are several alternative ways to approach material.

Using the Jump Option

The J (*Jump)* option allows you to jump directly to a lesson by its heading number, without having to walk back and forth through the menus. This feature is particularly useful when you are already familiar with C++.

Imagine that you wanted to find out more about overloading the << operator so it will work with your custom-designed objects. You look at the course map found in this manual and find that the discussion on overloading the << and >> operators is in Chapter 14, Section 9. After starting Master C++, while sitting at any menu, invoke the Jump option. When asked to enter the lesson or section number, enter 14.9 (note that each of the lesson and section numbers must be separated by a period).

When you complete the lesson to which you jumped, Master C++ will return you to your starting point.

Using the Glossary

It is possible to use Master C++ in a more direct manner than studying its contents lesson by lesson. You can look up a specific concept or keyword in the Glossary, then jump to the location in Master C++ where that concept or keyword is covered. Master C++ doesn't just jump from the keyword to a specific concept. Rather it locates only those screens that are relevant to the keyword or concept and presents them so you can choose where to go next. The Glossary can be helpful when you want to study or review a particular concept in depth.

Using the Review Lessons

The main menu for most chapters in Master C++ contains a heading called *Review* which can be accessed by typing its item number. If you are somewhat familiar with C++ programming or you want to test your knowledge before embarking on detailed study in all the lessons, you can use this Review item.

As you work through the material, you will be presented with information and asked to answer questions. Whenever you answer a question incorrectly, after prompting by Master C++, you will be taken to the parts of earlier lessons where you are weak. This is a quick way to let Master C++ diagnose your problems and structure an individualized review.

When you complete a Review lesson, your success will be posted to the originating menu. The label on the parent menu will show REVIEWED. This is Master C++'s way of showing the difference between completing all lessons in a menu or only the review lesson.

Making a Hard Copy of Master C++ Screens

If you have a printer, you can study a Master C++ screen away from the computer by using the print screen command of DOS to capture the screen to paper. On an old-style PC keyboard (SHIFT)-(PRTSCR) are the keys to press to cause the Master C++ screen to be printed. On a newer AT-style keyboard you can press just the (PRTSCR) key to capture a screen to paper. Some users like to build their own personal book of C++ notes this way.

Embarking on Your Own

We have outlined a number of features of Master C++, and suggested a number of strategies for accessing information. The designers of Master C++ know that everyone doesn't learn in the same way. We invite you to experiment to find the learning approach that best suits your needs. The best approach for many users is to use a combination of these techniques, reading sections in a sequence; alternating with reading the book; jumping into specific lessons via the Glossary, studying just the Review sections. The next chapter of this manual presents the course map—an overview of the material covered in the course.

CHAPTER 5
➤ COURSE MAP

This chapter provides a "map" of the material covered by Master C++. You can use the accompanying lesson overviews to get a broad sense of the topics involved in mastery of the C++ language. You can use the topic list for each chapter to zero in on a topic of particular interest. Then, you can use Master C++'s *Jump* item on the Option Bar to go directly to a lesson in the desired section. Or, you can read more about a topic by reading the corresponding chapter in The Waite Group's *Object-Oriented Programming in Turbo C++*. Within Master C++ you can use the Jump item on the Option Bar to go directly to a lesson on the desired section.

HOW MASTER C++ IS ORGANIZED

The Master C++ CBT is made up of 14 chapters which, as you have seen, are presented on the main menu screen. Table 5-1 shows all 14 lessons and the estimated time for the average student to cover each lesson. Remember that the lesson numbers correspond to the chapter numbers in *Object-Oriented Programming in Turbo C++*.

Chapter	Lesson Title	Hours
1	The Big Picture	1.25
2	Using Turbo C++	0.5
3	C++ Programming Basics	2.5
4	Loops and Decisions	3.0
5	Structures	1.5
6	Functions	3.0
7	Objects and Classes	2.25
8	Arrays	1.75
9	Operator Overloading	2.0
10	Inheritance	2.25
11	C++ Graphics	1.75
12	Pointers	3.0
13	Virtual Functions and Other Subtleties	2.0
14	Files and Streams	1.5
	Total:	28.25

Table 5-1. Master C++ lessons and course time requirements

1: The Big Picture

Overview of Contents

C++ is a superset of the C language—that is, it includes all of C's features and syntax and adds many features of its own. But C++ is not merely an improved C with added features. Rather, C++ is designed to be a vehicle for *object-oriented programming (OOP)*—a new way to think about data and the things you need to do with data. OOP came as a response to the problems increasingly encountered in trying to manage large programs written in traditional *procedural* languages such as BASIC, Pascal, and C. Although these languages provide features for breaking down large programs into smaller pieces, they do not provide an effective mechanism for controlling access to data and hiding irrelevant details.

Thus while the *function*—a set of instructions for manipulating certain data in a specified way—is the building block in C, C++ programs are organized as a set of *classes*. A class represents an *object* that the program needs to work with—for example, a geometric figure, a bank account, or a screen window. Each class *encapsulates* the necessary data items and functions. A class also provides controlled access to the data from other parts of the program, making the overall program easier to understand (and thus to maintain). Additionally, the mechanism of *inheritance* allows specialized classes to be *derived* from more general ones. The C++ language thus provides easy *reusability* of well-tested code as well as *extensibility* because the new data types and operators you define become integral parts of the language. Finally, the *polymorphism* of C++ allows operators and functions to work appropriately under different circumstances.

Objectives

> Putting the C++ language in perspective
> Gaining a broad overview of object-oriented programming and its advantages
> Learning about the main characteristics of object-oriented languages
> Comparing C and C++ to see how C++ is in many ways an entirely new language

Topics

1.1	Introduction
1.2	The Object-Oriented Approach
1.3	Characteristics of Object-Oriented Languages
1.4	C++ and C
1.5	Review

Time Requirements: 1.25 hours

2: Using Turbo C++

Overview of Contents

The *segmented* architecture used by the Intel 80X86 processors on the IBM PC complicates programming by requiring that a decision be made about how memory will be divided among program code, the stack (used to pass data to and from functions), and *near* and *far* data areas. Standard configurations called *memory models* are provided to meet most needs. Fortunately, the *small* memory model should be quite adequate for learning C++.

After this overview of some of the programming realities of the PC world you are introduced to the components and features of Turbo C++ and Borland C++. The *integrated development environment (IDE)* provided by the Borland compilers (and others such as Zortech's) makes it easy to write, compile, link, run, and debug C++ programs.

Objectives

➤ Understanding how C++ compilers for the IBM PC such as Turbo C++ and Borland C++ organize memory

➤ Stepping through the process of creating and running a program in Turbo C++ or Borland C++

Topics

2.1	Memory Models in Turbo C++
2.2	Compiling, Linking, Running in Turbo C++
2.3	Review

Time Requirements: 0.5 hour

3: C++ Programming Basics

Overview of Contents

In this chapter you will learn how to put together simple but complete C++ programs. Each C++ program must have a function called *main()*, which is the point at which execution begins. By following simple rules you construct a series of program *statements* that define what each function does. Each statement must end with a semicolon. Statements often contain *expressions*, which use variables, constants, and operators to express values.

You use *preprocessor directives* to give the compiler special instructions. The *#include* directive gives your program access to the rich library of ANSI C functions and C++ classes that comes with Borland/Turbo C++ and other modern compilers. You will begin to use the simple output facilities C++ provides through the IOSTREAM.H header file.

You will also learn how to create and name variables, using the basic data types to represent numbers and characters, and performing calculations with arithmetic operators. You will learn the rules C++ uses for converting one type of variable to another, and how to use *type casts* to convert a value to a specific type.

Objectives

➤ Learning how a C++ program is organized

➤ Using the preprocessor to control compilation and processing of your program

> ➤ Understanding the structure and use of the fundamental numeric and character data types
> ➤ Computing values using the standard arithmetic operators
> ➤ Using header files and library files to bring needed functionality into your program

Topics

3.1	Basic Program Construction
3.2	Preprocessor Directives and Comments
3.3	Integer Variables
3.4	Character Variables
3.5	Floating Point Variables
3.6	Manipulators
3.7	Variable Type Summary
3.8	Arithmetic Operators
3.9	Header Files and Library Files
3.10	Review

Time Requirements: 2.5 hours

4: Loops and Decisions

Overview of Contents

In most real-world processes decisions must be made on the basis of changing conditions. In this chapter you will learn how to have your program test for one or more specified conditions. Based on the result of the test, the program can perform some other specified action (via a *decision statement*). A *loop* allows for the conditional or unconditional repetition of an operation.

C++ provides three loop statements: *for, while,* and *do while.* You generally use the *for* loop when you know how many times a particular operation should be performed. The *while* and *do while* loops are "open ended," running until some specified condition is either met or fails to be met. The *while* loop may not be executed at all (if the condition is never met), but the *do while* statement is always executed at least once. The *break* and *continue* statements can be used to interrupt a loop if a specified situation arises during execution.

The *if* and *if else* statements test one or more conditions and perform the specified actions if the conditions are met. The *if else* construct allows several alternatives to be considered in the same statement, but the *switch* statement is easier to use and clearer to read when there are many conditions being tested.

You can use *logical operators* to express complex conditions that have two or more parts. The *AND* and *OR* operators test two conditions and are true if both (*AND*) or at least one *(OR)* of them is true. The *NOT* operator can be used to negate (reverse) the truth of a condition.

Objectives

- ➤ Using relational operators to compare data values
- ➤ Controlling repeated program actions with the *for while*, and *do while* loops
- ➤ Deciding how the program will test and respond to data
- ➤ Making simple and complex branching decisions with the *if* and *if else* statements
- ➤ Using the *switch* statement for multi-way branching
- ➤ Employing logical operators to express complex conditions

Topics

Time Requirements: 3.0 hours

5: Structures

Overview of Contents

This chapter begins the exploration of structures and classes in C++ by introducing simple structures that group together related data items. Many applications deal with data that is organized into individual "records" that describe sets of data such as customer information, the status of an account, the location and size of a graphics figure, and so on.

You will learn to define simple data *structures* and access individual "fields" or *members* within the structure. A simple card game will illustrate the manipulation of structures. You will also learn how to use *enumerated variables* to manipulate items that have a small number of possible values, such as the suits in a card deck.

Objectives

➤ Learning how to use structures to group related items of data together
➤ Accessing and changing data in a structure
➤ Using enumerated variables to specify items that have one of a specified list of values

Topics

5.1	An Introduction
5.2	Other Structure Features
5.3	Structures Within Structures
5.4	A Card-Game Example
5.5	Enumerated Data Types
5.6	Review

Time Requirements: 1.5 hours

6: Functions

Overview of Contents

Now that you've learned how to represent and organize data into simple variables and structures, it is time to define functions to manipulate the data. You will learn how to define a function and how to specify its *arguments* (data in the form of variables or constants being passed to the function for processing). You specify the behavior of the function in a *prototype* and then write an actual *definition* in the form of executable statements that perform the function's work.

A function can return only a single data value, but that value can be a complete structure or array of data. Alternately, a function can work with *references* to actual variables, rather than just using a copy of the data. Passing a reference allows the function to change the actual value of the variable. C++ provides a more convenient syntax for references than the use of pointers in C.

You will also learn to use other convenient function features that C++ adds to C. By declaring a function to be *inline* you can have its code repeatedly inserted wherever the function is named, avoiding the processing delay caused by a function call. Because an inline function is a true function with a prototype, C++ can still check the types of values being passed to it. This gives the inline function a significant advantage over the preprocessor macros used in C for this purpose. You will also learn how to define functions that set default values for certain variables. This can make function calls easier to write.

Finally you will survey the *storage classes*, which determine which parts of a program can use a variable and how long values stored in the variable are kept. Variables defined in a function are normally *automatic* and exist only while the function is running. However, such variables can be made *static* instead, so that they will retain their value between function calls. *External* variables defined outside functions exist as long as the program is running.

Objectives

- ➤ Defining simple functions
- ➤ Passing values to a function for processing
- ➤ Getting results back from a function
- ➤ Using references to pass actual variables to a function for modification
- ➤ Defining inline functions for faster processing
- ➤ Establishing default values for data being passed to a function
- ➤ Understanding storage classes and visibility of variables

Topics

Time Requirements: 3.0 hours

7: Objects and Classes

Overview of Contents

Now that you've mastered data and functions it's time to put them together into classes and objects—the heart of object-oriented programming. A *class* defines a specific type of *object* and normally includes both data items and functions to work with the data. You can control what other parts of a program will be able to access the data and function members of a class. *Private* members can be accessed only by an object of the class. *Public* members can be accessed by other functions in the program. Just as with simple variables, objects can be sent to a function or used as a return value.

Each class has two special member functions—a *constructor* that creates new objects of the class on demand, and a *destructor* that specifies how objects no longer being used by the program will be removed. C++ provides default, built-in constructors and destructors, but if your object is complex you will sometimes have to define your own.

Classes provide a powerful tool for representing the data your program works with and the operations that must be performed on the data. There are few hard and fast rules for defining appropriate classes, so object-oriented programming is more of an art than a science.

Objectives

➤ Understanding the parts of a class and how a class defines objects

➤ Using constructors and destructors to create and manage objects

➤ Giving class objects to a function and returning an object from a function

➤ Understanding how a C++ program manages the use of memory by objects

Topics

Time Requirements: 2.25 hours

8: Arrays

Overview of Contents

A structure or class is the best way to group together different kinds of data that describe a particular entity, such as a person's name, address, and phone number. When you have many instances of the same kind of data item (for example, test scores or positions of graphics objects), an *array* is the appropriate organizational tool. With an array, an individual items can be searched, sorted, or copied easily by manipulating a value called the *index*, a number that points to a particular item or *element* of the array. An array can have more than one *dimension*, thus you can have an array of arrays. For example, a calendar can be represented as an array of 12 months, with each month being an array of days.

Arrays can be used in the same ways as simple data types. The array name stands for the starting address of the array. You can thus pass an array to a function for modification. You can have an array of any sort of data object—simple numeric variables, characters, strings, or class objects.

A string is actually an array of characters. An array of strings is particularly useful for storing and manipulating text. As you work through the more complex and interesting examples you will learn more about the string formatting capabilities of the C++ Streams library and the useful string manipulation functions inherited from the C library. Finally you will begin to develop a string object that improves on the traditional way of working with strings.

Objectives

➤ Using arrays to hold collections of similar data items
➤ Creating arrays of arrays (multidimensional arrays)
➤ Using structures and objects in arrays
➤ Defining a string array
➤ Mastering the string manipulation functions in the standard library
➤ Including strings as members of a class

Topics

8.1	Array Fundamentals
8.2	Multidimensional Arrays
8.3	Arrays of Structures
8.4	Arrays of Objects
8.5	Strings
8.5.1	String Variables and Constants
8.5.2	Reading Multiple Lines
8.5.3	Copying a String the Easy Way
8.5.4	Arrays of Strings
8.5.5	Strings as Class Members
8.6	Review

Time Requirements: 1.75 hours

9: Operator Overloading

Overview of Contents

The ability to redefine or *overload* operators is a key feature of C++. You can take many of the standard operators (such as +) and make them work with objects of classes. Thus you can extend the language to include syntax such as *string1* + *string2* to combine two strings, or *C1* + *C2* to add two complex numbers. You could use *Obj1* > *Obj2* to check whether one graphics object is farther from the center of the screen than the other. You redefine operators by providing an appropriate *operator function* as part of the class whose objects you want to work with.

Redefining operators requires understanding the difference between *unary* operators that take only one operand and *binary* operators that use two operands. You must also make sure that the operations you define have a meaning analogous to the ordinary use of the operator so the expressions you write will make sense to the reader of your program.

You will often need to convert between your defined objects and real-world data expressed in different units. (For example, you may need to convert between polar and Cartesian coordinates.) You will learn how to use constructors to convert values when initializing objects, and how to write conversion functions that can convert your objects into other specified units.

Objectives

- Understanding the difference between unary and binary operators
- Redefining (overloading) operators to work with the new objects you define
- Defining useful operations such as string concatenation and comparison
- Dealing with issues involving type conversion.

Topics

9.1	Introduction
9.2	Overloading Unary Operators
9.3	Overloading Binary Operators
9.4	Concatenating Strings
9.5	Comparison Operators
9.6	Arithmetic Assignment Operators
9.7	Data Conversion
9.7.1	Between Basic Types
9.7.2	Between Objects and Basic Types
9.7.3	When to Use What
9.8	Review

Time Requirements: 2.0 hours

10: Inheritance

Overview of Contents

Most programs require more than one class to represent the real-world objects being manipulated. Inheritance provides a way to express the relationship between classes. For example, a graphics circle can be *derived* from the *base class* called Point by adding a radius data member to the X and Y coordinates it receives from the Point class.

You can control the access derived classes have to the data in the base class. The keyword *protected* specifies that a derived class can access data or functions from the base class but they cannot be accessed from the outside. You can also control access by making the class derivation *public* (allowing access to the base class's public members) or *private* (prohibiting such access). Access control makes it possible to safely distribute classes without losing control of their internal structure.

When you create a hierarchy of classes you must understand how constructors and destructors are called for an object of a derived class. When an object is created the base constructor is called first (or more than one base constructor in the case of multiple inheritance). When the object is destroyed, however, the derived destructor is called first, then the base destructor. When working with a class hierarchy you can use the *scope resolution operator* to explicitly call a member function at a particular point in the hierarchy.

In addition to the inheritance relationship, you can also put one class inside another, expressing *containership*. While derivation says in effect "B is a kind of A" containership says "A has a B."

Objectives

➤ Understanding the concept of class inheritance and how it can help you represent a hierarchy of concepts
➤ Learning how to derive a new class from an existing one
➤ Controlling access to inherited class members
➤ Using multiple inheritance, where one class can share characteristics from two "parent" classes
➤ Containing one class inside another
➤ Exploring issues in program design with classes

Topics

Time Requirements: 2.25 hours

11: C++ Graphics

Overview of Contents

The material in this lesson is specific to the IBM PC in general and the Borland/Turbo C++ compilers in particular, although other IBM PC compilers will have similar graphics functions. (The graphics capabilities available under UNIX will likely be organized quite differently.) There are two types of "graphics" on the IBM PC: one uses ASCII text characters (including the special extended character set), while the other uses true graphics constructed from individual points (pixels).

Borland/Turbo C++ inherits a rich library of text and graphics functions from Turbo C. You can use any of these functions in your C++ program, and several examples are given in this lesson. The best way to handle graphics in C++, however, is to create a class hierarchy of graphics objects, and this chapter teaches you how to create and use such graphics classes. Along the way you will also learn how to add sound to your program and how to use random number functions to make simulations and games more interesting.

Objectives

> Working with text mode graphics in Borland/Turbo C++

> Defining and using text windows

> Creating figures in graphics mode

> ➤ Using classes and inheritance to model graphics objects
> ➤ Adding sound to your programs and using random numbers to vary output

Topics

Time Requirements: 1.75 hours

12: Pointers

Overview of Contents

Pointers hold the addresses where values are stored. By adding to or subtracting from a pointer you can quickly retrieve a series of values stored together in memory, such as array elements or characters in a string. The * (asterisk) operator is used to *dereference* a pointer and return the value stored at the address in the pointer.

Pointers can be used to pass an actual variable (rather than only its value) to a function. In this respect pointers are an alternative to the C++ reference operator. Strings and arrays can be accessed either using *array notation* (with an index value) or through dereferencing a pointer. Class objects can also be referenced with pointers. Giving a class a pointer member that points to another object of the same class makes it possible to have linked data structures such as stacks and lists. You can even have pointers to other pointers.

While pointers offer great flexibility it is easy to make mistakes in working with them, and complex expressions involving pointers may be hard to read. We therefore offer some suggestions for debugging pointer problems.

Objectives

➤ Understanding pointers and how to access addresses and the value stored at an address
➤ Using pointers as an alternate way to access arrays
➤ Using pointers to pass variables to a function
➤ Manipulating values with pointers inside a function
➤ Using pointers to access strings
➤ Using pointers with class objects
➤ Debugging common problems involving pointers

Topics

Time Requirements: 3.0 hours

13: Virtual Functions and Other Subtleties

Overview of Contents

When you have a hierarchy of derived classes, C++ uses the type of the object to determine which classes' member functions to call. This can cause problems when a program is using a reference or pointer of the base type that refers to an object of a derived type. By default the member function from the base type will be called, losing the added functionality in the derived type. A solution to this problem is the use of a *virtual* base function: with a virtual function the correct call will be made at runtime.

Sometimes you will create a class that needs to access members of two classes that aren't otherwise related. In this situation you can make your new function or class a *friend* to the existing one, allowing access to private members. Friends are typically defined to allow the streams to work with overloaded functions from user-defined classes.

If a class has data values shared by all of its objects (for example a "flag" used to indicate a mode of processing), you can define and access such common data through *static* functions.

Assignment operators and copy constructors can be overloaded in order to manage the creation of a new copy of an object during assignment. This is often necessary when memory must be allocated for a complex object.

You can use the predefined *this* pointer to refer to "the object itself" within a member function. This allows you to return the object itself from a function.

Objectives

- ➤ Using virtual functions for run-time flexibility
- ➤ Defining friend functions to allow controlled access to unrelated classes
- ➤ Using static functions to manage data values common to all objects of a class
- ➤ Understanding problems involved with creation of copies of objects during assignment
- ➤ Having an object refer to itself with the *this* pointer

Topics

13.1   Virtual Functions
13.2   Pure Virtual Functions

Time Requirements: 1.5 hours

14: Files and Streams

Overview of Contents

As you will have seen earlier, C++ provides a Streams library of I/O functions that can replace the traditional C I/O facilities. C++ streams are often more efficient because you can put together the components you need rather than relying on a few large "all purpose" I/O and formatting functions. You will first review I/O with the keyboard and screen (*cin* and *cout*) and then look at I/O with disk files.

Stream I/O can also be combined with operating system facilities such as the command-line processing and I/O redirection available with MS-DOS and UNIX. This can enable you to write programs that can be used flexibly at the command line.

By overloading the << and >> operators you can tailor I/O operations to work with the class objects you design.

Objectives

➤ Understanding how the C++ Streams library provides facilities for input and output (including access to files)

➤ Using streams for input and output of single characters and strings

➤ Reading and writing data from files

➤ Dealing with errors in file processing

➤ Redirecting file input and output and sending output to a printer

➤ Processing command-line arguments

➤ Overloading the << and >> operators to work with new classes

Topics

14.1   Streams

14.2   String I/O

14.3   Character I/O

14.4   File Pointers

14.5   Error Handling

14.6   Redirection

14.7   Command-Line Arguments

14.8   Printer Output

14.9   Overloading the << and >> Operators

14.10   Review

Time Requirements: 1.5 hours

CHAPTER 6
➤ IN CASE OF TROUBLE

Master C++ has been thoroughly tested with a number of different PC configurations. In 99% of the cases Master C++ should install and run without problems. But just in case something is wrong, we present here some answers to common questions about running Master C++.

TROUBLESHOOTING MASTER C++

For convenience we've divided the possible problems involving Master C++ into two categories. First we will deal with problems that might prevent proper installation of the software, and then we will talk about problems that might occur while you are using Master C++.

Installation Problems

The first step in dealing with installation problems is to review Chapter 2, which discusses the steps involved in Master C++. You may find that you accidentally skipped a step, and you can start over and complete the installation successfully. If that is not the case, look for the question in the following section that most closely describes your problem.

I've copied Master C++ to my hard disk but it won't run.

You cannot run Master C++ directly from the distribution disks. Nor can you run it by copying the files to your hard disk. The Master C++ files are compressed and have to be processed by the INSTALL program.

Why won't the Install program work?

Check to make sure you have at least 2.2 MB of space available on your hard disk. You can do this by typing **CHKDSK** at the DOS prompt and looking for the line that says:

```
XXXXXX bytes available on disk
```

(where XXXXXX is the number of bytes left.)

(DOS 5 users can type **DIR** to determine free disk space.)

Make sure you have your serial number (from the Master C++ disks) handy. You must enter a valid serial number before installation will continue.

If Master C++ reports that it can't update your CONFIG.SYS file, this may mean that your CONFIG.SYS file has been given a read-only status for some reason. In this case we recommend that you first make a backup copy of your CONFIG.SYS file, then type the DOS command

```
ATTRIB -R C:\CONFIG.SYS <Enter>
```

to remove the read-only status. You should now be able to install Master C++.

If you are still having problems installing Master C++ try running INSTALL with the /i switch:

INSTALL /I

The INSTALL program doesn't run or quits prematurely. When I check the hard disk I find no Master C++ files there.

There may be rare cases (involving unusual hardware configurations) where the installation program doesn't run, or seems to run but doesn't actually copy the Master C++ programs to your hard disk. If the INSTALL program doesn't work properly, you can install Master C++ manually using the following steps.

(Note that we show DOS prompts such as C:\MCPP> to help you orient yourself. Your DOS prompt may vary depending on the drive, directory, and DOS configuration in use. Do not type the DOS prompt. You can type any DOS command in lowercase or uppercase. The (ENTER) after each command means to press the (ENTER) key.)

1. Change drives to the destination hard disk:

```
A:\>C: <Enter>
C:\>
```

2. Make a directory for Master C++ on the hard disk. For example:

```
C:\>MD MCPP <Enter>
```

(You can use a different directory name if you wish. If you do, substitute your directory name for MCPP in the instructions that follow. Note that if the directory already exists DOS won't let you make it. In that case skip this step.)

3. Change to that directory:

```
C:\>CD MCPP <Enter>
C:\MCPP>
```

4. Make a subdirectory called REGISTER in your Master C++ directory:

```
C:\MCPP>MD REGISTER <Enter>
```

5. Copy all the files on Master C++ Disk One to the Master C++ directory. Assuming your Master C++ disk is in drive A: you would type:

```
C:\>MCPP>COPY A:*.* <Enter>
```

(Change the A: to B: here and below if your Master C++ disk is in drive B:)

6. Copy all the files on Master C++ Disk Two to the directory:

```
C:\MCPP>COPY A:*.* <Enter>
```

7. Copy all the files on Master C++ Disk Three to the directory:

```
C:\MCPP>COPY A:*.* <Enter>
```

8. Decompress the Master C++ files by typing:

```
C:\MCPP>PKUNZIP *.ZIP <Enter>
```

9. Rename the file called INSTALL.EXE to MCPP.EXE:

```
C:\MCPP>REN INSTALL.EXE MCPP.EXE <Enter>
```

10. Copy the file NANSI.SYS to the root directory:

```
C:\MCPP>COPY NANSI.SYS \ <Enter>
```

11. Make sure that your CONFIG.SYS file contains the line:

```
DEVICE=NANSI.SYS
```

My machine has only 3.5" drives. How do I install Master C++?

Master C++ comes with 360 K 5.25" disks. These disks are not copy-protected. If you know someone who has a PC that has both 5.25" and 3.5" drives, you can copy the Master C++ disks from the supplied 5.25" disks to

720 K or 1.44 MB 3.5" disks with the DOS COPY command. (Note that you can't use the DOS DISKCOPY command with different-sized disk drives.) Just copy each distribution disk to a separate floppy, label the floppies with the corresponding disk numbers, and use the copies for installation. Remember, though, that your license doesn't allow the use of the same Master C++ package on more than one PC at a time.

Problems While Running Master C++

Suppose you've installed Master C++ and it runs when you start it from the DOS command line. But the screen doesn't look right and you can't see some of the features we describe in Chapters 3 and 4. Or perhaps Master C++ runs fine but you want to use it in a special operating environment such as DesqView or Microsoft Windows. Check the following questions for help in these situations.

I've installed Master C++ but it won't run.

Check the hardware requirements for Master C++ listed at the beginning of Chapter 2. Check to make sure you have at least 384 K of free RAM. You can do this by typing CHKDSK at the DOS prompt and looking at the end of the listing, for example:

    655360 total bytes memory
    582544 bytes free

Suppose you don't have enough memory? One reason may be that you are running Master C++ from a DOS "shell" program or from an "exit to DOS" command from some other program. To gain more memory, run Master C++ directly from the command line (type **MCPP** at the command prompt).

Assuming you have enough memory, try running Master C++ from the provided batch file MC.BAT. Just change to the Master C++ directory by typing **CD \MCPP** and type **MC** at the DOS prompt. (This batch file offers no special features—it's just provided to help cope with some unusual configurations.)

Master C++ starts up but the screen is full of weird "garbage."

Master C++ uses a device driver to control output to the screen. If you see a host of strange characters displayed immediately after the logo screen, the device driver has not been loaded.

Your package comes with a screen driver called NANSI.SYS, and this will be copied to your hard disk by the INSTALL program. A reference to this driver will also be added to your CONFIG.SYS file. To correct the strange character problem you may only have to restart your computer, since device drivers are loaded into the computer from the hard disk only when the computer is first started.

If the problem persists after restarting the computer, you may have to adjust your CONFIG.SYS file directly. Or you may have another device driver which is in conflict. Use your editor to check CONFIG.SYS. Ensure that the following line is included:

DEVICE = NANSI.SYS *or* DEVICE = ANSI.SYS

Of course, there will probably be many other statements in the CONFIG.SYS file, all of which should be left unaltered. Save the file and try restarting the computer again.

Note that if you prefer to keep your screen driver in a directory other than the root directory, you are free to do so. Just correct the statement in your CONFIG.SYS file so that it gives the correct pathname for the screen driver. For example, if you keep NANSI.SYS in a SYS directory that is a subdirectory of your DOS directory, change the line in CONFIG.SYS so that it reads:

DEVICE=C:\DOS\SYS\NANSI.SYS

If your system has a hard disk but you boot it from a floppy, you can run Master C++ on such a system. You must, however, have NANSI.SYS (or ANSI.SYS) on your boot floppy, and the boot floppy must have a CONFIG.SYS file that loads the driver.

Note that while Master C++ will work with either ANSI.SYS or NANSI.SYS there is no reason to install both drivers. Since NANSI.SYS is fully compatible with ANSI.SYS and runs faster as well, you may prefer to make NANSI.SYS your regular screen driver.

I get disk errors during installation or while running Master C++.

If you get a disk error when installing or running Master C++, try starting the INSTALL process over. Disk errors are almost always caused by a difference in drive alignments. If reinstalling fails, try copying the disks one at a time to a second floppy disk drive. If this doesn't work try copying the disks one at a time on a different computer system. Often one computer will read disks that are slightly out of alignment and the process of rewriting them to a floppy will produce a copy that will be less out of alignment than the originals.

I'm running Master C++ and it runs into a problem with not having "enough files."

Master C++ isn't finding enough available "slots" for opening the files that it uses. (For example, if you use the Glossary and "jump" to a related lesson Master C++ has to keep some temporary files open.) Make sure that your CONFIG.SYS file has a FILES setting of at least 20 in it. Look for the line:

FILES=20

(or some higher number). If the number is less than 20, change it to 20.

I can't read the characters on the screen very well.

Master C++ assumes you have a color display (CGA or higher resolution) connected to your computer. However, some IBM PC compatible computers (especially laptops) use amber, gray, blue, or green displays. Because

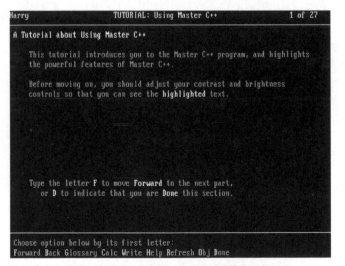

Figure 6-1. Adjusting the brightness of highlighted text

Master C++ uses colors that may be incompatible with certain monochrome displays, you may find that Master C++ will not initially display bright and non-bright characters properly. If you find your text screen is difficult to read, the problem can be corrected by simply switching Master C++ to the monochrome display mode. To do this first press the H key to enable the *Help* window. (H is one of several commands in the Option Bar area at the bottom of the screen.) When the *Help* window is open, press the C key to open the Color palette menu. Choose option 2

on this menu if you have a monochrome display. If you have a color display, you can experiment with the other two palette choices to see what looks best to you.

I can't tell which text is highlighted.

As you learned in Chapter 3, Master C++ uses highlighting to call your attention to certain parts of a lesson or to parts of the program code that are under discussion. (Figure 6-1 shows a sample screen with several parts highlighted.) If you cannot see a difference between regular and highlighted text, you may have to work with the brightness and contrast controls—adjusting one a little, then the other—until a suitable balance is obtained. If this does not work, you may have one of the rare displays that does not support highlighting.

In general, feel free to experiment with the colors available from the color palette item on the Help menu. Taking a few moments now to set things up for comfortable viewing will help make the process of learning C++ more pleasant.

I have an old DOS version and Master C++ won't run.

Master C++ will NOT work with any version of DOS 2 or lower. Only DOS 3 and up are compatible with Master C++. Upgrade your DOS—and with the new memory-saving features of DOS 5.0, you'll be glad you did!

I'm using an IBM 3270 terminal or terminal emulator and I can't run C++.

Master C++ will not work with an IBM 3270 terminal or an IBM 3270 terminal emulator.

I'd like to use Master C++ with DesqView so I can run other programs while I work.

Master C++ works fine with DesqView, but you have to take a few extra steps to set it up. DesqView does not recognize any ANSI.SYS/NANSI.SYS device drivers, even when they are specified correctly in the CONFIG.SYS file.

DesqView provides an executable file called DVANSI.COM.

This file provides all the functionality of an ANSI.SYS/NANSI.SYS device driver, but it must be run as an executable program just before Master C++ is run. To do this, you might want to create a .BAT file named: DVMC.BAT. In it you might put the following lines of code:

```
ECHO OFF
CLS
C:\DV\DVANSI > NUL
MCPP
EXIT
```

The first two lines just keep the screen from being cluttered with messages. The third line invokes the DesqView code which will provide ANSI.SYS/NANSI.SYS functionality (the messages which are output from the program DVANSI.COM are suppressed by redirecting output to the device NUL—essentially discarding them). The fourth line, of course, just invokes Master C++. The last line is required to return you to the DesqView environment.

You can add Master C++ to the DesqView main menuing system as you would any other application. When it asks for the program name to execute, you must provide it with the .BAT file you have just created. (In our case, the file named DVMC.BAT.) The basic options can be set to:

```
Memory Size (in K): 256
Writes text directly to screen . . . N
Displays graphics information  . . . N
Virtualize text/graphics . . . . . . Y
Uses serial ports  . . . . . . . . . N
Requires floppy diskette . . . . . . N
```

The advanced options should have two additional sets of changes.

```
Window Position:
   Maximum Height: 25    Starting Height: 25
Starting Row  : 0
   Maximum Width:  80    Starting Width:  80
Starting Row  : 0
Uses its own colors . . . . . . . . Y
```

Can I run Master C++ with Microsoft Windows?

Master C++ is not a Windows application, but it does run fine as a DOS application under Windows. Set it up like any other DOS application, by choosing the desired group in the Program Manager and selecting New from the File menu. Select New Program Item and enter a brief description such as "Master C++." Under Filename type the actual path to the main Master C++ program (this will usually be C:\MCPP\MCPP.EXE). Since Master C++ uses no graphics, it can be run in a small window in Windows 386 Enhanced Mode, but the Note and Example items on the Option Bar may not blink in this case. We thus recommend running Master C++ in a full screen window.

Working With C++

CHAPTER 7
➤ DEVELOPING C++ PROGRAMS

Once you've completed the Master C++ lessons, you will have a good grasp of the elements of the C++ language and the mechanics of writing a C++ program. But learning a programming language is like learning a foreign language in this respect: There's no substitute for experience. If you work through the questions and exercises in Chapter 8, you'll have a chance to sharpen your new programming skills. After that, the next step in learning C++ is to try out the language on a variety of small to medium-sized projects of your own choosing. Only by writing lots of code will you figure out what works and what doesn't.

You obviously need a C++ compiler to develop C++ programs. Which one should you buy? You may also have some questions about developing C++ programs. What are the steps involved in using a C++ compiler? What features and tools are provided to help you? What resources can you draw upon in writing a program that interfaces both to the operating system (such as for file or device I/O) and to the user (perhaps via a graphical user interface with menus, windows, and dialog boxes)? What considerations are forced on you by the constraints of the operating system?

We can't tell you which compiler to buy, and we won't be able to answer all these questions definitively in this short chapter, but we *can* help you start thinking about them, and we can offer some advice about choosing and working with C++ compilers and other tools. And while our discussion will focus on the Borland/Turbo C++ compiler for DOS (the most popular C++ compiler and the most widespread operating system), most of the discussion will apply to other compilers (such as Zortech C++) and other operating systems (such as UNIX).

OVERVIEW OF PROGRAM DEVELOPMENT

If you have completed the CBT lesson for Chapter 2 you are familiar with the basic terms used in describing the program development process, and the steps you follow to write, compile, link, and run a program. Now is a good time to review these steps, which we have diagrammed in Figure 7-1.

Writing

Before you can do anything else you have to have a *source file*, which is an ordinary ASCII text file containing the statements that make up your C++ program. Since this is an ASCII file it can be created with any available text editor (or even with a word processor in ASCII text mode). Integrated products such as Borland/Turbo C++ provide built-in text editors. In some environments, however, you may have to use a separate text editor to write your program.

There are also specialized programming editors for DOS and other environments. These editors include features that make it easier to write your program, such as preformatted templates for class and function declarations.

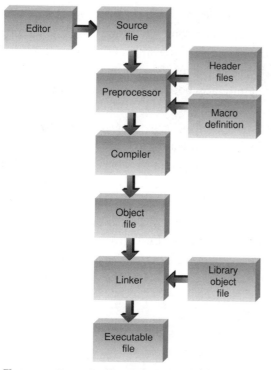

Figure 7-1. Steps in C++ program development

Preprocessing

Once you've written your program you invoke the compiler (either from the operating system's command line or from a menu provided by the compiler package). The compiler runs a *preprocessor*, which responds to any *preprocessor directives* that you have placed in the source code. There are two directives you will use the most. The *#include* directive, as you have seen, brings in additional source code from a *header file*. The *#define* directive can be employed to specify symbolic *constant values* and can also be used to define *macros*, which use a function-like syntax to substitute text.

Compiling

The compiler takes the source code (including additions and substitutions made by the preprocessor) and compiles it into the corresponding machine-language statements that will accomplish what your C++ program specifies. Although the topic is beyond our scope here, you should be aware that a given C++ statement usually translates into several machine instructions, and compilers must be carefully crafted to ensure that the machine code they generate not only correctly implements the C++ instructions, but does so as efficiently as possible in terms of execution speed and program size.

If the compiler encounters an error such as a statement with incomplete or incorrect syntax, an error message is given. Depending on how the compiler is set up, it may stop compiling or continue. Sometimes you will receive *warnings* for situations that the compiler detects that are not actual errors but may make the program unsafe to use (for example, certain data type conversions). Some warnings, however, may indicate actual errors. For example, if the compiler tells you that you declared a variable that was never used, it's time to examine your program logic!

When C++ first came on the scene it was desirable to provide facilities for developing C++ programs as quickly as possible. As a result, a number of C++ *translators* were developed. Rather than compiling the C++ source file to object code, a translator turns the C++ code into standard C code, which is then fed to a C compiler and linked to make an executable file. There are two main drawbacks to translation: it can be quite slow because of the additional step of running the C compiler, and the final object code will probably not be the optimal expression of the original intent of the C++ program. Therefore, most recent C++ packages compile directly to object code rather than creating intermediate C code.

Linking

The result of successful compilation is an *object file*. The linker is called on to create the actual executable program by combining the compiler's output with other object files. This additional step is needed because the object code generated from your source code has to be combined with the object code in the function or class libraries that you have called upon with your *#include* directives. (Remember that the preprocessor responds to an *#include* by adding the specified header file to your source file. But the header file contains only declarations of the functions or classes to be used. Their actual implementation is found in a *library file* containing the appropriate object code.) At minimum, a standard run-time library must be added to your executable program This provides the built-in code for such things as processing constructors and setting up virtual function tables. In addition, the

IBM PC and DOS require the use of memory models (with a separate library specific to each model), as well as libraries for carrying out floating-point calculations with or without a math coprocessor chip.

The Executable Program

The result of a successful linking operation is an *executable file*—that is, a program that can be run like any other from the command line (or by clicking on an icon in a graphical environment). Under DOS an executable file has the .EXE or occasionally .COM filename extension. (.COM files are limited to 64 K in size, but because they always load into a fixed location in memory they load faster than .EXE files, which can be flexibly moved around in memory.) Under UNIX there's no particular extension signifying an executable file, but traditionally UNIX compilers produce executables with the *.out* extension unless told otherwise.

Repeat Until Done

There is no guarantee of course that a correctly compiled and linked program will actually do the job for which it was intended. In fact, for a non-trivial program the odds are that one or more *bugs* (errors in program logic or specifications) are waiting to be discovered. The program therefore has to be run and tested under a variety of conditions, and given a range of input or commands that at least aproximates what the program will encounter in actual day-to-day use. As problems are discovered, changes are made in the source code, and the edit-compile-link-run cycle is repeated until the program is satisfactory.

PROGRAMMING ENVIRONMENTS

The steps we've discussed aren't all that complicated conceptually, but a serious programmer is going to spend a lot of time moving from editing to compiling to linking, with frequent detours for debugging and revising the source file to fix errors and problems. Therefore, the choice of a compiler package is an important one. The first step is to decide between two general ways of developing a program: command-line compilation or the use of an integrated development environment.

Command-Line Compilation

Command-line compilation, as the name suggests, means working at the DOS (or UNIX or another operating system) command line and typing in the necessary commands for each step of the program development process. For example, under UNIX you might create an executable program like this:

```
% vi myprog.C
% CC myprog.C
% a.out
```

Your first step is to run a text editor (we used one called *vi*). After writing the source file, you save the file to disk and exit the editor. Next, you run the C++ compiler (this one happens to be called *CC*, to contrast it with the traditional C compiler, *cc*). Most UNIX compilers automatically create an executable file with the name *a.out*. (Here we've assumed that the *CC* compiler includes both the compile and link steps, which is usual. If not, you'd have to follow the *CC* invocation with a command to run the linker on the file *myprog.o* (the object file made by the compiler), the result again being the file *a.out*.) Finally we ran the completed program by entering *a.out* at the UNIX prompt.

The very first DOS C compilers worked only on the command line in a way similar to that shown above. Even today's integrated compilers usually include a command-line compiler. Thus with Borland C++ you can develop *myprog* as follows:

```
C:\BORLANDC>edit myprog.cpp
C:\BORLANDC>bc myprog.cpp
```

Here we used the DOS 5.0 *edit* editor to write the source code, and then invoked the command-line C++ compiler.

Command-line compilation may not *look* that hard, but there are two things to note. First, if you want anything other than the default compiler or linker settings you have to remember to specify the appropriate command-line switches. If you have more than one source file (a common occurrence) you must specify all of the source files; you may also have to explicitly specify library files. Second, the inevitable mistakes are reported by the compiler, but since there is no connection between the editor and the compiler, when you return to the editor you have no indication of where the errors were

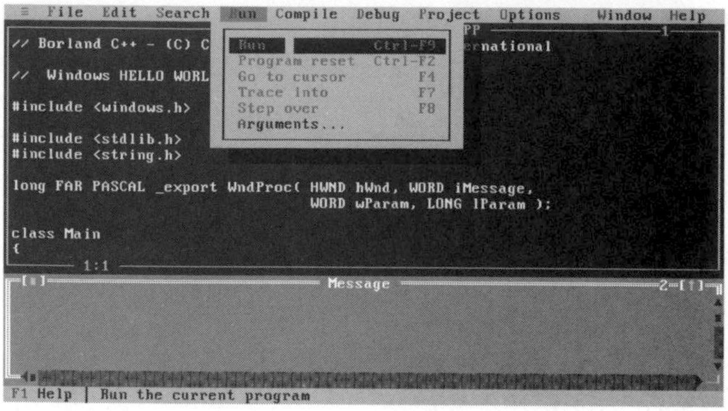

Figure 7-2. An integrated development environment

found, and you may no longer even have the text of the error messages to refer to, unless you arranged to print them or redirect them to a file.

Because of these difficulties, command-line compilation is generally used in only two cases: when, as with some UNIX installations, nothing better is available, and when you have to repeatedly rebuild large programs with many different compiler options and file names. In the latter case a UNIX shell script or DOS batch file used together with a "make" file (discussed later) can be used to make the whole process automatic, avoiding the need to retype lengthy commands.

Integrated Development Environments

Rather than relying on a separate editor and compiler at the command line, most programmers today prefer an *integrated development environment (IDE)* such as that provided by Borland/Turbo C++. As shown in Figure 7-2, the integration comes from having the editor, compiler, project manager, debugger, and other tools available from the same screen. Text is entered in a source code editor window, using cursor control and editing functions similar to those found in other full-screen editors. As you can see in the figure, menu commands control such operations as compiling the current source code, or compiling, linking, and running in one step (the Run command).

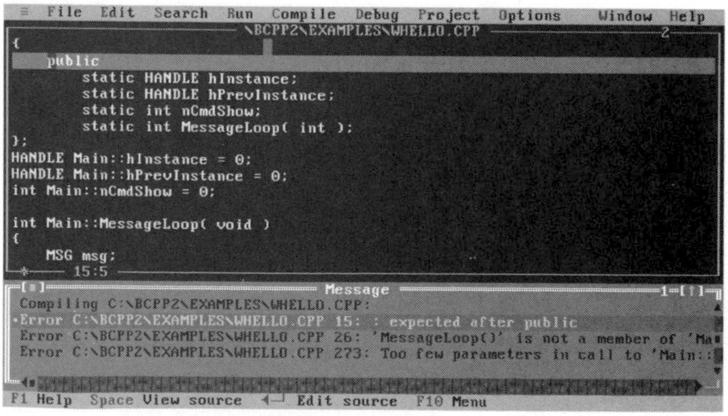

Figure 7-3. Fixing errors in an IDE

When you try to compile or run a program and encounter errors, the error messages are displayed in a separate window (see Figure 7-3). Both the source code and error message window are always in view; you can even select an error from the message window to move directly to the place in the source code where that error was encountered. It should be clear how much easier the process of writing, debugging, and refining a

Figure 7-4. Controlling the compiler in an IDE

Figure 7-5. An online help facility

program is in an integrated development environment as opposed to a command-line one.

Another important feature of an IDE is dialog boxes for controlling the operation of the compiler and other tools, and for performing other operations such as loading and saving files and searching for text. In a command-line environment options are set by typing in obscure combinations of dashes and letters. In an IDE it's all handled with pushbutton ease (see Figure 7-4).

IDEs also include an invaluable online *help* facility. Generally a help system allows you to select topics of interest from a contents list, pick topics from an alphabetical index, or get appropriate help simply by clicking on a keyword, function name, or other item in your source code with the mouse (see Figure 7-5).

PROGRAMMING TOOLS

The complexity of modern programming requires the use of tools besides the compiler and linker. A commercial application often has a dozen or more source files representing different aspects of a program's operation (for example, file-handling, text display, graphics display, and user interface). The problem becomes how to make sure that when, for example, you change a library file, the source files that include functions from that library are also recompiled to include the revised object code.

Make and Project Managers

There are two common solutions to this problem. The one inherited from the older command-line compilers is a utility usually called *make* (or *nmake* in Turbo C++). Its purpose is to allow you to specify which files are needed to build a complete program, and among the files, which ones depend on which others and thus must be recompiled when a change is made. The make file is an ASCII text file that contains the appropriate specifications. For example, a simple program might have this Turbo C++ make file:

```
myprog.exe: myprog.obj funcs.obj
  tlink myprog funcs
myprog.obj: myprog.cpp mydef.h
  tcc -c myprog.cpp
funcs.obj: funcs.cpp funcs.h
  tcc -c funcs.cpp
```

This example is divided into three make statements. Each statement consists of a *dependancy*, which lists a target file and the file or files that are needed to create that target. In other words, the target file is dependant on those other files. Each statement also has a *rule* that tells make how to re-build the target if any of the component files have changed. Thus the first make statement above says that *myprog.exe* (the executable file) depends on two object files, *myprog.obj* and *funcs.obj* (the latter being a function library). The rule part says to run the linker *tlink* with the two object files to link them.

Notice that the order of the statements in the make file is opposite from the order of the steps in program development. The first statement is really the last step (making an executable from object files). The next two statements specify how to build the object files; each depends on a source file and a header (include) file, and the rule used says to run the *tcc* compiler with the source file.

While the above example is simple, make files can actually be quite complicated, and specifying them by hand can be tedious. Thus IDEs usually include a *project* utility that lets you simply specify what files your program uses. The project facility then generates the actual make file by working out the dependencies and constructing the rules from your current compiler settings (see Figure 7-6).

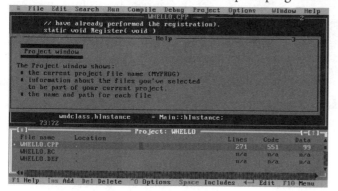

Figure 7-6. Using a project facility

Debuggers

Just about any integrated C++ compiler provides a *debugger* that allows you to display the changing value of one or more objects and to set *breakpoints*, or places where the program will automatically stop to allow you to examine it. (Stopping can also be made conditional on the value of an object.) Debuggers also let you *step through* your program statement by statement or object by object, observing and possibly changing values as you seek to isolate a problem.

Profilers

A program can be sound, correct, and reliable—and too slow for practical use. Some C++ compilers such as Borland C++ include a *profiler*—a utility that measures the execution of the blocks that make up your program (such as loop statements). The profiler's most important use is to tell you which parts of your program are executed the most frequently. Once you have identified these portions (typically less than 10% of the program statements) you know where to expend your effort at optimization. Ways to speed up these program sections can vary from writing your own assembly language code (if you think the compiler's code is inefficient), to thinking of a completely different *algorithm*, or plan for accomplishing the task.

Browsers

Since C++ programs are organized not into groups of functions but into a hierarchy of classes, C++ requires visualizing a program in a new way. On the one hand, one of the big advantages of object-oriented programming is that it hides much of the complexity of program implementation, allowing you to concentrate on the big picture: what objects does my program manipulate, and what are their characteristics and functions? On the other hand, the relationships between base classes and their offspring can be hard to visualize and to remember, particularly when multiple inheritance and friend classes and functions are involved.

To help with this structural complexity some of the latest C++ compilers provide a *browser* that allows you to display, search through, and inspect the hierarchy of classes, much in the way a modern file management utility lets you work with

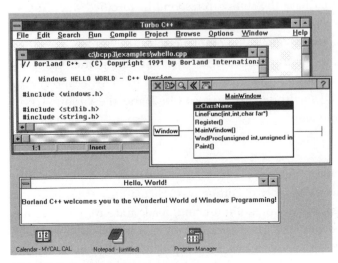

Figure 7-7. C++ browser

disk directories and subdirectories. Figure 7-7 shows the display of the member functions in the *Window* class of a Microsoft Windows application.

PROGRAMMING RESOURCES

Figure 7-7 also illustrates how a new generation of C++ compilers takes advantage of a *GUI* (graphical user interface) and a multitasking environment—in this case Microsoft Windows. When you use a product such as Borland C++ 3.0, the compiler is itself a Windows application and takes advantage of all the features of the environment, including a standard way to interact with windows, menus, and icons, and the ability to run several programs at the same time. Note, for example, that in addition to the source code for the Hello program and the *Browser* window you can also see other programs such as a daily calendar and notebook (represented by *icons* at the bottom of the screen). Indeed when you develop C++ under Windows you can easily create your own customized working environment, mixing and matching tools as needed.

Until recently, Windows was as difficult for programmers to write for as it is easy for users to work with. The creation and management of the graphical display interface involved calls to hundreds of different library functions. So much effort had to be spent on interfacing with the Windows environment that the program's actual functionality was sometimes neglected.

C++ comes to the rescue! Notice that we use much of the same terminology in referring to the C++ language and the Windows environment. Both focus on objects that have the ability to respond in specified ways. A C++ class responds to *messages* in the form of calls to its member functions. A graphical object in the Windows environment, such as a window, icon, button, or check box responds to user actions such as clicking or dragging the mouse. C++ and Windows therefore are a natural fit. This is also true of other modern GUI environments such as OS/2 and the various UNIX windowing environments.

Traditional Libraries

A modern application (especially one using a GUI) has to do much more than fulfill its primary purpose of editing text, calculating a spreadsheet, or updating a database. The program must find, load, and save files. It must also manage the menus and other aspects of the user interface. It would be wasteful, if not downright impossible, for a programmer to have to write new routines for each of these tasks. Instead, traditional C programmers draw upon the standard header files and function libraries, plus whatever "bonus" ones are provided by the compiler vendor.

C++ Class Libraries

While this wealth of library functions can make programming a lot easier, it is not organized in an object-oriented way. Increasingly, therefore, the support functions are being reorganized into *class libraries*. For example, instead of having to manage 20 separate functions for dealing with files, a class library might offer a *file* object with member functions for finding, copying, deleting, or renaming files. Through inheritance, a generic file object might be specialized into a binary file object, a text file object, and so on. Hiding details and providing a uniform syntax for member functions makes it easier to manage the inherent complexity.

Besides "repackaging" traditonal function libraries, C++ programmers are busy creating useful new objects such as stacks, lists, queues, and containers. Borland C++, for example, contains a rich library of such utility classes. As the years pass we should see much less reliance on the old C function library.

Borland and others are tackling the problem of dealing with the Windows API (application program interface) and its 500 or more functions by encapsulating the most commonly used ones in C++ classes—for example, classes representing windows, icons, graphic bitmaps, and other objects.

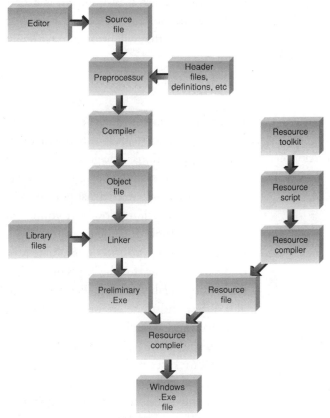

Figure 7-8. Windows program development

Windows Development and Resource Tools

As you can see from Figure 7-8, developing a program for Windows (or a similar graphic environment) is more complicated than developing a program for DOS or other traditional character-oriented operating systems. The basic program development process, shown on the left side of the figure, is still the same. The executable file created by the linker, however, is not yet ready for use.

When you write a Windows program you don't write functions to draw all the icons, bitmaps, and other graphic objects that the program will need to use. To do so would be a hit-or-miss process, not to mention an excruciatingly tedious one. Instead, modern Windows programmers use a *resource toolkit* such as the Whitewater Resource Toolkit or Borland's new Resource Workshop to design the graphical objects needed. As you can see on the right side of Figure 7-8, the resource toolkit is used to create the resources in the form of a *resource script*—a kind of "source program" whose statements describe the position, style, and behavior of the objects. The *resource compiler* creates a *resource file* and then combines the preliminary executable file from the standard compile-link process with the resource file to produce the executable program.

The resource toolkit is used interactively, which is easy since it is itself a Windows application. Figure 7-9 shows the Borland Resource Workshop being used to modify a "magnifying glass" icon that will be used to represent the "file search" feature of a program.

Summary

We have tried to show you the steps and issues involved in the development of modern C++ programs. Mastering C++ as a language is only the first part of mastering the development of quality applications. The good news is that a variety of increasingly powerful and easy-to-use tools are there to assist you in writing your application. Now that you know about these tools and their purposes, you will be in a better position to evaluate how important they are for the kinds of applications you will be writing. Peoples' needs will differ, and there are products ranging in power and complexity from a no-frills C++ compiler to a full-blown Windows development system. Like everything else, though, mastering C++ is done one step at a time, and we've tried to make sure that you are off to a good start.

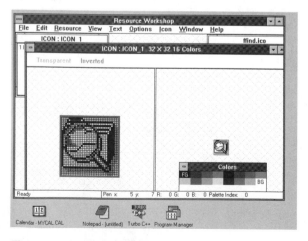

Figure 7-9. Editing resources

CHAPTER 8

➤ REVIEW EXERCISES

This chapter of exercises provides a valuable way to consolidate your understanding of C++. Each exercise corresponds to the lessons on the Master C++ disks. For each chapter there are a few simple exercises to test your fundamental knowledge of the material, and several more challenging ones to give you practice in applying the principles to more or less practical problems.

Use these exercises after you complete a Master C++ chapter to reinforce what you've learned. Try not to look at the solutions before you've tried the exercise yourself.

Note that when example programs are referred to as "Example X in Chapter N on the disk" we mean an example from the Master C++ disk tutorial. "Exercise X in Chapter N" means an exercise in this section.

Each exercise provides only one possible solution. Of course, there are many ways to implement each solution.

There are a few chapters that we feel did not require additional exercises. These are chapters 1, 2, and 11.

CHAPTER 3

Exercise 1

Write a program that displays your name and address on the screen, using a separate program statement to generate each line of the address.

```
// address1.cpp
// outputs name and address using three statements
#include <iostream.h>

void main()
   {
   cout << "\nIma Coder";
   cout << "\n2123 Object Ave.";
   cout << "\nClasstown, OP  10101";
   }
```

Exercise 2

Modify the ADDRESS1 exercise so that it uses only one program statement to display the entire address. Use a separate << operator for each line of the address.

```cpp
// address2.cpp
// outputs name and address using one statement
#include <iostream.h>

void main()
  {
  cout << "\nIma Coder"
       << "\n2123 Object Ave."
       << "\nClasstown, OP 10101";
  }
```

Exercise 3

Write a program that asks the user to input exactly three characters. The program should then print out the three characters in reverse order: last one first.

```cpp
// revlets.cpp
// reverses three characters
#include <iostream.h>

void main()
  {
  char first, second, third;

  cout << "\nInput first character: ";
  cin >> first;
  cout << "Input second character: ";
  cin >> second;
  cout << "Input third character: ";
  cin >> third;
  cout << "Reversed word is " << third << second << first;
 }
```

Exercise 4

Here's a handy program for astronomers. Write a program that converts light-years to inches. There are 5.878e12 (that is, 5,878,000,000,000) miles in a light-year, 5,280 feet in a mile, and 12 inches in a foot. The program should take a value in light-years input by the user, and generate the corresponding value in inches.

```cpp
// lightyrs.cpp
// converts inches to light-years
```

```
#include <iostream.h>

void main()
   {
   const float MPLY = 5.878e12;
   const float FPM = 5280;
   const float IPF = 12;
   float ltyears;

   cout << "Enter distance in light-years: ";
   cin >> ltyears;
   cout << "Distance in inches is ";
   cout << ltyears * MPLY * FPM * IPF;
   }
```

Exercise 5

Sometimes the increment operator (++) can produce surprising results. To test this, write a program that, in a single statement, prints the same variable three times. Each appearance of the variable should include a postfix increment operator (as in *joe++*).

```
// incagain.cpp
// demonstrates increment operator
#include <iostream.h>

void main()
   {
   int joe-10;
   cout << endl << joe++ << " " << joe++ << " " << joe++;
   }
```

Examine the output. Note that although the variables are printed from left to right, the increment operators are applied from right to left. The moral: operations are not always performed in the order you think they may be. In this case, be careful of using the increment (or decrement) operator more than once on the same variable in a given statement.

CHAPTER 4
Exercise 1

Write a program to see how fast your computer performs integer addition. Use two *for* loops, one nested inside the other. The inner loop should always cycle 32,767 times (the maximum for integers). The outer loop should cycle a number of times selected by the user, so it can be adjusted for different speed ranges. In the inner loop, add the two loop variables together and assign them to a dummy variable:

dummy = k + j;

This should be the only statement in the nested loops. Have the program wait for a keystroke before starting the test, and display "Done" when the test is over.

The variable that holds the sum is called a dummy variable because you don't really care about its value. However, you'll need to do something with this value following the loops, or the compiler will complain that "dummy is assigned a value that is never used." For instance, you can display its value when the test is over.

For comparison, a Compaq DeskPro 386/20e takes 20 seconds to run this test when the outer loop limit is 500.

```
// speedtst.cpp
// tests computer speed
#include <iostream.h>
#include <conio.h>    // for getch()

void main()
  {
  int cycles;        // number of times through outer loop
  int dummy;         // dummy variable for dummy arithmetic
  int j, k;          // loop variables
  const int MAX = 32767;  // maximum value of type int

  cout << "\nEnter the number of times to cycle: ";
  cin >> cycles;
  cout << "Press any key to begin: ";
  getch();
  cout << "\nRunning test...";
  for(j=0; j<cycles; j++)     // outer loop counts to cycles
    for(k=0; k<MAX; k++)      // inner loop counts to MAX
      dummy = k + j;          // dummy statement
  cout << "\nDone (dummy=" << dummy << ")";
  }
```

Exercise 2

Write a program that enables the computer to play the old game of NIM against a human opponent. In this game you start with a certain number of sticks, say 25. Two players alternate turns. Each can select either one, two, or three sticks from the pile. Whoever is forced to take the last stick is the loser. The program should make the human play first.

Assume that the original number of sticks is a special kind of number: 1 added to a multiple of 4, such as 25=1+(6*4). Then the winning strategy for the program is to subtract from 4 however many sticks the human chose, and take that many sticks. For example, if the human takes 3, the program should take 1; if the human takes 2, the program should take 2. This guarantees there will be one stick left on the human's last turn. Try the game on your friends as an example of the computer's infallibility. Use a *do* loop, which exits and prints the *You lose* message when the number of sticks equals 1.

```cpp
// nim.cpp
// plays the game of nim against a human player
#include <iostream.h>

void main()
   {
   int sticks=25;                 // multiple of 4, plus 1
   int human, machine;            // sticks to remove

   do
      {
         cout << "\nThere are " << sticks << " sticks.";
         cout << "\nYou can take 1, 2 or 3. Enter choice: ";
      cin >> human;               // get human move
      sticks -= human;            // subtract it from total
      machine = 4 - human;        // calculate machine move
         cout << "There are " << sticks << " sticks.";
         cout << "\nI'll take " << machine << " stick(s).";
      sticks -= machine;          // subtract it from total
      }
   while( sticks != 1 );          // quit if 1 stick left
   cout << "\nThere is 1 stick left, and you must take it."
         << " You lose.";
   }
```

Exercise 3

Write a program that calculates the greatest common divisor (GCD) of two numbers. This number has many uses. A common one is reducing a fraction to lowest terms by dividing the numerator and denomenator by their GCD. For example, to express 12/21 in lowest terms, find the GCD of 12 and 21. This turns out to be 3, since there is no larger number that divides into both 12 and 21 with no remainder. Dividing both numbers by 3 gives you 4/7, which is 12/21 reduced to lowest terms. Other examples: the GCD of 8 and 6 is 2, the GCD of 42 and 66 is 6, and the GCD of 387 and 153 is 9.

You can find the GCD using Euclid's Algorithm. Here's how it works. Get the two numbers from the user. If necessary, switch them so the first is larger. Subtract the second from the first, and assign the result to the first number. Again, switch if necessary, and subtract the second from the first. Repeat this process until the first and second numbers are equal. Both numbers now equal the GCD.

Use a *while* loop that terminates when the first and second numbers are equal. Use an assignment operator to perform the subtraction of the second number from the first, assigning the result to the first. You'll need a temporary variable to help with swapping.

```
// gcd.cpp
// computes the greatest common divisor of two numbers
#include <iostream.h>

void main()
   {
   long int first, second, temp;
   cout << "\nEnter two numbers: ";
   cin >> first >> second;
   while( first != second )       // done when they're equal
      {
      if( first < second )        // if first isn't bigger,
         {
         temp=first;              // swap them
         first=second;
         second=temp;
         }
      first -= second;            // first = first - second
      }
   cout << "Greatest Common Divisor is ";
   cout << first;
   }
```

Exercise 4

Write a program that simulates a TV remote-control channel-selector. The user should be able to type in a digit from 2 to 9 (don't worry about multidigit channel numbers), or press the 'u' key to increment the channel number or the 'd' key to decrement it. After each keypress the program should display the new channel number. You might use a *while* loop that encloses both an *if* statement to check for digits and a *switch* statement to check for 'u' and 'd'. Use the *getche()* function to read the digits.

```
// remote.cpp
// simulates TV remote-control channel-switcher
#include <iostream.h>
#include <conio.h>      // for getche()

void main()
```

```
   {
const int ESC = 27;         // ascii code for escape key
int channel=2;              // channel number
char ch;                    // character typed by user

while( (ch=getche()) != ESC)        // get the character
   {                                // exit on escape key
   if( ch<58 && ch>47 )             // if it's a digit
      channel = ch - 48;            // set channel to it
   else                             // otherwise
      switch(ch)                    // go up or down
        {
         case 'u': channel++; break;     // 'u' key
         case 'd': channel--; break;     // 'd' key
         default:  cout << "\nError";    // anything else
        }                                // display channel
   cout << "\nchannel=" << channel << endl;
   }
}
```

Exercise 5

Write a program that accepts individual digits in the form of characters (from *0* to *9*). These digits should be read in with *getche()* in a loop, and assembled into a number of type *int*. The program should accept digits that form any positive number up to 32,767, the maximum size for this type. The input part of the program should terminate on any non-digit character. The program should then print out the entire number using *cout* in the usual way.

You can create the number out of individual digits by starting with zero, multiplying by 10 whenever a new digit is typed (to shift the number one place left) and adding the new digit (thus inserting it in the one's column). The ASCII codes for the digits from 0 to 9 run from 48 to 57 (decimal).

```
// makenumb.cpp
// makes a number out of digits
#include <iostream.h>
#include <conio.h>          // for getche()

enum boolean { false, true };      // make a "true" value for loop

void main()
   {
   int numb = 0;                   // final number
   char ch;                        // character typed by user

   cout << "\nEnter a number: ";
   while( true )                   // loop ends with break
      {
```

```
    ch=getche();              // get character from user
    if( ch<48 || ch>57 )      // if it's not a digit
      break;                  // exit loop
    int digit = ch - 48;      // convert ASCII to digit
    numb *= 10;               // shift number one place left
    numb += digit;            // put digit in one's column
    }
  cout << "\nNumber is " << numb;
  }
```

The routine described here emulates, in part, such input routines as the one built into *cin* that accept digits from the user and create a multidigit number.

CHAPTER 5
Exercise 1

Create a structure to store time values. It should have three members of type *int*; one each for hours, minutes, and seconds. Also write a *main()* program that allows the user to input values for these three members, and then displays the result in the 12:59:59 format.

Don't worry about leading zeros in single-digit numbers; that is, 12:5:5 is all right.

```
// timestrc.cpp
// models time data type using structure
#include <iostream.h>

struct time                  // specify a structure template
   {
   int hrs;
   int mins;
   int secs;
   };

void main()
   {
   time t1;                  // define structure of type time

   cout << "Enter hours: ";  // get values from user
   cin >> t1.hrs;
   cout << "Enter minutes: ";
   cin >> t1.mins;
   cout << "Enter seconds: ";
   cin >> t1.secs;
   cout << "Time entered is ";
                             // display time (format 12:59:59)
   cout << t1.hrs << ":" << t1.mins << ":" << t1.secs << endl;
   }
```

Exercise 2

Create an enumerated data type called *change* that contains the U.S coins and their values. For instance, *nickel=5.* Use this in a program that makes change; that is, the user types an amount in cents, like 295, and the program tells how many pennies, nickels, dimes, quarters, half-dollars, and dollars this amount is equal to.

```
// changer.cpp
// makes change; uses enumerated type for coin values
#include <iostream.h>

enum change { penny=1, nickel=5, dime=10,
                        quarter=25, half=50, dollar=100 };

void main()
   {
   int cents, whole, remain;

   cout << "\n\nEnter an amount in cents: ";
   cin >> cents;

   whole = cents / dollar;    // find how many dollars
   cout << "\nThat's " << whole << " dollars, ";
   remain = cents % dollar;   // find how much left over

   whole = remain / half;     // find how many half-dollars
   cout << whole << " half-dollars, ";
   remain %= half;            // find how much left over

   whole = remain / quarter;  // find how many quarters
   cout << whole << " quarters, ";
   remain %= quarter;         // find how much left over

   whole = remain / dime;     // find how many dimes
   cout << whole << " dimes, ";
   remain %= dime;            // find how much left over

   whole = remain / nickel;   // find how many nickels
   cout << whole << " nickels, ";
   remain %= nickel;          // find how much left over

   cout << remain << " penneys.";    // penneys is what's left
   }
```

Exercise 3

A compass rose is the rotating circular card in a compass that has the directions, such as N, NE, E, and so on, printed on it. Create an enumerated data type called *rose* that holds eight such directions. Within the definition of the enumerated type, set each symbol equal to the number of degrees it represents. Degrees are measured clockwise from 0 around to 360, so N (north) is 0, NE (northeast) is 45, E (east) is 90, and so on through SE, S, SW, W, and NW, which is 315.

Write a program that allows the user to input a course in degrees, and then displays the course, using "N", "NE" and so on if the course is exactly equal to one of these directions, but simply displays the number of degrees if the course is some other direction, such as 10 degrees.

```cpp
// rose.cpp
// enumerated data type holds compass directions
#include <iostream.h>

enum rose { N=0, NE=45, E=90, SE=135,
            S=180, SW=225, W=270, NW=315 };

void main()
  {
  int degrees;

  while( degrees >= 0 )
    {
    cout << "\n\nEnter a course in degrees: ";
    cin >> degrees;
    cout << "Course is ";
    switch(degrees)
      {
      case N:  cout << "N";  break;
      case NE: cout << "NE"; break;
      case E:  cout << "E";  break;
      case SE: cout << "SE"; break;
      case S:  cout << "S";  break;
      case SW: cout << "SW"; break;
      case W:  cout << "W";  break;
      case NW: cout << "NW"; break;
      default: cout << degrees << " degrees";
      }
    }
  }
```

Exercise 4

Stock prices are usually presented in terms of a whole number and a fraction. For example, the closing price of General Motors stock on a certain day was thirty-six and five-eighths, written 36-5/8.

Create a structure called *fracpri* that holds the three parts of this price: the whole number (36 in the example shown above), the numerator of the fraction (5), and the denominator of the fraction (8).

Write a *main()* program that creates at least two *fracpri* structures, prompts the user to place values in them (three numbers for each one), and then displays the contents of each structure in the form "36-5/8".

```
// fracstr.cpp
// structure used to hold stock prices
#include <iostream.h>

struct fracpri                  // structure holds fractional prices
  {
  int whole;                    // whole number part of price
  int numer;                    // numerator (top) of fraction
  int denom;                    // denominator (bottom) of fraction
  };

void main()
  {
  fracpri fp1, fp2;             // make two structures
  char dummy;                   // for hyphen and slash

  cout << "\nEnter first price: ";          // get first
  cin >> fp1.whole;             // get whole number
  cin >> dummy;                 // get hyphen
  cin >> fp1.numer;             // get numerator
  cin >> dummy;                 // get slash
  cin >> fp1.denom;             // get denominator

  cout << "\nEnter second price: ";         // get second
  cin >> fp2.whole;             // get whole number
  cin >> dummy;                 // get hyphen
  cin >> fp2.numer;             // get numerator
  cin >> dummy;                 // get slash
  cin >> fp2.denom;             // get denominator

  cout << "\nFirst price is ";              // display first
  cout << fp1.whole << "-"
       << fp1.numer << "/"
       << fp1.denom;

  cout << "\nSecond price is ";             // display second
  cout << fp2.whole << "-"
       << fp2.numer << "/"
       << fp2.denom;
  }
```

Exercise 5

Suppose we're on a fishing boat, motoring through the fog, looking at the radar screen. The display shows other ships as spots of light, called blips. Each ship is a certain distance—called its range—away from our boat, and at a certain angle—called the bearing—to us. The bearing is measured in degrees, starting at 0 for a ship straight ahead of us, to 90 for a ship to the right, to 180 for a ship behind us, to 270 for a ship to the left. Bearings are never negative, and never exceed 360 degrees.

The range and bearing of a ship can be inferred by the position of its blip on the radar screen. Our own boat is in the center of the screen, and the up direction on the screen represents the forward direction for our boat. The range of a ship is shown by the distance of the blip from the center of the radar screen, and its bearing is shown by the direction of the blip. If the blip is above the center, the ship is in front of us, at 0 degrees. If the blip is to the right, the ship is to our right at 90 degrees, and so on.

Create a structure called *target* that contains members that represent the range and bearing of a blip. Use type *float* for the range (since a ship could be 2.4 miles away), and type *int* for the bearing (fractions of a degree are not necessary). Write a *main()* program that creates a target 10 miles away directly on our right. Now assume our boat can turn. Ask the user to type in the number of degrees we will turn. Positive numbers represent a right turn, and negative numbers represent a left turn. When we turn, the bearing of the target will change. Altar the target's bearing, and print the range and the new bearing.

```cpp
// radar.cpp
// structure models ship as seen on a radar set
#include <iostream.h>

struct target
   {
   float range;                // miles from our location
   int bearing;                // relative to our heading, from 0 to 360
   };

void main()
   {
   target t1 = { 10.0, 90 };   // 10 miles away, on our right
   int turn = 10;              // can't start at 0

   cout << endl << endl;
   while( turn != 0 )          // exit if no turn
      {
      cout << "Range and bearing of target 1 is "
          << t1.range << " miles, "
          << t1.bearing << " degrees.";

      cout << "\nEnter number of degrees to turn "
          << "(negative numbers indicate left turn): ";
      cin >> turn;             // get degrees to turn
```

```
   t1.bearing -= turn;       // subtract turn from bearing
   if(t1.bearing < 0)        // if result is negative,
      t1.bearing += 360;     // add 360 for positive bearing
   if(t1.bearing >= 360)     // if result 360 or more,
      t1.bearing -= 360;     // subtract 360
   }
}
```

CHAPTER 6
Exercise 1

An easy (but slow) way to clear the screen is to write 2000 spaces to it (for an 80x25 screen). Create a function called *clear()* that does this, and a *main()* program to test the function.

```
// clear.cpp
// clears screen by writing blank lines to it
#include <iostream.h>

void clear();               // prototype

void main()
   {
   clear();                 // clear the screen
   cout << "This message appears on an otherwise blank screen.";
   }

// clear()
// clears screen by writing 2000 spaces to it
void clear()
   {
   for(int j=0; j<2000; j++) // print a blank 2000 times
      cout << ' ';
   cout << endl;            // put cursor at beginning of line
   }
```

Exercise 2

Write a function that acts like the *getch()* library function, except that it returns 0 if the user presses the (ENTER) key. (This function can call *getch()* to get the character.) Like *getch()*, it should return any other character unchanged. Write a *main()* program that tests this function by using it in a loop. Note that it's easier to write the test condition for the loop with this function than it is *getch()*, since you don't need to test for equality with '\r', but only for truth (not zero).

```
// getachar.cpp
// places getch() in user-written function
#include <iostream.h>
#include <conio.h>                    // for getch()

char getachar();                      // prototype

void main()
   {
   char ch;

   while( ch=getachar() )             // get a character
     cout << ch;                      // display it
   }

// getachar()
// return character typed by user
char getachar()
   {
   char ch = getch();                 // get a character
   if( ch == '\r' )                   // if it's Enter,
     return 0;                        // return 0
   else                               // otherwise,
     return ch;                       // return the character
   }
```

Exercise 3

The FRACSTR exercise from the last chapter modelled stock prices, using a structure called *fracpri* to represent the three parts of the price: the whole number, the numerator of the fractional part, and the denominator of the fractional part.

Modify this program so that getting data from the user to put into the structure, and displaying the data from the structure, are handled by functions. You'll need to pass a structure variable to the function that displays the data, and return a structure from the function that gets the data from the user.

```
// fraction.cpp
// structure used to hold stock prices
#include <iostream.h>

struct fracpri                 // structure holds fractional prices
   {
   int whole;                  // whole number part of price
   int numer;                  // numerator (top) of fraction
   int denom;                  // denominator (bottom) of fraction
   };
```

```
void dispfrac(fracpri);      // prototypes
fracpri getfrac();

void main()
  {
  fracpri fp1, fp2;                // make two structures

  cout << "\nEnter first price: ";  // prices in fp1 and fp2
  fp1 = getfrac();
  cout << "\nEnter second price: ";
  fp2 = getfrac();
  cout << "\nFirst price is ";      // display fp1 and fp2
  dispfrac(fp1);
  cout << "\nSecond price is ";
  dispfrac(fp2);
  }

// dispfrac()
// displays fractional price, in form 37-1/8
void dispfrac(fracpri fp)
  {
  cout << fp.whole << "-"
       << fp.numer << "/"
       << fp.denom;
  }

// getfrac()
// function gets fractional price from user
// returns fracpri structure
fracpri getfrac()
  {
  fracpri temp;            // make a temporary structure
  char dummy;              // for hyphen and slash

  cin >> temp.whole;       // get whole number
  cin >> dummy;            // get hyphen
  cin >> temp.numer;       // get numerator
  cin >> dummy;            // get slash
  cin >> temp.denom;       // get denominator
  return temp;             // return temp structure
  }
```

Exercise 4

The data for a company's stock, shown in the newspaper each day, includes the number of shares traded, the closing or last price of the day, and the change in price from the day before. Create a structure that holds these three values. Use the *fracpri* structure from the FRACTION exercise in this chapter to hold the *last* and *change* prices. Use type *long int* to hold *sales*, the number of shares traded (which is the actual number divided by 100).

Write a *main()* program that creates at least two structures to hold stock data, asks the user for the data for the stocks, fills it in, and displays it. You'll need the functions used with the *fracpri* structure in the FRACTION exercise as well as the structure itself.

```cpp
// stocks.cpp
// uses structure to hold stock data
#include <iostream.h>

struct fracpri                  // structure holds fractional prices
   {
   int whole;                   // whole number part of price
   int numer;                   // numerator (top) of fraction
   int denom;                   // denominator (bottom) of fraction
   };

struct stock                    // structure holds stock data
   {
   long sales;                  // number of shares sold (div by 100)
   fracpri last;                // closing price
   fracpri chng;                // change from previous day
   };

void dispfrac(fracpri);         // prototypes
fracpri getfrac();
void dspstock(stock);
stock getstock();

void main()
   {
   stock stk1, stk2;                        // create two stocks

   cout << "\nEnter data for first stock";  // get data
   stk1 = getstock();
   cout << "\nEnter data for second stock";
   stk2 = getstock();
   cout << "\nFirst stock: ";               // display data
   dspstock(stk1);
   cout << "\nSecond stock: ";
   dspstock(stk2);
   }

// dspstock()
// displays data for one stock
void dspstock(stock s)
   {
   cout << "sales=" << s.sales;     // display sales
   cout << ", last=";               // display closing price
   dispfrac(s.last);
   cout << ", change=";             // display change
   dispfrac(s.chng);
   }
```

```
// getstock()
// get stock data from user,
// return data in stock structure
stock getstock()
   {
   stock temp;

   cout << "\n   Enter sales: ";          // get sales
   cin >> temp.sales;
   cout << "   Enter closing price";      // get closing price
   temp.last = getfrac();
   cout << "   Enter change";             // get change
   temp.chng = getfrac();
   return temp;                           // return stock struct
   }

// dispfrac()
// displays fractional price, in form 37-1/8
void dispfrac(fracpri fp)
   {
   cout << fp.whole << "-"                 // display whole number
       << fp.numer << "/"                  // display top of fract
       << fp.denom;                        // display bottom
   }

// getfrac()
// function gets fractional price from user
// returns price in fracpri structure
fracpri getfrac()
   {
   fracpri temp;  // make a temporary structure

   cout << "\n      Enter whole number part of price: ";
   cin >> temp.whole;
   cout << "      Enter top of fraction: ";
   cin >> temp.numer;
   cout << "      Enter bottom of fraction: ";
   cin >> temp.denom;
   return temp;
   }
```

Exercise 5

Combine the MAKENUMB and REMOTE exercises from Chapter 4 so the user can enter multidigit channel numbers. The MAKENUMB program should be made into a subroutine that is called from the modified REMOTE program at the appropriate point.

```
// remote2.cpp
// simulates TV remote-control channel-switcher
// accepts multidigit channel numbers
```

```
#include <iostream.h>
#include <conio.h>              // for getche()

enum boolean { false, true };
int makenumb(char);            // prototype

void main()
   {
   const int ESC = 27;             // ascii code for escape key
   int channel=2;                  // channel number
   char ch;                        // character typed by user

   cout << "\nchannel=" << channel << endl;
   while( (ch=getche()) != ESC)         // get the character
      {                                 // exit on escape key
      switch(ch)
         {
         case 'u': channel++; break;    // 'u' key; go up
         case 'd': channel--; break;    // 'd' key; go down
         default:                       // might be number
            if( ch>47 && ch<58 )        // if digit,
               channel = makenumb(ch);  // get complete number
            else                        // otherwise,
               cout << "\nError";       // error
         }                              // display channel
      cout << "\nchannel=" << channel << endl;
      }
   }

// makenumb()
// makes a number out of digits
int makenumb(char c)           // enter with first digit
   {
   int numb = c-48;            // put first digit in number

   while( true )              // loop ends with break
      {
      c=getche();              // get next char from user
      if( c<48 || c>57 )       // if it's not a digit
         break;                // exit loop
      numb *= 10;              // shift number one place left
      numb += c-48;            // put digit in one's column
      }
   return(numb);               // return final number
   }
```

Exercise 6

To the FRACTION exercise in this chapter, add a function that adds two fractions of type *fracint*. Adding two fractions involves first representing both fractions with a common denominator, and then adding the numerators, as you learned in grade school.

```cpp
//addfracs.cpp
// adds two fraction structures
#include <iostream.h>

struct fracpri                 // structure holds fractional prices
   {
   int whole;                  // whole number part of price
   int numer;                  // numerator (top) of fraction
   int denom;                  // denominator (bottom) of fraction
   };

void dispfrac(fracpri);                     // prototypes
fracpri getfrac();
fracpri addfracs(fracpri, fracpri);

void main()
   {
   fracpri fp1, fp2, fp3;                   // make three structures

   cout << "\n\nEnter first price: ";       // prices in fp1 and fp2
   fp1 = getfrac();
   cout << "Enter second price: ";
   fp2 = getfrac();

   fp3 = addfracs(fp1, fp2);                // fp3 = fp1 and fp2

   cout << "\nSum of fp1 and fp2 is ";
   dispfrac(fp3);
   }

// dispfrac()
// displays fractional price, in form 37-1/8
void dispfrac(fracpri fp)
   {
   cout << fp.whole;                  // print whole number
   if( fp.numer )                     // if not 0, print fraction
      cout << "-" << fp.numer << "/" << fp.denom;
   }

// getfrac()
// function gets fractional price from user
// returns fracpri structure
fracpri getfrac()
   {
   fracpri temp;         // make a temporary structure
   char dummy;           // for hyphen and slash

   cin >> temp.whole;         // get whole number
   cin >> dummy;              // get hyphen
   cin >> temp.numer;         // get numerator
   cin >> dummy;              // get slash
   cin >> temp.denom;         // get denominator
   return temp;               // return temp structure
   }
```

```
// addfracs()
// adds two fractions sent as arguments, returns sum
// (for comments, assume f1 = 7-2/3, f2 = 11-3/4)
fracpri addfracs(fracpri f1, fracpri f2)
   {
   fracpri temp;
   int newnum1, newnum2, newnumer, carry;

   temp.whole = f1.whole + f2.whole;        // 18 = 7 + 11
   temp.denom = f1.denom * f2.denom;        // 12 = 3 * 4
   newnum1 = f1.numer * f2.denom;           // 8 = 2 * 4
   newnum2 = f2.numer * f1.denom;           // 9 = 3 * 3
   newnumer = newnum1 + newnum2;            // 17 = 8 + 9
   carry = newnumer / temp.denom;           // 1 = 17 / 12
   temp.whole += carry;                     // 19 = 18 + 1
   temp.numer = newnumer % temp.denom;      // 5 = 17 % 12
   return temp;                             // return 19-5/12
   }
```

Exercise 7

Write a function called *fraclow()* that reduces a fraction to lowest terms (that is, it changes 20/32 to 5/8). You can do this by dividing both numerator and denominator by their greatest common divisor, which can be calculated using the algorithm of the GCD exercise from Chapter 4.

Use reference arguments, so that the original fraction in the calling program is reduced to lowest terms. Write a *main()* program that allows the user to input values for a fraction, which is then stored, reduced to lowest terms by calling *fraclow()*, and displayed.

Before beginning Euclid's algorithm, you might want to check that the user didn't enter a 0 for the numerator, since the algorithm will cycle endlessly in this case. If the numerator is 0, set the fraction to 0/1.

```
// fraclow.cpp
// reduces fraction to lowest terms
#include <iostream.h>

void fraclow(long& numerator, long& denominator);      // prototype

void main()
   {
   long numerator, denominator;
   char dummy;                              // for slash

   cout << "\nEnter fraction: (format 20/32): ";
   cin >> numerator >> dummy >> denominator;    // get fraction
   fraclow(numerator, denominator);             // to lowest terms
   cout << "In lowest terms that's "            // display
        << numerator << '/' << denominator;
   }
```

```
// fraclow()
// reduces fraction to lowest terms, uses reference arguments
void fraclow(long& numer, long& denom)
   {
   if( numer == 0 )                   // check for special case of
     { denom=1; return; }             // zero numerator

   long first=numer;                  // find greatest common divisor
   long second=denom;                 // of numerator and denominator
   long temp;                         // (compute with local vars)

   while( first != second )           // done when they're equal
     {
     if( first < second )             // if first isn't bigger,
       {
       temp=first;                    // swap them
       first=second;
       second=temp;
       }
     first -= second;                 // first=first-second
     }
                                      // first is now gcd
   numer /= first;                    // divide both numer and denom
   denom /= first;                    // by gcd to get lowest terms
   }
```

CHAPTER 7
Exercise 1

Convert the structure from the TIMESTRC example of Chapter 5 to an object. Member functions should display the time and get the time from the user.

```
// timclass.cpp
// models time data type using class
#include <iostream.h>

class time
   {
   private:
     int hrs;
     int mins;
     int secs;
   public:
     void gettime()              // get time from user
       {
       char dummy;
       cout << "\nEnter time (format 12:12:59): ";
       cin >> hrs >> dummy >> mins >> dummy >> secs;
       }
     void disptime()             // display time (format 12:59:59)
```

```
    {
    cout << hrs << ":" << mins << ":" << secs;
    }
  };

void main()
  {
  time t1, t2;                    // create two objects of class time

  cout << "\nTime number 1: ";      // get two times from user
  t1.gettime();
  cout << "\nTime number 2: ";
  t2.gettime();

  cout << "\nTime number 1 is ";    // display two times
  t1.disptime();
  cout << "\nTime number 2 is ";
  t2.disptime();
  }
```

Exercise 2

Add a constructor to the *time* class in exercise TIMCLASS so that objects of this class can be initialized when they are created, using statements of the form

time t1(10,59,59);

```
// timconst.cpp
// adds constructor to time class
#include <iostream.h>

class time
  {
  private:
    int hrs;
    int mins;
    int secs;
  public:
    time()                         // constructor
      { }
    time(int h, int m, int s)      // constructor initializes time
        { hrs=h; mins=m; secs=s; }
    void gettime()                 // get time from user
        {
        char dummy;
        cout << "\nEnter time (format 12:12:59): ";
        cin >> hrs >> dummy >> mins >> dummy >> secs;
        }
    void disptime()              // display time (format 12:59:59)
        {
        cout << hrs << ":" << mins << ":" << secs;
        }
  };
```

```
void main()
  {
  time t1;              // create a time but don't initialize it
  time t2(10,33,45); // create another time and initialize it

  cout << "\nTime number 1: ";     // get time 1 from user
  t1.gettime();

  cout << "\nTime number 1 is ";    // display both times
  t1.disptime();
  cout << "\nTime number 2 is ";
  t2.disptime();
  }
```

Exercise 3

Use a class to represent the TV remote control unit from the REMOTE2 exercise in Chapter 6. It should have the same capabilities, but encapsulate the channel number as data, and the input and display routines as member functions. It should also have a constructor that initializes each channel object to channel 2. (Note: the member function that gets input cannot be inline if it incorporates a *switch* statement.)

```
// remclass.cpp
// uses class to simulate TV remote-control channel-switcher
#include <iostream.h>
#include <conio.h>            // for getche()

enum boolean { false, true };
int makenumb(char);          // prototype

class remote
  {
  private:
    int channel;             // channel number
  public:
    remote()                 // initialize channel to 2
      { channel = 2; }
    void displaychan()       // display current channel
      { cout << "\nchannel=" << channel << endl; }
    int getchan();           // get user input
  };

int remote::getchan()
  {
  const int ESC = 27;        // ascii code for escape key
  char ch;                   // character typed by user

  ch=getche();               // get the character
  if( ch == ESC)             // return 0 if it's ESC key
    return 0;
```

```
    switch(ch)
      {
      case 'u': channel++; break;        // 'u' key; go up
      case 'd': channel--; break;        // 'd' key; go down
      default:                           // might be number
        if( ch>47 && ch<58 )             // if digit,
          channel = makenumb(ch);        // get complete number
        else                             // otherwise,
          cout << "\nError";             // error
      }
    return 1;                            // return non-zero
    }

void main()
  {
  remote rem;                    // create a remote object

  cout << endl << endl;          // skip two lines
                                 // get channel from user
  while( rem.getchan() )         // cycle until zero
    rem.displaychan();           // display channel
  }

// makenumb()
// makes a number out of digits
int makenumb(char c)             // enter with first digit
  {
  int numb = c-48;               // put first digit in number

  while( true )                  // loop ends with break
    {
    c=getche();                  // get next char from user
    if( c<48 || c>57 )           // if it's not a digit
      break;                     // exit loop
    numb *= 10;                  // shift number one place left
    numb += c-48;                // put digit in one's column
    }
  return(numb);                  // return final number
  }
```

Exercise 4

Create a *fracint* class based on the *fracint* structure from the FRACTION example in Chapter 6. Give it the same capabilities called for in that program. A fraction should be able to display itself, and get a value for itself from the user.

```
// fraclass.cpp
// class used to hold stock prices
#include <iostream.h>

class fracpri                    // class for fractional prices
```

```
    {
    private:
       int whole;             // whole number part of price
       int numer;             // numerator (top) of fraction
       int denom;             // denominator (bottom) of fraction
    public:
       void dispfrac()        // display fraction (format 31-3/8)
          {
          cout << whole << "-"
               << numer << "/"
               << denom;
          }
       void getfrac()         // get fraction from user
          {
          char dummy;         // for hyphen and slash

          cin >> whole;       // whole number
          cin >> dummy;       // hyphen
          cin >> numer;       // top part of fraction
          cin >> dummy;       // slash
          cin >> denom;       // bottom part of fraction
          }
    };

void main()
    {
    fracpri fp1, fp2;                    // make two objects

    cout << "\nEnter first price: ";  // prices in fp1 and fp2
    fp1.getfrac();
    cout << "\nEnter second price: ";
    fp2.getfrac();
    cout << "\nFirst price is ";       // display fp1 and fp2
    fp1.dispfrac();
    cout << "\nSecond price is ";
    fp2.dispfrac();
    }
```

Exercise 5

Use a class to represent the NIM game in the NIM example of Chapter 4. It should hold the number of counters remaining as private data, and have member functions to get the human's move and display the machine move. The machine-move routine can return the number of sticks remaining so the *main()* program can issue appropriate messages, such as *you lose* if there is only one stick remaining.

```
// nimclass.cpp
// plays the game of nim against a human player
#include <iostream.h>
```

```
class nim                     // class holds state of nim
   {
   private:
      int sticks;             // number of sticks left
   public:
      nim()                   // constructor
         {
         sticks = 25;         // initialize to 25 sticks
         }
      void humanmove()        // get human move
         {
         int human;
         cout << "\nThere are " << sticks << " sticks.";
         cout << "\nYou can take 1, 2 or 3. Enter choice: ";
         cin >> human;        // get human move
         sticks -= human;     // subtract it from total
         }
      int machinemove()       // calculuate machine move
         {
         int machine;
         machine = (sticks+3) % 4;  // calculate machine move
         cout << "There are " << sticks << " sticks.";
         cout << "\nI'll take " << machine << " stick(s).";
         sticks -= machine;   // subtract it from total
         return sticks;       // return remaining sticks
         }
   };

void main()
   {
   nim n;                     // make object n of class nim

   do
      {
      n.humanmove();          // get human move
      } while( n.machinemove() != 1 );  // quit if 1 stick left
   cout << "\nThere is 1 stick left, and you must take it."
      << " You lose.";
   }
```

Exercise 6

Use a class to represent an object of type *target* that represents a radar target's position in terms of range and bearing, as seen in the RADAR example of Chapter 5. Member functions should display the current target and alter its bearing if the ship turns.

```
// rbclass.cpp
// class models range and bearing of radar targets
#include <iostream.h>

class target
   {
```

```
   private:
     float range;  // miles from our location
     int bearing;  // relative to our heading, from 0 to 360
   public:
     target(float ra, int be)      // initialize target info
        { range=ra; bearing=be; }
     void display()                // display target info
        {
        cout << range << " miles, "
           << bearing << " degrees.";
        }
     void rotate(int turn)         // rotate target
        {
        bearing -= turn;           // subtract turn from bearing
        if(bearing < 0)            // if result is negative,
           bearing += 360;         // add 360 for positive bearing
        if(bearing >=360)          // if result is 360 or more,
           bearing -= 360;         // subtract 360
        }
   };

void main()
   {                         // initialize targets
   target t1(10.0, 90);      // 10 miles away, on our right
   target t2(4.5, 0);        // 4.5 miles away, straight ahead
   int turn = 10;            // (can't start at 0 degrees)

   cout << endl << endl;
   while( turn != 0 )        // exit if no turn
      {
      cout << "\nTarget t1: ";    // display targets'
      t1.display();               // range and bearing
      cout << "\nTarget t2: ";
      t2.display();

      cout << "\nEnter number of degrees to turn "
         << "(negative numbers indicate left turn): ";
      cin >> turn;                // get degrees to turn
      t1.rotate(turn);           // tell the targets to rotate
      t2.rotate(turn);
      }
   }
```

Exercise 7

Extend the *fracint* class in the FRACLASS example in this chapter so that two fractions can be added together. That is, a member function will add two fractions given it as arguments, and set itself to the sum. The addition routine from the ADDFRACS example in Chapter 6 can be used. Another member function should reduce the resulting fraction to lowest terms. You can use the *fraclow()* function from the FRACLOW exercise of Chapter 6 to do this. Note, however, that as a member function, the new *fraclow()* need not take any arguments, reference or otherwise.

```cpp
// fracladd.cpp
// add two fractions, reduce result to lowest terms
#include <iostream.h>

class fracpri                   // class for fractional prices
   {
   private:
      int whole;                // whole number part of price
      int numer;                // numerator (top) of fraction
      int denom;                // denominator (bottom) of fraction
   public:
      void dispfrac()           // display fraction (format 31-3/8)
         {
         cout << whole << "-"
              << numer << "/"
              << denom;
         }
      void getfrac()            // get fraction from user
         {
         char dummy;            // for hyphen and slash
         cin >> whole >> dummy >> numer >> dummy >> denom;
         }
      void addfracs(fracpri, fracpri);     // add two fractions
      void fraclow();           // reduce ourself to lowest terms
   };

// addfracs()
// member function adds two fractional prices
void fracpri::addfracs(fracpri f1, fracpri f2)  // this=f1+f2
   {
   int newnum1, newnum2, newnumer, carry;

   whole = f1.whole + f2.whole;        // find new whole number
   denom = f1.denom * f2.denom;        // find new denominator
   newnum1 = f1.numer * f2.denom;      // cross multiply
   newnum2 = f2.numer * f1.denom;
   newnumer = newnum1 + newnum2;       // add the new numerators
   carry = newnumer / denom;           // find how much to carry
   whole += carry;                     // add to whole number part
   numer = newnumer % denom;  // find new numerator
   }

// fraclow()
// member function reduces fraction to lowest terms
void fracpri::fraclow()
   {
   if( numer == 0 )            // check for special case of
      { denom=1; return; }     // zero numerator

   long first=numer;           // find greatest common divisor
```

```
   long second=denom;        // of numerator and denominator
   long temp;                // (compute with local vars)

   while( first != second )  // done when they're equal
      {
      if( first < second )   // if first isn't bigger,
         {
         temp=first;         // swap them
         first=second;
         second=temp;
         }
      first -= second;       // first=first-second
      }                      // first is now gcd
   numer /= first;           // divide both numer and denom
   denom /= first;           // by gcd to get lowest terms
   }

void main()
   {
   fracpri fp1, fp2, fp3;    // make three objects

   cout << "\n\nEnter first price: ";      // get prices for fp1, fp2
   fp1.getfrac();
   cout << "Enter second price: ";
   fp2.getfrac();

   fp3.addfracs(fp1, fp2);   // fp3 = fp1 + fp2;

   fp3.fraclow();            // fp3 to lowest terms
   cout << "Sum is ";        // display fp3
   fp3.dispfrac();
   }
```

CHAPTER 8
Exercise 1

Write a function *getmax()* that finds the maximum value in an array of integers passed to it as an argument. (The number of valid elements in the array may be passed as the second argument.)

A *main()* program should first fill an array with test scores entered by the user, then call *getmax()* to find the highest score, and finally display this score.

```
// scores.cpp
// find highest score from array of scores
#include <iostream.h>

int getmax(int[], int);
const int SIZE = 100;        // size of array
```

```
void main()
  {
  int scores[SIZE];        // array of scores
  int sc;                  // score entered by user
  int j=0;                 // array index

  cout << endl;
  while(1)
    {
    cout << "Enter score: ";
    cin  >> sc;            // get a score
    if( sc < 0 )           // if negative entry,
      break;               // no more entries
    scores[j++] = sc;      // put entry in array
    }
  int m = getmax(scores, j);// return maximum score
  cout << "\nMaximum score is " << m;
  }

// getmax()
// function to find maximum score
int getmax(int arr[], int n)
  {
  int max=0;               // holds maximum value
  int k;                   // array index

  for(k=0; k<n; k++)       // if any array element
    if( arr[k] > max )     // is greater than max,
      max = arr[k];        // max becomes that element
  return max;
  }
```

Exercise 2

Write a function called *compstr()* that compares two strings sent to it as arguments. Use a character-by-character comparison to determine if the strings match. Return a 1 if the strings are the same, and a 0 if they are different.

Write a *main()* program that tests this function by inviting the user to compare two strings. You can use the *cin.gets(str, MAX)* function to get the string; this enables you to read strings with imbedded blanks. Unfortunately, this function leaves a delimiter in the *istream* after use, so insert *cin.ignore()* between calls to *cin.gets()* to get rid of the delimiter.

```
// compstr.cpp
// function compares two strings passed as arrays
#include <iostream.h>
#include <string.h>          // for strlen(), etc.

const int MAX = 80;          // maximum length of words
```

```
int compstr(char string1[], char string2[]);      // prototype

void main()
   {
   char s1[MAX], s2[MAX];

   cout << "\nEnter first string:  ";
   cin.get(s1, MAX);
   cin.ignore();              // clear istream

   cout << "Enter second string: ";
   cin.get(s2, MAX);
   if( compstr(s1, s2) )
      cout << "These strings are the same.";
   else
      cout << "These strings are different.";
   }

// compstr.cpp
// compares two strings passed as arguments
// returns 0 if different, 1 if the same
int compstr(char s1[], char s2[])
   {
   int j;                     // loop variable
   int len1 = strlen(s1);     // get string lengths
   int len2 = strlen(s2);

   if( len1 != len2 )         // if different lengths,
      return 0;               // strings not the same
   for(j=0; j<len1; j++)      // step through characters
      if( s1[j] != s2[j] )    // if any mismatch,
         return 0;            // strings not the same
   return 1;                  // otherwise they are the same
   }
```

Exercise 3

Create a class of addresses called *address*. There should be three items of data in this class: a string holding the street number and name, a string holding the city and state, and a long integer holding the zip code. A member function *putaddr()* should display the address, and a member function *getaddr()* should prompt the user to type in a new address.

Write a *main()* program that creates an array of *address* objects, prompts the user to enter as many addresses as desired, and then displays all the addresses.

```
// addrarr.cpp
// create an array of address objects
#include <iostream.h>
#include <conio.h>              // for getche()

const int MAX = 80;            // length of input buffer
```

```
class address
   {
   private:
      char street[MAX];        // street number and name
      char city[MAX];          // city and state
      long zip;                // zip code
   public:
      void putaddr()           // display address
         {
         cout << "\n   " << street
              << "\n   " << city
              << "  " << zip;
         }
      void getaddr()           // get address from user
         {
         cout << "\n   Enter street name and number: ";
         cin.get(street, MAX);
         cin.ignore();         // clear istream
         cout << "   Enter city and state: ";
         cin.get(city, MAX);
         cout << "   Enter zip code: ";
         cin >> zip;
         }
   };

void main()
   {
   address adlist[100];        // array of 100 address objects
   int j=0;                    // set to start of array
   char ch;                    // for user choice

   do
      {
      cout << "\nEnter address number " << j+1;
      adlist[j++].getaddr(); // get address, put it in array
      cout << "Input another (y/n)? ";
      ch = getche();
      cin.ignore();           // clear istream
      }
   while( ch == 'y' );        // cycle until user types 'n'

   cout << "\n\nAddress list:";
   for(int k=0; k<j; k++)     // display array of addresses
      {
      cout << "\n\nAdress number " << k+1;
      adlist[k].putaddr();
      }
   }
```

Exercise 4

Modify the FRACLADD exercise from Chapter 7 so that you can store objects of type *fracpri* in an array. Get a series of fractions from the user, and store them in the array. Then total the contents of the array, using the *addfracs()* member function and keeping a running total. Finally, display this result.

```
// fracarr.cpp
// adds elements in array of fraction objects
#include <iostream.h>
#include <conio.h>          // for getche()

class fracpri                // class for fractional prices
   {
   private:
     int whole;              // whole number part of price
     int numer;              // numerator (top) of fraction
     int denom;              // denominator (bottom) of fraction
   public:
     fracpri()               // initialize to 0 (except denom!)
       { whole=numer=0; denom=1; }
     void dispfrac()         // display fraction (format 31-3/8)
       {
       cout << whole << "-" << numer << "/" << denom;
       }
     void getfrac()          // get fraction from user
       {
       char dummy;           // for hyphen and slash
       cin >> whole >> dummy >> numer >> dummy >> denom;
       }
     void addfracs(fracpri, fracpri);  // add two fractions
     void fraclow();         // reduce ourself to lowest terms
   };

void fracpri::addfracs(fracpri f1, fracpri f2)  // add fracs
   {
   int newnum1, newnum2, newnumer, carry;

   whole = f1.whole + f2.whole;     // find new whole number
   denom = f1.denom * f2.denom;     // find new denominator
   newnum1 = f1.numer * f2.denom;   // cross multiply
   newnum2 = f2.numer * f1.denom;
   newnumer = newnum1 + newnum2;    // add the new numerators
   carry = newnumer / denom;        // find how much to carry
   whole += carry;                  // add to whole number part
   numer = newnumer % denom;        // find new numerator
   }

void fracpri::fraclow()     // reduce to lowest terms
   {
   if( numer == 0 )         // check for special case of
     { denom=1; return; }   // zero numerator

   long first=numer;        // find greatest common divisor
   long second=denom;       // of numerator and denominator
   long temp;               // (compute with local vars)
```

```
  while( first != second )   // done when they're equal
    {
    if( first < second )     // if first isn't bigger,
      { temp=first; first=second; second=temp; }      // swap
    first -= second;         // first=first-second
    }                        // first is now gcd
    numer /= first;          // divide both numer and denom
    denom /= first;          // by gcd to get lowest terms
  }

void main()
  {
  fracpri fracarr[100];      // make array of fractions
  fracpri total;             // total amount (set to 0)
  int j = 0;                 // array index

  do
    {
    cout << "\nEnter price (format 31-3/8): ";
    fracarr[j++].getfrac();        // get price, put in array
    cout << "   Do another (y/n)? ";
    } while( getche() == 'y' );    // repeat until 'n'

  for(int k=0; k<j; k++)           // total=total+fracarr[k];
    total.addfracs(total, fracarr[k]);
  total.fraclow();                 // total to lowest terms
  cout << "\nTotal is ";           // display total
  total.dispfrac();
  }
```

Exercise 5

A queue is like a stack except that when you take an item out of a queue, it is the first item that was placed in the queue, rather than the last. It's like the line at the checkout counter in the supermarket: it operates on a first in, first out (FIFO) basis, as opposed to a stack, which operates on a last in, first out (LIFO) basis.

Create a class called *Queue* that models a queue, using an array to hold the data, which can consist of integers (assumed to be positive). This is slightly more complicated than a stack, because you need two indexes into the array: *head* points to the place where the next input will be placed, and *tail* points to the place where the next output will be taken. Both these indices move forward through the ARRAY. When either one reaches the end of the array, it must be reset to the beginning. This gives the effect of a circular buffer. If the tail catches the head it should return an error code (such as a minus number) to indicate there is no more data to read.

Write a *main()* program to test this class by letting the user choose whether to put an item in the queue, or take it out. This way the user can experiment with the queue, seeing how it works under different circumstances. Try putting in a few items, then taking them out. When you have put in MAX items (even if some have been taken out) you've reached the end of the buffer and the head pointer goes back to the beginning.

Don't worry about such unusual cases as when the head catches up with itself and writes over data that has not yet been read by the tail.

```cpp
// queue.cpp
// models a queue, using an array
#include <iostream.h>
#include <process.h>          // for exit()
#include <conio.h>            // for getche()

const int MAX = 10;           // size of array for queue
const int ESC = 27;           // ascii code for 'Esc' key

class Queue                   // class models FIFO queue
   {
   private:
      int queue[MAX];         // array holds queue
      int head;               // array index for input
      int tail;               // array index for output
   public:
      Queue()                 // constructor
         {
         head=tail=0;         // initialize head and tail
         }
      void put(int var)       // put item in queue
         {
         queue[head++] = var; // put item in array
         if( head >= MAX )    // if head past end of array,
            head = 0;         // reset it to beginning
         }
      int get()               // take item from queue
         {
         if( tail >= MAX )    // if tail past end of array,
            tail = 0;         // reset it to beginning
         if( tail == head )   // if tail catches head,
            return(-1);       // return "error code"
         return queue[tail++];        // normally, return item at tail
         }
   };

void main()
   {
   Queue Q;                             // make a queue
   int item;                            // item to put in queue
```

```
    char choice;                      // user's choice: get or put

  while(1)
    {
    cout << "\nEnter p to put item in queue, g to get an item: ";
    choice = getche();
    switch(choice)
      {
    case 'p':
      cout << "\nEnter item to put in queue: ";
      cin >> item;
      Q.put(item);
      break;
    case 'g':
      cout << "\nItem is " << Q.get();
      break;
    case ESC:
      exit(1);
    default:
      cout << "\nType 'p' or 'g'";
      }
    }
  }
```

CHAPTER 9
Exercise 1

Sometimes it's necessary to bump a counter; that is, increase it by a number larger than 1. This might represent a tour-group arriving all at once in a bank teller's line, rather than individual people arriving.

Modify the COUNTPP3 example from Chapter 9 so that it adds an integer value to a *Counter* object. Overload the '+' operator so you can do this with an expression like

$$c2 = c1 + 9;$$

where *c1* and *c2* are *Counter* objects. The *Counter* object should not modify its own value; only that of the unnamed temporary object that it returns.

```
// countadd.cpp
// add integer to count variable with '+' operator
#include <iostream.h>

class Counter
  {
  private:
    unsigned int count;                 // count
  public:
    Counter()      { count = 0; }       // constructor  no args
```

```
    Counter(int c)   { count = c; }        // constructor, one arg
    int get_count()  { return count; }     // return count

    Counter operator + (int i)             // add integer to Count
       {
       return Counter(count+i);            // return temp Count
       }                                   // initialized to sum
   };

void main()
   {
   Counter c1(2), c2;                      // c1=2, c2=0

   cout << "\nc1=" << c1.get_count();      // display
   cout << "\nc2=" << c2.get_count();

   c2 = c1 + 17;                           // add 17 to c1,
                                           // put result in c2
   cout << "\nc1=" << c1.get_count();      // display: c1=2
   cout << "\nc2=" << c2.get_count();      // c2=19
   }
```

Exercise 2

Suppose you want to know whether two *Counter* objects are equal. Overload the '==' operator so you can compare two *Counters* with an expression like

$$if(c1 == c2)$$

Write a *main()* program to test this operator by creating several *Counter* objects with the same and different values, and comparing them in an *if* expression.

```
// countcmp.cpp
// overload '==' operator to compare two counters
#include <iostream.h>

enum boolean { false, true };

class Counter
   {
   private:
     unsigned int count;               // count
   public:
     Counter()        { count = 0; }        // constructor  no args
     Counter(int c)   { count = c; }        // constructor, one arg
     int get_count()  { return count; }     // return count

     boolean operator == (Counter c)        // compare two Counters
        {
        if( count == c.count )              // if count data is
```

```
        return true;              // equal, then the
      else                        // Counters are equal
        return false;
      }
  };

void main()
  {
  Counter c1(27), c2(27), c3(33);     // initialize
  cout << "\nc1=" << c1.get_count();
  cout << "\nc2=" << c2.get_count();
  cout << "\nc3=" << c3.get_count();

  if( c1 == c2 )
    cout << "\nc1 equals c2";
  else
    cout << "\nc1 not equal to c2";

  if( c2 == c3 )
    cout << "\nc2 equals c3";
  else
    cout << "\nc2 not equal to c3";
  }
```

Exercise 3

Modify the FRACLADD exercise of Chapter 7 so that the overloaded '+' operator is used in the *main()* part of the program to add two fractions (*fracpri* objects). That is, the statement

$$fp3 = fp1 + fp2;$$

should add the fractions *fp1* and *fp2* and assign the result to *fp3*. You may need to add a three-argument constructor to the *fracpri* class so that the '+' operator can create a temporary *fracpri* object whose value it can return.

```
// fracplus.cpp
// overloads '+' operator to add two fractions
#include <iostream.h>

class fracpri                 // class for fractional prices
  {
  private:
    int whole;                // whole number part of price
    int numer;                // numerator (top) of fraction
    int denom;                // denominator (bottom) of fraction
  public:
    fracpri()                          // constructor, no args
      { whole=numer=0; denom=1; }
    fracpri(int w, int n, int d)    // constructor, 3 args
      { whole=w, numer=n, denom=d; }
```

```
   void dispfrac()            // display fraction (format 31-3/8)
      {
      cout << whole << "-"
           << numer << "/"
           << denom;
      }
   void getfrac()             // get fraction from user
      {
      char dummy;             // for hyphen and slash
      cin >> whole >> dummy >> numer >> dummy >> denom;
      }
   fracpri operator + (fracpri);  // add two fractions
   void fraclow();            // reduce ourself to lowest terms
   };

// overloaded '+' operator adds this fraction to argument,
// returns the sum as a fraction
fracpri fracpri::operator + (fracpri farg)        // ans=this+farg
   {
   int w, d, n;                 // three parts of temp frac
   int newnum1, newnum2, newnumer, carry;

   w = whole + farg.whole;        // find new whole number
   d = denom * farg.denom;        // find new denominator
   newnum1 = numer * farg.denom;  // cross multiply
   newnum2 = farg.numer * denom;
   newnumer = newnum1 + newnum2;  // add the new numerators
   carry = newnumer / d;          // find how much to carry
   w += carry;                    // add to whole number part
   n = newnumer % d;              // find new numerator
   return fracpri(w, n, d);       // return temporary fraction
   }

// fraclow()
// member function reduces this fraction to lowest terms
void fracpri::fraclow()
   {
   if( numer == 0 )          // check for special case of
      { denom=1; return; }   // zero numerator

   long first=numer;         // find greatest common divisor
   long second=denom;        // of numerator and denominator
   long temp;                // (compute with local vars)

   while( first != second )  // done when they're equal
      {
      if( first < second )   // if first isn't bigger,
      { temp=first; first=second; second=temp; } // swap'em
      first -= second;       // first=first-second
      }                      // first is now gcd
      numer /= first;        // divide both numer and denom
      denom /= first;        // by gcd to get lowest terms
   }
```

```
void main()
  {
  fracpri fp1, fp2, fp3;              // make three objects

  cout << "\nEnter first price: ";  // get prices for fp1, fp2
  fp1.getfrac();
  cout << "Enter second price: ";
  fp2.getfrac();

  fp3 = fp1 + fp2;            // add fp1 and fp2
                             //    put result in fp3
  fp3.fraclow();             // set fp3 to lowest terms
  cout << "Sum is ";         // display fp3
  fp3.dispfrac();
  }
```

Exercise 4

Modify the RBCLASS exercise of Chapter 7 so that the overloaded '∗' operator is used in the *main()* part of the program to rotate a target. That is the statement

t1 ∗ *turn;*

should rotate the target *t1* by *turn* degrees (remember that a right turn causes the target to rotate left).

```
// rbtimes.cpp
// overloads '*' operator to rotate target
#include <iostream.h>

class target
  {
  private:
    float range;              // miles from our location
    int bearing;              // relative to our heading, from 0 to 360
  public:
    target(float ra, int be)  // initialize target info
      { range=ra; bearing=be; }
    void display()            // display target info
      {
      cout << range << " miles, "
           << bearing << " degrees.";
      }
    void operator * (int turn)  // rotate target
      {
      bearing -= turn;          // subtract turn from bearing
      if(bearing < 0)           // if result is negative,
        bearing += 360;         // add 360 for positive bearing
      if(bearing >=360)         // if result is 360 or more,
        bearing -= 360;         // subtract 360
```

```
      }
  };
void main()
  {                            // initialize targets
  target t1(10.0, 90);         // 10 miles away, on our right
  target t2(4.5, 0);           // 4.5 miles away, straight ahead
  int turn = 10;               // (can't start at 0 degrees)

  cout << endl << endl;
  while( turn != 0 )           // exit if no turn
     {
     cout << "\nTarget t1: ";       // display targets'
     t1.display();                  // range and bearing
     cout << "\nTarget t2: ";
     t2.display();

     cout << "\nEnter number of degrees to turn "
          << "(negative numbers indicate left turn): ";
     cin >> turn;              // get degrees to turn
     t1 * turn;                // tell the targets to rotate
     t2 * turn;
     }
  }
```

Exercise 5

Modify the FRACPLUS exercise from this chapter so that it compares two fractions using the overloaded '<' operator. That is, the expression

   fp1 < fp2

should evaluate to 1 (true) if *fp1* is numerically less than *fp2*, and to 0 otherwise. Test this operator with a *main()* program that lets the user type in two fractions, and then reports whether the first is smaller than the second.

```
// fracomp.cpp
// overloads '<' operator to compare two fractions
#include <iostream.h>

enum boolean { false, true };

class fracpri                 // class for fractional prices
  {
  private:
    int whole;                // whole number part of price
    int numer;                // numerator (top) of fraction
    int denom;                // denominator (bottom) of fraction
  public:
    void dispfrac()           // display fraction (format 31-3/8)
       {
```

```
         cout << whole << "-"
              << numer << "/"
              << denom;
         }
      void getfrac()            // get fraction from user
         {
         char dummy;            // for hyphen and slash
         cin >> whole >> dummy >> numer >> dummy >> denom;
         }
      boolean operator < (fracpri);  // compare two fractions
   };

// overloaded '<' operator compares this fraction with argument
// returns 1 if this is less than arg, 0 if not less than
// (assumes fractions are in lowest terms)
boolean fracpri::operator < (fracpri farg)
   {
   if( whole < farg.whole )  // if whole number less,
      return 1;              // then fraction irrelevent
   if( whole > farg.whole )  // if whole number greater,
      return 0;              // then fraction irrelevent
                             // whole numbers are equal
   int newnum1 = numer * farg.denom; // cross multiply
   int newnum2 = farg.numer * denom;
   if( newnum1 < newnum2 )   // compare new numerators
      return 1;              // first is less
   else
      return 0;              // second is less or equal
   }

void main()
   {
   fracpri fp1, fp2;         // make two fractions

   cout << "\nEnter first price: "; // get prices for fp1, fp2
   fp1.getfrac();
   cout << "Enter second price: ";
   fp2.getfrac();

   if( fp1 < fp2 )           // compare the fractions
      cout << "First price is less than second.";
   else
      cout << "First price not less than second.";
   }
```

Exercise 6

Modify the *fracpri* class so it can convert floating point (decimal) numbers into fractions, and fractions into floating point numbers. That is, it should figure out that 7.3 is 7-9/64, and that 2-7/8 is 2.875.

You can assume that the denominator of a fraction need never be smaller than 64. Thus any decimal number evaluates to some number of sixty-fourths, reduced to lowest terms if necessary.

```cpp
// fraconv.cpp
// converts fractions to real numbers and back again
#include <iostream.h>

void fraclow(int&, int&);    // prototype (not a member func)

class fracpri                // class for fractional prices
   {
   private:
      int whole;             // whole number part of price
      int numer;             // numerator (top) of fraction
      int denom;             // denominator (bottom) of fraction
   public:
      fracpri()                      // constructor, no args
         { whole=numer=0; denom=1; }
      fracpri(float flo)             // constructor, 1 arg
         {                           //   (float to fraction)
         flo += 0.0078125;           // adjust: add 1/128
         whole = int(flo);           // whole is integer part
         float flofrac = flo - whole; // frac is what's left
         numer = flofrac * 64;       // how many 64ths?
         denom = 64;                 // denominator always 64
         fraclow(numer, denom);      // to lowest terms
         }
      void dispfrac()        // display fraction (format 31-3/8)
         {
         cout << whole << "-" << numer << "/" << denom;
         }
      void getfrac()         // get fraction from user
         {
         char dummy;         // for hyphen and slash
         cin >> whole >> dummy >> numer >> dummy >> denom;
         }
      operator float()       // conversion function
         {                   //   (fraction to float)
         return whole + float(numer)/denom;
         }
   };

// fraclow()
// function reduces fraction to lowest terms (not a member func)
void fraclow(int& numer, int& denom)
   {
   if( numer == 0 )          // check for special case of
      { denom=1; return; }   // zero numerator

   long first=numer;         // find greatest common divisor
   long second=denom;        // of numerator and denominator
```

```
    long temp;                  // (compute with local vars)

    while( first != second )    // done when they're equal
       {
       if( first < second )     // if first isn't bigger,
          {
          temp=first;           // swap them
          first=second;
          second=temp;
          }
       first -= second;         // first=first-second
       }                        // first is now gcd
    numer /= first;             // divide both numer and denom
    denom /= first;             // by gcd to get lowest terms
    }

void main()
   {
   fracpri fp1;                 // create fraction
   float decimal;               // create decimal number

   cout << "\nEnter decimal number (format 7.75): ";
   cin >> decimal;

   fp1 = decimal;               // convert decimal to fraction

   cout << decimal << " = ";    // display fraction
   fp1.dispfrac();

   decimal = fp1;               // covert back to decimal

   cout << " = " << decimal;    // display decimal
   }
```

CHAPTER 10
Exercise 1

Instead of adding the overloaded '+' operator to the *Count* class as a member function, as was done in the COUNTADD exercise in Chapter 9, add this operator to the *Count* class using inheritance, by creating a derived class called *Countadd* that contains this operator. In *main()* add an integer to an object of type *Countadd* instead of type *Count*.

```
// counplus.cpp
// add integer to count variable using inheritance
#include <iostream.h>

class Counter
   {
   protected:                              // note: not private
```

```
    unsigned int count;                  // count
  public:
    Counter()        { count = 0; }      // constructor  no args
    Counter(int c)   { count = c; }      // constructor, one arg
    int get_count() { return count; }    // return count
  };

class Countadd : public Counter
  {
  public:
    Countadd() : Counter()               // constructor, no args
      { }
    Countadd(int c) : Counter(c)         // constructor, 1 arg
      { }
    Countadd operator + (int i)          // add integer to Count
      {
      return Countadd(count+i);          // return temp Count
      }                                  // initialized to sum
  };

void main()
  {
  Countadd c1(2), c2;                    // c1=2, c2=0

  cout << "\nc1=" << c1.get_count();     // display
  cout << "\nc2=" << c2.get_count();

  c2 = c1 + 17;                          // add 17 to c1,
                                         //    put result in c2

  cout << "\nc1=" << c1.get_count();     // display: c1=2
  cout << "\nc2=" << c2.get_count();     // c2=19
  }
```

Exercise 2

Imagine that you're running a hardware store in Hayfork, Idaho. You need a database program to keep track of your inventory. Start with a base class called *item* that includes data for the name of the item (a string) the price (type *float*) and the quantity in stock (type *int*). From this derive four other classes, called *pipe, lightbulb, tool,* and *paint.* The *pipe* class should add data for the length (expressed in feet, type *float*), the size (the diameter in inches, type *float*) and the type (galvanized, ABS, and so on, a string). The *lightbulbs* class should add data for the wattage of the bulb (type *int*). The *tool* class doesn't need any additional data. The *paint* class should add data for the size in pints (type *int*) and the color (a string).

Write a *main()* program to get data from the user for several items of different types, and then display these items. (See the EMPLOY program in Chapter 10 on the disk for an approach to this situation.)

```
// hardware.cpp
// models hardware store inventory using inheritance
#include <iostream.h>

const int LEN = 80;          // maximum length of names

class item                   // base class for all items
  {
  private:
    char name[LEN];          // item name
    float price;             // item price
    int quantity;            // number in stock
  public:
    void getdata()           // get data from user
      {
      cout << "\n   Enter item name: ";
      cin >> name;
      cout << "   Enter price (format 12.95): ";
      cin >> price;
      cout << "   Enter quantity in stock: ";
      cin >> quantity;
      }
    void putdata()           // display data
      {
      cout << "\n   Name: " << name;
      cout << "\n   Price: " << price;
      cout << "\n   Quantity: " << quantity;
      }
  };

class pipe : public item     // pipe class
  {
  private:
    float length;            // length of pipe
    float size;              // size of pipe
    char type[LEN];          // type of pipe
  public:
    void getdata()           // get data from user
      {
      item::getdata();
      cout << "   Enter length: "; cin >> length;
      cout << "   Enter size: ";   cin >> size;
      cout << "   Enter type: ";   cin >> type;
      }
    void putdata()                // display data
      {
      item::putdata();
      cout << "\n   Length: " << length;
      cout << "\n   Size: " << size;
      cout << "\n   Type: " << type;
      }
  };
class lightbulbs : public item        // lightbulbs class
```

```
   {
   private:
      int watts;                      // wattage of light bulbs
   public:
      void getdata()                  // get data from user
         {
         item::getdata();
         cout << "   Enter wattage: "; cin >> watts;
         }
      void putdata()                  // display data
         {
         item::putdata();
         cout << "\n   Wattage: " << watts;
         }
   };

class tools : public item            // tool class
   {                                  // (no additional data)
   };

class paint : public item            // paint class
   {
   private:
      int size;                       // size in pints
      char color[LEN];                // color of paint
   public:
      void getdata()                  // get data from user
         {
         item::getdata();
         cout << "   Enter size (pints): "; cin >> size;
         cout << "   Enter color: "; cin >> color;
         }
      void putdata()                  // display data
         {
         item::putdata();
         cout << "\n   Size: " << size;
         cout << "\n   Color: " << color;
         }
   };

void main()
   {
   pipe p1;                           // make one item
   lightbulbs b1;                     // of each class
   tools t1;
   paint pnt1;

   cout << endl;
   cout << "\nEnter data for pipe item ";   // get data for
   p1.getdata();                            // items

   cout << "\nEnter data for light bulb item";
   b1.getdata();
```

```
   cout << "\nEnter data for tool item";
   t1.getdata();

   cout << "\nEnter data for paint item";
   pnt1.getdata();

   cout << "\nItem 1";                    // display data for
   p1.putdata();                          // items

   cout << "\nItem 2";
   b1.putdata();

   cout << "\nItem 3";
   t1.putdata();

   cout << "\nItem 4";
   pnt1.putdata();
   }
```

Exercise 3

Use inheritance to add the capability to handle negative fractions to the *fracpri* class from the FRACLASS.CPP exercise for Chapter 7. The derived class can be called *signfrac*. In this class a no-argument constructor should set the sign to positive and call the no-argument constructor in *fracpri*. A four-argument constructor should set the sign to '+' or '-' and call the three-argument constructor in *fracpri*. A *dispfrac()* function should display the sign "(+)" or "(-)", and call *dispfrac()* in *fracpri*; and a *getfrac()* function should get the sign ('+' or '-') from the user and call the *getfrac()* function in *fracpri*. Don't worry about how to add signed fractions.

```
// negfrac.cpp
// uses inheritance to add sign ('+' or '-') to fractions
#include <iostream.h>

class fracpri                  // class for fractional prices
   {
   private:
     int whole;                // whole number part of price
     int numer;                // numerator (top) of fraction
     int denom;                // denominator (bottom) of fraction
   public:
     fracpri()                 // constructor, no args
        { whole=numer=0; denom=1; }
     fracpri(int w, int n, int d)          // constructor, 3 args
        { whole=w, numer=n, denom=d; }
     void dispfrac()           // display fraction (format 31-3/8)
         {
```

```
            cout << whole << "-"
                 << numer << "/"
                 << denom;
               }
       void getfrac()              // get fraction from user
           {
           char dummy;          // for hyphen and slash
           cin >> whole >> dummy >> numer >> dummy >> denom;
           }
       fracpri operator + (fracpri);        // add two fractions
       void fraclow();           // reduce ourself to lowest terms
   };

enum posneg { pos, neg };     // values for sign

// new class derived from fracpri
class signfrac : public fracpri              // adds sign to fracpri
   {
   private:
     posneg sign;
   public:
       signfrac() : fracpri()          // constructor, no args
         { sign = pos; }
                                     // constructor, 4 args
       signfrac(posneg s, int w, int n, int d) : fracpri(w, n, d)
         { sign = s; }
       void dispfrac()              // display sign and fraction
         {
         cout << ((sign==pos) ? "(+)" : "(-)");      // display sign
         fracpri::dispfrac();                        // rest of frac
         }
       void getfrac()              // get sign and fraction
         {
         char ch;                              // get sign
         cout << "(format +31-3/8 or -31-3/8): ";
         cin >> ch;
         sign = (ch=='-') ? neg : pos;         // set sign
         fracpri::getfrac();                   // rest of frac
         }
   };

void main()
   {
   signfrac fp1;                      // make signed fraction
   signfrac fp2( neg, 1, 7, 8 );      // initialize signed frac

   cout << "\nEnter price ";         // get price for fp1
   fp1.getfrac();

   cout << "\nfp1 = "; fp1.dispfrac();      // display signed
   cout << "\nfp2 = "; fp2.dispfrac();      // fractions
   }
```

Exercise 4

Start with the ENGLEN example in Chapter 10 on the disk, that adds a sign ('+' or '-') to the *Distance* class using inheritance. Assume that you don't like the input and output routines. You would prefer distances to be entered by the user using the format +3'4" or -3'4", rather than answering individual questions for feet, inches, and the sign. You also would like distances output in the same format, rather than with a hyphen between the feet and inches and parentheses around the sign.

Create a third generation class, derived from the *DistSign* class (which is derived from the *Distance* class) that incorporates new versions of the *getdist()* and *showdist()* member functions to allow for input and output in this new format. Don't modify *Distance* and *DistSign* (except for one small item). Assume the user will always type a sign before the feet and inches, whether '+' or '-'. Don't forget that when you use the single quote (') or double quote (") in string or character constants they must be preceded by a backslash (e.g. \' and \").

```
// engliop.cpp
// modify I/O routines by deriving new class
#include <iostream.h>

class Distance                        // English Distance class
   {
   protected:                         // note: can't be private
     int feet;
     float inches;
   public:
     Distance()                       // constructor (no args)
         { feet = 0; inches = 0.0; }
     Distance(int ft, float in)       // constructor (two args)
         { feet = ft; inches = in; }
     void getdist()                   // get length from user
         {
         cout << "\nEnter feet: ";  cin >> feet;
         cout << "Enter inches: ";  cin >> inches;
         }
     void showdist()                  // display distance
         { cout << feet << "\'-" << inches << '\"'; }
   };

enum posneg { pos, neg };             // for sign in DistSign

class DistSign : public Distance      // adds sign to Distance
   {
   protected:                         // note: can't be private
     posneg sign;                     // sign is pos or neg
   public:
```

```
                                  // constructor  (no args)
      DistSign() : Distance()     // call base constructor
        { sign = pos; }           // set the sign to +

                                  // constructor (2 or 3 args)
      DistSign(int ft, float in, posneg sg=pos) :
            Distance(ft, in)      // call base constructor
        { sign = sg; }            // set the sign

      void getdist()              // get length from user
        {
        Distance::getdist();      // call base getdist()
        char ch;                  // get sign from user
        cout << "Enter sign (+ or -): ";  cin >> ch;
        sign = (ch=='+') ? pos : neg;
        }

      void showdist()             // display distance
        {
        cout << ( (sign==pos) ? "(+)" : "(-)" );    // show sign
        Distance::showdist();                       // ft and in
        }
   };

class DistIO : public DistSign
   {
   public:
      DistIO()                    // one-arg constructor
        { }                       // 2- or 3-arg constructor
      DistIO(int f, float i, posneg s=pos) : DistSign(f, i, s)
        { }
      void getdist()              // get distance from user
        {                         // format +7'4" or -7'4"
        char ch, dummy;
        cin >> ch                 // get sign   (in DistSign)
            >> feet               // get feet   (in Distance)
            >> dummy              // get feet mark (')
            >> inches             // get inches (in Distance)
            >> dummy;             // get inches mark (")
        sign = (ch=='-') ? neg : pos;
        }
      void showdist()             // display distance
        {                         // format -7'4" or +7'4"
        cout << ( (sign==pos) ? '+' : '-'  )
             << feet << '\''
             << inches << '\"';
        }
   };

void main()
   {
   DistIO alpha;                  // no-arg constructor
   cout << "\n\nEnter distance (format +7\'4\"): ";
```

```
alpha.getdist();                 // get alpha from user

DistIO beta(11, 6.25);           // 2-arg constructor

DistIO gamma(100, 5.5, neg);     // 3-arg constructor

                                 // display all distances
cout << "\nalpha = ";  alpha.showdist();
cout << "\nbeta = ";   beta.showdist();
cout << "\ngamma = ";  gamma.showdist();
}
```

Exercise 5

Start with the ENGLEN example in Chapter 10 (on the disk), that adds a sign ('+' or '-') to the *Distance* class. Then add a new overloaded '+' routine to the *DistSign* class so that two signed distances can be added together.

To do this you may want to add the routine for the overloaded '+' operator from the ENGLPLUS example and the routine for the overloaded '<' operator from the ENGLESS example, both in Chapter 9 (on the disk), to the *Distance* class. Also, you will want to write a member function that overloads the '-' operator so you can subtract two *Distance* objects. Finally, you may find that you need a constructor for the *DistSign* class that takes two arguments: a *Distance* and a sign.

When signed quantites (call them *a* and *b*) are added, there are several possible results, depending on the signs of *a* and *b*. If they are both positive, they are added and given a positive sign. If both are negative, they are added and given a negative sign. If the signs are different, and *a* is less than *b*, then *a* is subtracted from *b* and the result is given the sign of the larger quantity. If *a* is greater than *b*, then *b* is subtracted from *a* and the result is given the sign of the larger quantity. The new addition routine in *DistSign* will need to consider these possibilites by examining the signs of the *DistSign* objects and by using the overloaded '<' operator in *Distance*. It can then call the overloaded '+' and '-' routines in *Distance* to carry out the arithmetic.

```
// negengl.cpp
// use inheritance to add sign ('+' or '-') to Distance class,
// modify overloaded '+' operator to work with signed Distances
#include <iostream.h>

enum boolean { false, true };

class Distance               // English Distance class
   {
   protected:                // NOTE: can't be private
```

```
      int feet;
      float inches;
   public:
      Distance()               // constructor (no args)
         { feet = 0; inches = 0.0; }
      Distance(int ft, float in)          // constructor (two args)
         { feet = ft; inches = in; }
      void getdist()           // get length from user
         {
          cout << "\n   Enter feet: ";  cin >> feet;
          cout << "   Enter inches: ";  cin >> inches;
         }
      void showdist()          // display distance
         { cout << feet << "\'-" << inches << '\"'; }
      Distance operator + (Distance);       // add Distances
      Distance operator - (Distance);       // subtract Distances
      boolean operator < (Distance);        // compare Distances
   };
                              // add this Distance to d2
Distance Distance::operator + (Distance d2)   // return the sum
   {
   int f = feet + d2.feet;     // add the feet
   float i = inches + d2.inches;            // add the inches
   if(i >= 12.0)               // if total exceeds 12.0,
      {                        // then decrease inches
      i -= 12.0;               // by 12.0 and
      f++;                     // increase feet by 1
      }                        // return a temporary Distance
   return Distance(f,i);       // initialized to sum
   }
                              // subtract d2 from this Dist
Distance Distance::operator - (Distance d2)      // return difference
   {                           // (assume this > d2)
   int f = feet - d2.feet;     // subtract feet
   float i = inches - d2.inches;            // subtract inches
   if( i < 0 )                 // if carry needed,
      {                        // increase inches by 12.0
      i +=12.0;                // and
      f--;                     // decrease feet by 1
      }
   return Distance(f,i);       // return difference
   }
                              // compare this with d2
boolean Distance::operator < (Distance d2)        // true or false
   {
   float bf1 = feet + inches/12;
   float bf2 = d2.feet + d2.inches/12;
   return (bf1 < bf2) ? true : false;
   }

enum posneg { pos, neg };     // for sign in DistSign

// class inherited from Distance
class DistSign : public Distance            // adds sign to Distance
```

```
    {
    private:
      posneg sign;               // sign is pos or neg
    public:
                                  // constructor (no args)
      DistSign() : Distance()         // call base constructor
        { sign = pos; }               // set the sign to +
                                      // constructor (Distance+sign)
      DistSign(Distance d, posneg sg) : Distance(d)
        { sign = sg; }
                                      // constructor (2 or 3 args)
      DistSign(int ft, float in, posneg sg=pos) :
            Distance(ft, in)          // call base constructor
        { sign = sg; }                // set the sign

      void getdist()                  // get length from user
        {
        Distance::getdist();          // call base getdist()
        char ch;                      // get sign from user
        cout << "  Enter sign (+ or -): ";  cin >> ch;
        sign = (ch=='+') ? pos : neg;
        }

      void showdist()                 // display distance
        {
        cout << ( (sign==pos) ? "(+)" : "(-)" );    // show sign
        Distance::showdist();                       // ft and in
        }
      DistSign operator + (DistSign);       // add signed Distances
    };

DistSign DistSign::operator + (DistSign d2)       // add signed dists
    {
    posneg tsign;
    Distance t1(feet, inches);        // Distance version of this
    Distance t2(d2);                  // Distance version of d2
    Distance sum;                     // Distance to hold sum
    // (need these so we can use Distance arithmetic functions)

    if( sign==pos && d2.sign==pos )   // if both signs positive
      {                               // add Distances
      sum = t1 + t2;                  // sign is positive
      tsign = pos;
      }
    else if( sign==neg && d2.sign==neg )    // if both signs neg
      {                               // add Distances
      sum = t1 + t2;                  // sign is negative
      tsign = neg;
      }                               // signs are different
    else if( t1 < t2 )
      {                               // if this < d2
      sum = t2 - t1;                  // subtract this from d2
      tsign = (d2.sign==pos) ? pos : neg;   // use sign of larger
```

```
      }
   else                         // if d2 < this
      {
      sum = t1 - t2;            // subtract d2 from this
      tsign = (sign==pos) ? pos : neg;      // use sign of larger
      }                         // return sum
    return DistSign(sum, tsign);         //    in DistSign form
   }

void main()
   {
   DistSign a, b, c;            // make 3 signed distances

   cout << "\n\nEnter Distance a: ";      // get values for two
   a.getdist();
   cout << "Enter Distance b: ";
   b.getdist();
   c = a + b;                   // add two signed distances
   cout << "Sum is ";
   c.showdist();                // display the sum
   }
```

CHAPTER 12

Exercise 1

Here's a program that lets you see in a different way how pointers work.

Start by creating five integer variables, and initializing them to constants like 1, 2, 3, 4, and 5. Create a pointer to *int*. Set the pointer to point to the middle variable. Now, in a loop, allow the user to enter either 'i' or 'd', to increment or decrement the pointer (as in *ptr++* and *ptr--*). Quit the loop by pressing the ⒠ key.

Also in the loop, print out the address pointed to, and the contents of that address. Now the user can roam back and fourth in the program's data, examining the data items and their corresponding addresses. Notice that you can easily go beyond the program's data. Such out-of-bounds data won't mean much, since it is program code or garbage left over from other programs. Remember that local data is stored in descending order in memory, with the highest address getting the first data item, while global data is stored in ascending order.

```
// ptrtest.cpp
// allows user to increment and decrement address pointer
#include <iostream.h>
#include <conio.h>

const char ESC = 27;
```

```
void main()
  {
  int avar = 111;                    // five integer
  int bvar = 222;                    // variables,
  int cvar = 333;                    // initialized
  int dvar = 444;
  int evar = 555;

  char ch;
  int* ptr = &cvar;                  // set ptr to cvar

  while( ch != ESC )                 // quit on Esc key
    {
    cout << "\n\nContents of " << ptr << " = " << *ptr;
    cout << "\nType i to increment address, "
        << "or d to decrement address: ";
    ch = getche();                   // get character
    if( ch == 'i' )
       ptr++;          // increment ptr
    if( ch == 'd' )
       ptr--;          // decrement ptr
    }
  }
```

Exercise 2

It is said that a woman's ideal weight can be found by multiplying her height in inches by 3.5 and subtracting 110 from the result. (This and all such formulas should be taken with a grain of salt.) Write a function that takes two arguments: a height in inches, and a pointer to a weight. The function should calculate the ideal weight based on this recipe, and insert it into the appropriate variable in the calling program, using the pointer. You can use type *int* throughout. See the PASSPTR example from Chapter 12 (on the disk) for the general idea.

```
// weight.cpp
// passing one argument by pointer
#include <iostream.h>

void main()
  {
  void ideal(int, int*);    // prototype

  int height;
  int weight;

  cout << "\nEnter height in inches: ";
  cin >> height;
```

```
  ideal(height, &weight);   // send address of weight
  cout << "Ideal weight is " << weight;
  }

void ideal(int h, int* ptrw)
  {
  *ptrw = (3.5 * h) - 110;   // *ptrw is the same as weight
  }
```

Exercise 3

Using the COPYSTR example in Chapter 12 on the disk as a starting point, create a function that concatenates two strings to form a third. That is, if the first string is "cats" and the the second is " and dogs", the resulting string should be "cats and dogs". The prototype for the function should be of the form

void concastr(char* dest, char* src1, char* src2);

Within this function, move the source strings to the destination string on a character-by-character basis, using pointers. The destination string should already exist as an empty array, sized large enough to hold the concatenated strings.

```
// concat.cpp
// concatenates two strings to form a third; uses pointers
#include <iostream.h>

void main()
  {
  void concastr(char*, char*, char*);     // prototype

  char* str1 = "\nThe quality of mercy ";  // Shakespeare
  char* str2 = "is not strained;";
  char str3[80];                           // empty string

  concastr(str3, str1, str2);              // concatenate str1 and str2
  cout << endl << str3;                    // display str3
  }

void concastr(char* dest, char* src1, char* src2)
  {
  while( *src1 )                  // until null character,
     *dest++ = *src1++;           // copy chars from src1 to dest
  while( *src2 )                  // until null character,
     *dest++ = *src2++;           // copy chars from src2 to dest
  *dest = '\0';                   // terminate dest
  }
```

Exercise 4

Write a member function for the *String* class from the NEWSTR example in Chapter 12 on the disk. This function should take take two *String* objects as arguments, and concatenate them to make a new string in the *String* object of which it is a member. The function will need to erase whatever string its object currently holds, copy the first *String* object into its object, and concatenate the second *String* object.

```cpp
// stringca.cpp
// concatenates two String objects
#include <iostream.h>
#include <string.h>                 // for strlen(), strcpy(), strcat()

class String                        // user-defined string type
   {
   private:
      char* str;                    // pointer to string
   public:
      String(char* s)               // constructor, one arg
         {
         int length = strlen(s);    // length of string argument
         str = new char[length+1];  // get memory
         strcpy(str, s);            // copy argument to it
         }
      ~String()                     // destructor
         {
         delete str;                // release memory
         }
      void display()                // display the String
         {
         cout << str;
         }
      void concat(String, String);  // concatenate strings
   };

void String::concat(String s1, String s2) // concatenate strings
   {
   delete str;                            // forget current string
   int len = strlen(s1.str) + strlen(s2.str);
   str = new char[len];                   // get space for both
   strcpy(str, s1.str);                   // copy first into space
   strcat(str, s2.str);                   // add the second
   }

void main()
   {
   String str1 = "Now is the time "; // initialize Strings
   String str2 = "for all good men.";
   String str3 = "";                 // empty String
```

```
    str3.concat(str1, str2);          // concatenate old Strings
    cout << endl << "str1 = ";
    str3.display();                   // display new String
    }
```

Exercise 5

Make an array of pointers to fractional price objects. Start with the *fracpri* class from the FRACLASS exercise from Chapter 7, and use the array of pointers to objects as seen in the PTROBJS example from Chapter 12 (on the disk).

```cpp
// ptrfracs.cpp
// array of pointers to fracpri (fraction) objects
#include <iostream.h>
#include <conio.h>              // for getche()

class fracpri                   // class for fractional prices
   {
   private:
      int whole;                // whole number part of price
      int numer;                // numerator (top) of fraction
      int denom;                // denominator (bottom) of fraction
   public:
      void dispfrac()           // display fraction (format 31-3/8)
         {
         cout << whole << "-" << numer << "/" << denom;
         }
      void getfrac()            // get fraction from user
         {
         char dummy;            // for hyphen and slash
         cin >> whole >> dummy >> numer >> dummy >> denom;
         }
   };

void main(void)
   {
   fracpri* fracPtr[100];       // array of pointers to fractions
   int n = 0;                   // number of fractions in array
   char choice;                 // user's choice

   do                                        // put fractions in array
      {
      cout << "\nEnter fractional price: ";
      fracPtr[n] = new fracpri;              // make new object
      fracPtr[n]->getfrac();                 // get fraction from user
      n++;                                   // count new fraction
      cout << "Enter another (y/n)? ";       // enter another
      choice = getche();                     //    fraction?
      }
   while( choice=='y' );                     // quit on 'n'
```

```
for(int j=0; j<n; j++)                    // display all fractions
   {
   cout << "\nFractional price number " << j+1 << " is ";
   fracPtr[j]->dispfrac();
   }
} // end main()
```

Exercise 6

Make a linked list of *person* objects. Start with the linked list structure from the LINKLIST example and the *person* class from the PERSORT example, both in Chapter 12 on the disk. You won't need to modify the *person* object, but you'll need to change the *additem()* and *display()* member functions in *linklist* so they call the appropriate routines in *person*, rather than getting data from an argument and displaying it directly. For example, the appropriate statement in *additem()* is

   newlink->data.setName();

and in *display()* it's

   current->data.printName()

Write a *main()* program that, in a loop, asks the user for a name, using the *setName()* member function from *person* (which is embedded in the *additem()* member function from *linklist*). The new *person* object should then be added to the linked list. When the user has added as many names as desired to the list, display all the names using the *printName()* member function in *person* (which is embedded in the *display()* member function from *linklist*).

Notice that the same linked list class can be used to hold data from different classes, with few modifications to the linked list class itself. Container class libraries are based on this principle.

```
// linkpers.cpp
// linked list with person objects
#include <iostream.h>
#include <conio.h>                    // for getche()

class person                          // class of persons
   {
   private:
      char name[40];                  // person's name
   public:
      void setName(void)              // set the name
         { cout << "\n   Enter name: "; cin >> name; }
      void printName(void)            // display the name
```

```
      { cout << endl << name; }
    char* getName()                   // return the name
      { return name; }
  };

struct link                           // one element of list
  {
  person data;                        // data item is a person
  link* next;                         // pointer to next link
  };

class linklist                        // a list of links
  {
  private:
    link* first;                      // pointer to first link
  public:
    linklist()                        // no-argument constructor
      { first = NULL; }               // no first link
    void additem();                   // add data item (one link)
    void display();                   // display all links
  };

void linklist::additem()              // add data item
  {
  link* newlink = new link;           // make a new link
  newlink->data.setName();            // person gets own data
  newlink->next = first;              // it points to next link
  first = newlink;                    // now first points to this
  }

void linklist::display()              // display all links
  {
  link* current = first;              // set ptr to first link
  while( current != NULL )            // quit on last link
    {
    current->data.printName();        // person shows own data
    current = current->next;          // move to next link
    }
  }

void main()
  {
  linklist li;                        // make linked list
  char ch;                            // for user choice
  do
    {
    cout << "\nEnter data for person";
    li.additem();                     // add person to list
    cout << "\nAdd another person (y/n)? ";
    ch = getche();
    }
  while(ch != 'n');                   // quite loop on 'n'

  li.display();                       // display persons on list
  }
```

CHAPTER 13
Exercise 1

Start with the VIRTPERS example from this chapter. Remove the *isOutstanding()* member function from both the *student* and *professor* classes, and substitute a *printData()* function that displays a student's GPA or a professor's number of publications. Make whatever other changes are necessary so that the *main()* program, using the same basic loop approach as in VIRTPERS, will display a list of students and professors, showing the name (using the *printName()* function) followed by either the GPA or the number of publications, as appropriate (using the *printData()* function).

```cpp
// virtpez.cpp
// virtual functions with person class
#include <iostream.h>
enum boolean { false, true };

class person                          // person class
  {
  protected:
    char name[40];                    // person's name
  public:
    void setName()                    // get name from user
      { cout << "   Enter name: "; cin >> name; }
    void printName()                  // display name
      { cout << "Name is: " << name << endl; }
    virtual void printData() = 0;     // pure virtual function
  };

class student : public person         // student class
  {
  private:
    float gpa;                        // grade point average
  public:
    void setData()                    // get GPA from user
      { cout << "   Enter student's GPA: "; cin >> gpa; }
    void printData()                  // display GPA
      { cout << "   GPA is: " << gpa << endl; }
  };

class professor : public person       // professor class
  {
  private:
    int numPubs;                      // number of papers published
  public:
    void setData()                    // get number of papers from user
      {
      cout << "   Enter number of professor's publications: ";
      cin >> numPubs;
      }
```

```
      void printData()        // display number of papers
        { cout << "  Number of pubs is: " << numPubs << endl; }
   };

void main(void)
   {
   person* persPtr[100];      // list of pointers to persons
   student* stuPtr;           // pointer to student
   professor* proPtr;         // pointer to professor
   int n = 0;                 // number of persons on list
   char choice;               // user's choice

   do
      {
      cout << "Enter student or professor (s/p): ";
      cin >> choice;
      if(choice=='s')                 // it's a student
         {
         stuPtr = new student;        // make new student
         stuPtr->setName();           // set student name
         stuPtr->setData();           // set GPA
         persPtr[n++] = stuPtr;       // put pointer in list
         }
      else                            // it's a professor
         {
         proPtr = new professor;      // make new professor
         proPtr->setName();           // set professor name
         proPtr->setData();           // set number of pubs
         persPtr[n++] = proPtr;       // put pointer in list
         }
      cout << "  Enter another (y/n)? ";    // do another person?
      cin >> choice;
      } while( choice=='y' );         // cycle until not 'y'

   for(int j=0; j<n; j++)             // for each person,
      {
      persPtr[j]->printName();        // display name
      persPtr[j]->printData();        // display GPA or pubs
      }
   } // end main()
```

Exercise 2

Start with the HARDWARE exercise from Chapter 10. Your goal is to create a list in which you can store items from the four hardware categories: pipe, lightbulbs, tools, and paint. Each of these categories corresponds to a class derived from the *item* class. The program should repeatedly ask the user to select one of these four categories, and then prompt the user to fill in the specifics of the item, which depend on the category (you ask for the length and size of pipe, for example, but the color of paint).

The *main()* part of the program should create an array of type pointer-to-*item*, as in the VIRTPERS example from Chapter 13, on the disk. This array will hold pointers to items from the derived classes. In a loop the program should ask the user what category a new item should be, and then create the item using *new*. The pointer to the item should be placed on the list, where it can be used to ask the user for the details of the item. When the user has finished inputting items, the program, in a *for* loop, should display all the items, using the pointers stored in the array.

Only two lines need to be changed in the *item* class, and no changes are necessary in the derived classes *pipe*, *lightbulbs*, *tools*, and *paint*.

```cpp
// virthard.cpp
// virtual functions in hardware store inventory
#include <iostream.h>
#include <conio.h>                    // for getche()

const int LEN = 80;                   // maximum length of names

class item                           // base class for all items
   {
   private:
      char name[LEN];                 // item name
      float price;                    // item price
      int quantity;                   // number in stock
   public:
      virtual void getdata()          // get data from user (virtual)
         {
         cout << "\n   Enter item name: ";
         cin >> name;
         cout << "   Enter price (format 12.95): ";
         cin >> price;
         cout << "   Enter quantity in stock: ";
         cin >> quantity;
         }
      virtual void putdata()          // display data (virtual)
         {
         cout << "\n   Name: " << name;
         cout << "\n   Price: " << price;
         cout << "\n   Quantity: " << quantity;
         }
   };

class pipe : public item             // pipe class
   {
   private:
      float length;                   // length of pipe
      float size;                     // size of pipe
      char type[LEN];                 // type of pipe
   public:
      void getdata()                  // get data from user
         {
```

```
      item::getdata();
      cout << "   Enter length: "; cin >> length;
      cout << "   Enter size: ";   cin >> size;
      cout << "   Enter type: ";   cin >> type;
      }
   void putdata()                  // display data
      {
      item::putdata();
      cout << "\n   Length: " << length;
      cout << "\n   Size: " << size;
      cout << "\n   Type: " << type;
      }
   };

class lightbulbs : public item      // lightbulbs class
   {
   private:
      int watts;                   // wattage of light bulbs
   public:
      void getdata()               // get data from user
         {
         item::getdata();
         cout << "   Enter wattage: "; cin >> watts;
         }
      void putdata()               // display data
         {
         item::putdata();
         cout << "\n   Wattage: " << watts;
         }
   };

class tools : public item          // tool class
   {                               // (no additional data)
   };

class paint : public item          // paint class
   {
   private:
      int size;                    // size in pints
      char color[LEN];             // color of paint
   public:
      void getdata()               // get data from user
         {
         item::getdata();
         cout << "   Enter size (pints): "; cin >> size;
         cout << "   Enter color: "; cin >> color;
         }
      void putdata()               // display data
         {
         item::putdata();
         cout << "\n   Size: " << size;
         cout << "\n   Color: " << color;
         }
   };
```

```
void main()
   {
   item* itemPtr[100];        // array of pointers to items
   pipe* pipePtr;             // pointer to pipe
   lightbulbs* bulbPtr;       // pointer to lightbulbs
   tools* toolPtr;            // pointer to tools
   paint* paintPtr;           // pointer to paint
   int n=0;                   // number of items on list
   int nchoice;               // user's choice (1, 2, 3, or 4)
   char cchoice;              // user's choice (y or n)

   do
      {
      cout << "\n1--Pipe\n2--Lightbulbs\n3--Tools\n4--Paint";
      cout << "\nEnter number for category: ";
      cin >> nchoice;
      switch(nchoice)
         {
         case 1:
            pipePtr = new pipe;        // make ptr to new pipe
            itemPtr[n] = pipePtr;      // put ptr in array
            itemPtr[n++]->getdata();   // use it to get data
            break;
         case 2:
            bulbPtr = new lightbulbs;  // make ptr to new bulb
            itemPtr[n] = bulbPtr;      // put ptr in array
            itemPtr[n++]->getdata();   // use it to get data
            break;
         case 3:
            toolPtr = new tools;       // make ptr to new tool
            itemPtr[n] = toolPtr;      // put ptr in array
            itemPtr[n++]->getdata();   // use it to get data
            break;
         case 4:
            paintPtr = new paint;      // make ptr to new paint
            itemPtr[n] = paintPtr;     // put ptr in array
            itemPtr[n++]->getdata();   // use it to get data
            break;
         }
      cout << "\nEnter another (y/n)? ";
      cchoice = getche();
      cin.ignore();
      } while( cchoice != 'n' );

   for(int j=0; j<n; j++)
      {
      cout << "\nItem number " << j+1;      // use ptrs from array
      itemPtr[j]->putdata();                // to display data
      }                                     // for all items
   }
```

Exercise 3

Modify the FRACPLUS exercise from Chapter 9 so that you can execute statements of the form

fp2 = floatvar + fp1;

where *floatvar* is a variable of type *float*. You'll need to add the one-argument constructor from the FRACONV exercise of Chapter 9, so you can convert from type *float* to type *fracpri*. You'll also need to change the form of the overloaded '+' operator, otherwise you'll get the discouraging *Operator cannot be applied to these operand types* error message.

```cpp
// fracfren.cpp
// uses friend function to add two fractions
#include <iostream.h>

class fracpri                   // class for fractional prices
   {
   private:
     int whole;                 // whole number part of price
     int numer;                 // numerator (top) of fraction
     int denom;                 // denominator (bottom) of fraction
   public:
     fracpri()                           // constructor, no args
                          { whole=numer=0; denom=1; }
     fracpri(float flo)             // constructor, 1 arg
        {                           //   (float to fraction)
        flo += 0.0078125;          // adjust: add 1/128
        whole = int(flo);          // whole is integer part
        float flofrac = flo - whole;// frac is what's left
        numer = flofrac * 64;      // how many 64ths?
        denom = 64;                // denominator always 64
        fraclow();                 // to lowest terms
        }
     fracpri(int w, int n, int d)   // constructor, 3 args
        { whole=w, numer=n, denom=d; }
     void dispfrac()                // display fraction (format 31-3/8)
        {
        cout << whole << "-"
             << numer << "/"
             << denom;
        }
     void getfrac()             // get fraction from user
        {
        char dummy;            // for hyphen and slash
        cin >> whole >> dummy >> numer >> dummy >> denom;
        }
```

```
                              // add two fractions
     friend fracpri operator + (fracpri, fracpri);
     void fraclow();          // reduce ourself to lowest terms
   };

// friend function
// overloaded '+' operator adds two arguments, returns sum
fracpri operator + (fracpri farg1, fracpri farg2)
   {                              // ans=farg1+farg2
   int w, d, n;                   // three parts of temp frac
   int newnum1, newnum2, newnumer, carry;

   w = farg1.whole + farg2.whole;        // find new whole number
   d = farg1.denom * farg2.denom;        // find new denominator
   newnum1 = farg1.numer * farg2.denom;  // cross multiply
   newnum2 = farg2.numer * farg1.denom;
   newnumer = newnum1 + newnum2;    // add the new numerators
   carry = newnumer / d;            // find how much to carry
   w += carry;                      // add to whole number part
   n = newnumer % d;                // find new numerator
   return fracpri(w, n, d);         // return temporary fraction
   }

// fraclow()
// member function reduces this fraction to lowest terms
void fracpri::fraclow()
   {
   if( numer == 0 )               // check for special case of
      { denom=1; return; }        // zero numerator
   long first=numer;              // find greatest common divisor
   long second=denom;             // of numerator and denominator
   long temp;                     // (compute with local vars)

   while( first != second )       // done when they're equal
      {
      if( first < second )        // if first isn't bigger,
         { temp=first; first=second; second=temp; }      // swap'em
      first -= second;            // first=first-second
      }                           // first is now gcd
      numer /= first;             // divide both numer and denom
      denom /= first;             // by gcd to get lowest terms
   }

void main()
   {
   fracpri fp1, fp2, fp3;         // make three objects
   float decipri;                 // decimal price

   cout << "\nEnter fractional price: ";    // get price for fp1
   fp1.getfrac();
   cout << "Enter decimal price: ";         // get decimal price
   cin >> decipri;
```

```
fp2 = fp1 + decipri;          // add fp1 and float
fp3 = decipri + fp1;          // add float and fp1

fp2.fraclow();                // set fp2 to lowest terms
fp3.fraclow();                // set fp3 to lowest terms
cout << "Adding decimal to fraction gives ";
fp2.dispfrac();               // display fp2
cout << "\nAdding fraction to decimal gives ";
fp3.dispfrac();               // display fp3
}
```

Exercise 4

One reason to write your own function for an overloaded '=' operator is to monitor the amount of memory used by objects in your program. For example, suppose that you need to create a class of objects that hold a great deal of data. Let's call this the *bigdata* class. For simplicity, assume that the amount of data is the same for all *bigdata* objects, say 5000 integers.

Let's further suppose that it's sometimes desirable to create an object without actually allocating memory space for its data. For instance, if you use a no-argument constructor, you might want to bring an object into existence, so you can refer to it by name in the program, but not actually allocate memory at that time. We can call an object with no data an empty object. You would allocate memory for data when, for instance, the object was set equal to another object that did contain data (a full object).

This exercise models such a *bigdata* class. Its private data should consist only of a pointer that can point to a block of memory 5000 *ints* long. The class should have a no-argument constructor that creates an object but does not allocate memory for any data. Also, it should have a *putdata()* member function that creates memory space using *new* and fills it with data, thus changing the object from empty to full. (This can be arbitrary data, such as the integers from 0 to 4999. In a real application the data would come from an external source, such as a disk file.)

Finally, there should be an overloaded '=' operator to set the data in an empty object equal to the data in a full object. The empty object goes on the left of the equal sign and the full object on the right. The '=' operator should allocate memory and copy the data into this space from the full object.

Since it's easy to exceed the size of memory with large data items, you should add code to the overloaded '=' sign, and to the *putdata()* function, to check that there is still enough memory left in the system for 5000 integers. You can use the *coreleft()* Borland library function, which returns the memory space remaining. (This library function requires the ALLOC.H header file.) In the Small memory model, which we'll assume you're using, the data space available starts at somewhat less than 65,536 bytes. If there isn't enough memory, the user should be notified and the program should exit. Without this check, program or system code may be overwritten by the new data, causing a system crash.

In the *main()* program, create an object of type *bigdata* (call it *abig*) and initialize its data with *putdata()*. Then create an array of pointers to *bigdata* objects. For each one, create a *bigdata* object with *new*, and (using its pointer) set the object equal to *abig*, with a statement like

> **bigPtr[j] = abig;*

Let the user decide whether to create each new object. Since each object takes 10,000 bytes, you should run out of memory after the sixth object. If the user tries to create too many objects, the error message in the overloadedd '=' operator should be triggered.

```
// bigequal.cpp
// overloads assignment operator to avoid memory crash
#include <iostream.h>
#include <conio.h>          // for getche()
#include <alloc.h>          // for coreleft()
#include <process.h>        // for exit()

const unsigned int SIZE = 5000;      // data size in bigdata object

class bigdata
  {
  private:
    int* ptr;                // pointer to memory for data
  public:
    bigdata()                // no-arg constructor
      { }
    bigdata(int* p)          // one-arg constructor
      { ptr = p; }
    void putdata();          // fill memory with data
    void operator = (bigdata&);   // overloaded '=' operator
  };

void bigdata::putdata()                 // put data in memory
  {
  if( coreleft() > sizeof(int[SIZE]) )    // check memory
    {
    ptr = new int[SIZE];                  // get big chunk of memory
    for(unsigned k=0; k<SIZE; k++)        // fill it with dummy data
      *(ptr+k) = k;                       // (0, 1, 2, 3...)
    }
```

```
else                              // not enough memory
   {
   cout << "\nCan't create more data, memory is full";
   exit(1);
   }
}

void bigdata::operator = (bigdata& bg)    // overloaded '='
   {
   if( coreleft() > sizeof(int[SIZE]) )    // check memory
      {
      ptr = new int[SIZE];                 // get big chunk of memory
      for(unsigned k=0; k<SIZE; k++)       // copy data from bg
        *(ptr+k) = *(bg.ptr+k);
      }
   else                              // not enough memory
      {
      cout << "\nCan't create more data, memory is full";
      exit(1);
      }
   }

void main()
   {
   bigdata* bigPtr[10];       // array of ptrs to bigdata objects
   int j = 0;                 // count the objects created so far
   cout << "\nSize of data = " << sizeof(int[SIZE]);
   bigdata abig;              // create a bigdata object
   abig.putdata();            // fill it with data

   while(1)
      {
      cout << "\nj=" << j << " coreleft = "
           << (unsigned long)coreleft();
      cout << "\nCreate another object(y/n)? ";
      char choice;             // get permission from
      choice = getche();       // user to create
      if( choice == 'n' )          // another object
         exit(1);
      bigPtr[j] = new bigdata;     // make a new bigdata object
      *(bigPtr[j++]) = abig;       // set it equal to abig
      }
   }
```

Exercise 5

Modify the BIGEQUAL exercise from this chapter to include an overloaded copy constructor for the *bigdata* class. You can use this to create new *bigdata* objects with the statement

bigPtr[j] = new bigdata(abig);

which uses the copy constructor to initialize the new object pointed to by *bigPtr[j]*.

```cpp
// bigcopy.cpp
// overloads copy constructor to avoid memory crash
#include <iostream.h>
#include <conio.h>          // for getche()
#include <alloc.h>          // for coreleft()
#include <process.h>        // for exit()

const unsigned int SIZE = 5000;      // data size in bigdata object

class bigdata
   {
   private:
     int* ptr;                   // pointer to data
   public:
     bigdata()                   // no-arg constructor
        { }
     bigdata(int* p)             // one-arg constructor
        { ptr = p; }
     bigdata(bigdata&);          // copy constructor
     void putdata();             // fill memory with data
   };

void bigdata::putdata()         // put data in memory
   {
   if( coreleft() > sizeof(int[SIZE]) )     // check memory
      {
      ptr = new int[SIZE];             // get big chunk of memory
      for(unsigned k=0; k<SIZE; k++)   // fill it with dummy data
        *(ptr+k) = k;                  // (0, 1, 2, ...)
      }
   else                         // not enough memory
      {
      cout << "\nCan't create more data, memory is full";
      exit(1);
      }
   }

bigdata::bigdata(bigdata& bg)       // overloaded copy constructor
   {
   if( coreleft() > sizeof(int[SIZE]) )     // memory available?
      {
      ptr = new int[SIZE];             // get big chunk of memory
      for(unsigned k=0; k<SIZE; k++)   // copy data from bg
        *(ptr+k) = *(bg.ptr+k);
      }
   else                              // not enough memory
      {
      cout << "\nCan't create more data, memory is full";
      exit(1);
      }
   }
```

```
void main()
  {
  bigdata* bigPtr[10];      // array of ptrs to bigdata objects
  int j = 0;                // count the objects created so far
  cout << "\nSize of data = " << sizeof(int[SIZE]);

  bigdata abig;             // create a bigdata object
  abig.putdata();           // fill it with data

  while(1)
    {
    cout << "\nj=" << j << " coreleft = "
        << (unsigned long)coreleft();
    cout << "\nCreate another object(y/n)? ";
    char choice;            // get permission from
    choice = getche();      // user to create
    if( choice == 'n' )     // another object
      exit(1);
                            // make new bigdata object
    bigPtr[j++] = new bigdata(abig);  // initialize it with
    }                       // copy constructor
  }
```

CHAPTER 14

Exercise 1

In this exercise you write an array of *fracint* objects to the disk. Use the *fracint* class from the FRACLASS exercise in Chapter 7. In the *main()* program have the user enter an arbitrary number of objects of this type. Then store them in an array, and write them to the disk with a single statement. Write only as many objects as there are in the array; don't write any empty array spaces. You may want to precede this data with the number of fractions that will be written; having this number (an integer) in the disk file will simplify things for a program that must read this file.

```
// fracout.cpp
// writes array of fractions to a disk file
#include <fstream.h>       // for file streams
#include <conio.h>         // for getche()

class fracpri               // class for fractional prices
  {
  private:
    int whole;             // whole number part of price
    int numer;             // numerator (top) of fraction
    int denom;             // denominator (bottom) of fraction
  public:
    void dispfrac()        // display fraction (format 31-3/8)
```

```
      {
      cout << whole << "-" << numer << "/" << denom;
      }
   void getfrac()            // get fraction from user
      {
      char dummy;
      cin >> whole >> dummy >> numer >> dummy >> denom;
      }
   };

void main(void)
   {
   fracpri farray[100];             // array of fractions
   int n = 0;                       // number of fracs in array
   char ch;                         // user's response
   do
      {
      cout << "\nEnter fraction: ";
      farray[n++].getfrac(); // get frac, put in array
      cout << "Enter another (y/n)? ";
      ch=getche();
      }
   while(ch != 'n' );               // loop until user types 'n'

   ofstream outfile("FRACA.DAT");   // create file for output
                                    // write number of fracs
   outfile.write( (char*)&n, sizeof(int) );
                                    // write array from 0 to n
   outfile.write( (char*)&farray, n * sizeof(fracpri) );
   }
```

Exercise 2

Write a program that reads the file generated by the FRACOUT exercise in this chapter. It should first read the integer that tells how many fractions there are in the file. Then, in a single statement, it should read all the fractions into an array. It can then use a *for* loop to display all the fractions from the array.

```
// fracin.cpp
// reads fractions from a disk file into an array
#include <fstream.h>           // for file streams

class fracpri                  // class for fractional prices
   {
   private:
      int whole;               // whole number part of price
      int numer;               // numerator (top) of fraction
      int denom;               // denominator (bottom) of fraction
   public:
      void dispfrac()          // display fraction (format 31-3/8)
         {
```

```
      cout << whole << "-" << numer << "/" << denom;
      }
   void getfrac()            // get fraction from user
      {
      char dummy;
      cin >> whole >> dummy >> numer >> dummy >> denom;
      }
};

void main(void)
   {
   fracpri farray[100];             // array of fractions
   int n;                           // number of fracs in array

   ifstream infile("FRACA.DAT");    // open file for input
   infile.read( (char*)&n, sizeof(int) );   // read number into n
                                    // read file into array
   infile.read( (char*)&farray, n * sizeof(fracpri) );

   for(int j=0; j<n; j++)           // for each of n fractions
      {
      cout << "\nFraction " << j << " is ";
      farray[j].dispfrac();         // display it
      }
   }
```

Exercise 3

Write a program that compares two text files (such as .CPP files) that are entered as command-line arguments. If there is a mismatch in the files the program should display some characters following the mismatch so the user can figure out where the error is in the file. If the files match, the program should say so.

```
// ocomp.cpp
// compares two text files, displays difference
#include <fstream.h>        // for file functions
#include <process.h>        // for exit()

void main(int argc, char* argv[] )
   {
   char ch1, ch2;           // characters to read
   ifstream file1, file2;   // files for input
   char buffer[100];        // buffer for input

   if( argc != 3 )
      {
      cerr << "\nFormat: ocomp file1 file2";
      exit(-1);
      }
```

```
    file1.open( argv[1] );     // open file 1
    if( !file1 )               // check for errors
      { cerr << "\nCan't open " << argv[1]; exit(-1); }

    file2.open( argv[2] );     // open file 2
    if( !file2 )               // check for errors
      { cerr << "\nCan't open " << argv[2]; exit(-1); }

                               // read a character
    while( (file1.get(ch1) != 0) && (file2.get(ch2) != 0)  )
      if( ch1 != ch2 )                  // if mismatch
        {                               // display file 1
        cout << "\n\nFile 1:\n---------------\n";
        file1.read( (char*)&buffer, 70);
        buffer[70] = '\0';
        cout << ch1 << buffer;          // display file 2
        cout << "\n\nFile 2:\n---------------\n";
        file2.read( (char*)&buffer, 70);
        buffer[70] = '\0';
        cout << ch2 << buffer;
        exit(0);                        // exit program
        }
    cout << "\nFiles match.";
    }
```

Exercise 4

The idea in this exercise is to modify the *linklist* class from the LINKLIST example in Chapter 12 on the disk so a linklist object can write itself to a disk file, or add objects to itself by reading them from a disk file. Add *read()* and *write()* member functions to the *linklist* class that will carry out these activities. Write a *main()* program that creates a linked list, adds some data items to it, and writes the resulting list to a disk file. It should then create a second linked list, read the disk file back in, and display the list. Hint: the *read()* and *write()* functions are somewhat similar to the *display()* and *additem()* functions, at least as far as the interaction with the list itself is concerned.

```
// linkdisk.cpp
// reads and writes linked list to disk
#include <fstream.h>                // for file streams

struct link                         // one element of list
  {
  int data;                         // data item
  link* next;                       // pointer to next link
  };

class linklist                      // a list of links
```

```
     {
     private:
        link* first;                    // pointer to first link
     public:
        linklist()                      // no-argument constructor
           { first = NULL; }            // no first link
        void additem(int d);            // add data item (one link)
        void display();                 // display all links
        void write(char*);              // write this list to file
        void read(char*);               // add file to this list
     };

void linklist::additem(int d)          // add data item
     {
     link* newlink = new link;         // make a new link
     newlink->data = d;                // give it data
     newlink->next = first;            // it points to next link
     first = newlink;                  // now first points to new
     }

void linklist::display()               // display all links
     {
     link* current = first;            // set ptr to first link
     while( current != NULL )          // quit on last link
        {
        cout << endl << current->data; // print data
        current = current->next;       // move to next link
        }
     }
void linklist::write(char* fname)      // write this list to file
     {
     ofstream outfile;                 // make file
     outfile.open(fname);              // open file
     link* current = first;            // set ptr to first link
     while( current != NULL )          // quit on last link
        {                                       // write link to file
        outfile.write( (char*)&current->data, sizeof(int) );
        current = current->next;       // move to next link
        }
     outfile.close();
     }

void linklist::read(char* fname)           // add file to this list
     {
     int tempint;
     ifstream infile;                      // make file
     infile.open(fname, ios::nocreate);    // open it
     while( 1 )
        {                                  // read data
        infile.read( (char*)&tempint, sizeof(int) );
        if( infile.eof() )                 // break on eof
           break;
        additem(tempint);                  // insert data in list
```

```
      }
  }
void main()
  {
  linklist list1;             // make linked list

  list1.additem(25);          // add items to list
  list1.additem(36);
  list1.additem(49);
  list1.additem(64);
  list1.write("LIST.DAT");    // write items from list to disk

  linklist list2;             // make another linked list
  list2.read("LIST.DAT");     // read items from disk into list
  list2.display();            // display list
  }
```

Exercise 5

Here's a generalization of the LINKLIST exercise above. Create a class, called *objfile*, that models a disk file that can hold objects of any class. For each *objfile*, all the objects are from the same class, and are thus of the same size. The *objfile* class should have a member function that adds an object to the file, and another member function that reads back an object at an arbitrary record number in the file. For example, if you write five objects to the file, you should be able to read back the third one without reading the first or second.

You'll need to give each *objfile* object you create a file name, and you may want to tell it the size of the objects that will be read from it or written to it. A statement to create or "open" an object of class *objfile* might be

objfile ob1.("NAME.EXT", sizeof(testclass));

When you add or "write" an object to an *objfile* object you'll need to tell the routine the address of the object to be added, as in

ob1.add(&testobj);

When you read an object from an *objfile* object you'll need to tell it not only the address where you want the object placed (the address of an empty object), you'll need to specify which object in the file you want to read: 1 for the first, 2 for the second, and so on. A statement to read the third object might be

ob1.get(&emptytestobj, 3);

In the *main()* program, create a class that can be used to test the *objfile* class. As a minimum this test class should be able to create objects with initialized data, and should have a member function to display that data. (Alternatively, you could use an object from a class in this section, such as the *person* or *fracpri* class.) Create an object of class *objfile* and store several test objects in it. Then read them back from the disk and display them in an arbitrary order.

```
// objfile.cpp
// a class of disk files
#include <fstream.h>                // for file streams
#include <string.h>                // for strcpy()

class objfile                      // models disk file
   {
   private:
      char fname[80];              // file name
      int size;                    // size of objects in file
   public:
      objfile(char* fn, int s)     // two-arg constructor
         {
         size = s;                 // set size
         strcpy(fname, fn);
         }
      void add(void*);             // get object from buffer
      void get(void*, int);        // get object, put in buffer
   };
void objfile::add(void* buff)      // get object from buffer
   {
   ofstream outfile;               // create file for output
   outfile.open(fname, ios::app);  // open file for append
   outfile.write( (char*)buff, size );     // append object
   }
void objfile::get(void* buff, int p)      // get object at position p
   {
   ifstream infile;                // create file for input
   infile.open(fname);             // open it
   infile.seekg( (p-1)*size );     // go to record (object) p
   infile.read( (char*)buff, size );       // read object
   }

class test                        // typical class
   {
   private:
      float flo;                   // arbitrary data
      int int1;
      int int2;
   public:
      test()
         { }
      test(float f, int i1, int i2)  // initialize data
```

```
      { flo=f; int1=i1; int2=i2; }
    void display()                    // display data
      { cout << flo << " " << int1 << " " << int2; }
  };

void main(void)
  {
  test t1(14.5, 2, 1);               // make and initialize
  test t2(29.8, 4, 2);               // three test objects
  test t3(33.6, 6, 3);               // and
  test tempty;                       // an empty one

                                     // make objfile object
  objfile objf1( "TEST.DAT", sizeof(test) );
  objf1.add(&t1);                    // put test ojects
  objf1.add(&t2);                    // in file
  objf1.add(&t3);

  objf1.get(&tempty, 3);             // get object 3
  cout << "\nobject 3: ";
  tempty.display();                  // display it
  objf1.get(&tempty, 1);             // get object 1
  cout << "\nobject 1: ";
  tempty.display();                  // display it
  objf1.get(&tempty, 2);             // get object 2
  cout << "\nobject 2: ";
  tempty.display();                  // display it
  }
```

CHAPTER 9
➤ REFERENCE OVERVIEW

The printed reference materials for Master C++ are divided into two major parts: Chapter 9—a reference overview and Chapter 10—a detailed alphabetical listing. This chapter briefly introduces each of the following elements of C++ that are covered in the detailed reference:

➤ Language keywords, such as *char*, *while*, and *class*

➤ Operators, such as +, ::, and *sizeof*

➤ Preprocessor directives, such as *#include* and *#define*

➤ Predefined values, such as *_DATE_* and *BUFSIZ*

➤ Predefined data types, such as *time_t* and *va_list*

➤ Predefined standard classes such as *istream* and *ostream*, and their most commonly used member functions

➤ Character escape sequences, such as \n and \t

➤ Functions from the ANSI C library, such as *fopen()* and *printf()*

This overview presents groups of related items and a summary of their use. Since mastering the use of the predefined streams classes and ANSI library functions is particularly important, the overview divides them into functionally related groups (such as C++ Streams, ANSI C Streams and Files, Process Control, and Data Conversion). Most groups of functions are presented with two tables: one that lists the functions in the group alphabetically, and one that organizes them according to the task performed, such as opening a file, reading data from a file, and writing data to a file.

The bulk of the reference is the alphabetical list in Chapter 10. If you are interested in a particular keyword, function, macro, class, data structure, or other item, you can go directly to its entry. Each entry includes a description of the item's purpose, a summary of its use, and often an illustrative example. Before using the alphabetical list for the first time, please read the note at the start of Chapter 10 on use of the reference.

C++, AN EMERGING STANDARD

Unlike the older C language, C++ does not yet have an ANSI standard. Master C++ is therefore based on the C++ language as embodied in AT&T C++ Release 2.1 (the de facto standard) and reflects the common features found in such C++ implementations as Borland C++, Turbo C++ (also by Borland), and available C++ compilers for UNIX.

C++ and ANSI C

C++ is largely a superset of ANSI C. That is, the language keywords and syntax of ANSI C are included in that of C++. Put another way, a legal ANSI C program should also be a legal C++ program. Since Master C++ is specifically about C++, no attempt is made to distinguish the elements of ANSI C from the important new features added in C++.

As with C, much of the power of C++ comes from the addition of pre-defined libraries that include the functionality needed to handle real-world hardware in areas such as file I/O, arithmetic, and graphics. While ANSI C offers a generous library of such predefined functions, C++ doesn't really have such a standard library, except in the important area of Stream I/O. Most C++ implementations, therefore, include the ANSI C function library, the Streams class library, and often additional proprietary class libraries. The Master C++ reference includes the ANSI C and Streams libraries: you will have to consult your compiler documentation for information about other included class libraries as well as any additions to the ANSI C library. (Borland C++, for example, includes both the extensive Borland C library (a superset of ANSI C) and a set of useful class libraries.) See Appendix B, *Further Reading* for recommended books on Borland C++ and the ANSI C library.

OVERVIEW OF LANGUAGE ELEMENTS

We can now look at each of the kinds of items that make up the C++ language and environment, and that are covered in the alphabetical reference.

Language Keywords

C++ language keywords are used to provide control structures (such as *if* and *while*), data types (such as *char* and *float*), structure types (such as *struct*, *class*, and terms used to specify class access and relationships), and qualifying terms that specify how data types or variables will be handled (such as *un-signed* and *volatile*). Keywords are also sometimes called "reserved words" because they are reserved for the use of the compiler—you can't use them as variable names. It is, however, all right to embed a keyword in a variable name—for example, *chaptr*. Table 9-1 lists the C++ keywords, each of which has its own entry in the alphabetic reference.

asm	double	new	switch
auto	else	operator	template
break	enum	private	this
case	extern	protected	throw
catch	float	public	try
char	for	register	typedof
class	friend	return	union
const	goto	short	unsigned
continue	if	signed	virtual
default	inline	sizeof	void
delete	int	static	volatile
do	long	struct	while

Table 9-1. C++ language keywords

Note that while all of the C++ keywords listed in Table 9-1 have entries in the alphabetical reference, some of them are not covered in Master C++ because they are esoteric or not yet implemented in most C++ compilers.

Operators and Precedence

Operators are language elements that manipulate variables or data in some way, such as by adding data items together, getting the address of a variable, comparing the size of two numbers, and so on. Each operator has an entry in the alphabetical reference. Because all of the operators except *sizeof, new,* and the type cast (*<type>*) consist of non-alphabetic characters, we have placed all the non-alphabetic operators in the reference chapter in a sequence that *precedes* the letter *A*. Remember that in C++ you can also use the mechanism of *overloading* to extend the meaning of operators so that they handle objects of classes that you define. Table 9-2 lists all of the predefined C++ operators, grouped by category.

Operator	Name	Example	Explanation
Arithmetic Operators			
*	Multiplication	x*y	Multiply x and y
/	Division	x/y	Divide x by y
%	Modulo	x%y	Remainder of x divided by y
+	Addition	x+y	Add x and y
–	Subtraction	x–y	Subtract y from x
++	Increment	x++	Increment x after use
--	Decrement	--x	Decrement x before use
–	Negation	–x	Negate the value of x
+	Unary Plus	+x	Positive value of x
Relational and Logical Operators			
>	Greater than	x>y	1 if x exceeds y, else 0
>=	Greater than or equal to	x>=y	1 if x is greater than or equal to y, else 0
<	Less than	x<y	1 if x is less than y, else 0
<=	Less than or equal to	x<=y	1 if x is less than or equal to y, else 0
==	Equal to	x==y	1 if x equals y, else 0
!=	Not equal to	x!=y	1 if x and y are unequal, else 0
!	Logical NOT	!x	1 if x is 0, else 0
||	Logical OR	x||y	0 if both x and y are 0, else 1
Assignment Operators			
=	Assignment	x=y;	put value of y into x
o=	Compound assignment	x+=y;	equivalent to x =assignment x oy; where o is one of the operators: + – * / - % << >> & ^ |
Data Access and Size Operators			
[]	Array element x	[0]	first element of array x
.	Member selection	s.x	member x in class or struct s
->	Member selection	p->x	member named x in a class or struct that p points to
->*	Class member selection	p->*x	member x of class pointed to by p>
.*	Class member selection	(c.*f)	pointer to member funciton f in class c
*	Indirection	*p	contents of location whose address is in p

Operator	Name	Example	Explanation
&x	Address of	&x	address of variable x
<type>& x=y	Reference to x	int& x=y	x refers to same location as y
sizeof	Size in bytes	sizeof(x)	size of x in bytes

Bitwise Operators

Operator	Name	Example	Explanation
~	Bitwise complement	~x	flip 1 bits to 0 and complement 0 bits to 1
&	Bitwise AND	x&y	bitwise AND of x and y
|	Bitwise OR	x|y	bitwise OR of x and y
^	Bitwise	x^y	value with 1's at exclusive OR bits where corresponding bits of x and y differ
<<	Left shift	x<<y	x shifted to the left (by y positions)
>>	Right shift	x>>y	x shifted to the right (by y bit positions)

Miscellaneous Operators

Operator	Name	Example	Explanation
()	Function call	sqr(10)	call sqr with argument 10
type()	Type cast	double(i)	convert i to double
(type)	Type cast	(double) i	converted to a double (older syntax)
? :	Conditional	x1 ? x2 : x3	if x1 is not 0, x2 is evaluated, else x3 is evaluated
,	Sequential Evaluation	i++, m++	first increment i, then increment m
::	Scope resolution	a::b()	call member function b of class a
new	Memory allocation	p=new int [10]	allocate new object of type x, return pointer
delete	Delete object	delete(x)	destroy (deallocate) object x
<<	Insert to stream	cout << x	put value of x to cout
>>	Extract from stream	cin >> x	put value of input stream in x

Table 9-2. Operators in C++

An important consideration in using operators is the precedence, or order in which operators take effect. Within a given level of precedence the order in which operators take effect is called "associativity." Table 9-3 gives both the precedence and associativity of all of the C++ operators.

Operator Type	Operators	Associativity
Expression	() [] . ->	Left to right
Unary	– + ~ ! * & ++ -- sizeof (type) * (dereference), typecast new, delete	Right to left
Member selection	., ->	Right to left
Pointer to member	.*, ->*	Right to left
Multiplicative	* / %	Left to right
Additive	+ –	Left to right
Shift	<< >>	Left to right
Relational (inequality)	< <= > >=	Left to right
Relational (equality)	== !=	Left to right
Bitwise AND	&	Left to right
Bitwise XOR	^	Left to right
Bitwise OR	|	Left to right
Logical AND	&&	Left to right
Logical OR	||	Left to right
Conditional	? :	Right to left
Assignment	= *= /= %= += –= <<= >>= &= |= ^=	Right to left
Sequential Evaluation	,	Left to right

Table 9-3. Operator precedence and associativity in C++

Thus the expression $a * b / c + d$ is evaluated by doing multiplication and division first, since they have a higher precedence than addition. Because the associativity for the multiplicative operators is from left to right, $a * b$ is performed first, then the result is divided by c. Finally d is added to the result. Of course you can use parentheses to override precedence: in the expression $(a * b) / (c + d)$ the multiplication and addition in parentheses are peformed first, and then the division.

As mentioned earlier, most C++ operators can be overloaded or redefined to work with new data types. Table 9-4 lists the operators that can be overloaded. Remember that overloading cannot change the nature (unary or binary), precedence, or associativity of the operator.

+	-	*	/	%	^	&	|
~	!	=	<	>	+=	-=	*=
/=	%=	^=	&=	|=	<<	>>	>>=
<<=	==	!=	<=	>=	&&	||	++
--	,	->*	->()	[]			

Table 9-4. Operators that can be overloaded

Preprocessor Directives and Macros

The preprocessor processes the source text of a program file and acts on commands, called "preprocessor directives," embedded in the text. These directives begin with the character #. Usually the compiler automatically invokes the preprocessor before beginning compilation, but most compilers will allow you to invoke the preprocessor alone by using compiler options. The preprocessor provides three important services that enable users to make their programs modular, more easily readable, and easier to customize for different computer systems. The services are: including the contents of a file into a C++ program (file inclusion); replacing one string with another (token replacement and macro processing); and compiling selected portions of a program (conditional compilation). Table 9-5 summarizes the preprocessor directives. Each preprocessor directive also has an entry in the alphabetical reference.

Directive	Meaning
# operator	String-izing operator
Example:	#define show(x) printf(#x)
	show(me); expands to printf("me");
## operator	Token-pasting operator
Example:	#define version(x) BC##x
	version(5) results in the token BC5
#define	Define a symbol or a macro (you can redefine a macro with the same expression as often as you want)
Example:	#define double(x) ((x)+(x))
	r=double(2.0); sets r to 4.0
#elif	Else if operator (see example for #if)
#else	Else operator (see example for #if)
#endif	Mark the end of an #if directive
#error	Produce diagnostic message

Table 9-5. continued

Directive	Meaning
Example:	#if defined(WRONG_OPTION)
	#error Recompile with correct option
	#endif
#if	Conditional directive
Example:	#if !defined(FILE_1_INCLUDED)
	#include <file1.h>
	#elif defined(INCLUDE_FILE_2)
	#include <file2.h>
	#else
	#include <file3.h>
	#endif
#ifdef	Equivalent to #if defined
#ifndef	Equivalent to #if !defined
#include	File inclusion
Example:	#include <stdio.h>
#line	Set the current line number
#pragma	Instruct the compiler
#undef	Remove the definition of a symbol

Table 9-5. C++ Preprocessor directives

C++ essentially inherits the preprocessor directives from ANSI C. (Note, however, that use of the CONST keyword is preferable to *#define* for creating constants, because constants created with CONST can be type-checked and the compiler will guard against the value of such a constant being changed. Similarly, the use of inline functions is preferred in C++ over traditional macros when it is desirable to avoid the overhead of function calls. Most C++ implementations include a number of standard predefined preprocessor symbols, as listed in Table 9-6. Note that the predefined macros begin with an underscore character (_). You can not use *#undef* to remove the definitions of these macros. Each of these macros also has an entry in the alphabetical reference.

Macro Name	Defined To Be
__cplusplus	Tells combined C and C++ compilers that the source file is for C++
DATE	The date of translation of the source file in the form of a string of the form "MMM DD YYYY" (such as "Jul 12 1992")
FILE	A string containing the name of the source file
LINE	The line number of the current source file, as a decimal constant
STDC	The decimal constant 1 to indicate that the compiler conforms to some specified standard
TIME	The time of translation of the source file as a string of the form "HH:MM:SS"

Table 9-6. Common predefined macros

Other Predefined Values and Data Types

C++ implementations also provide predefined values that allow the programmer to access implementation-dependent values, such as the minimum and maximum sizes for various character and numeric data types, the locale (national format) in use, and so on. There are also many data types defined in the header files for use by various library functions, such as file information, time, and date formats. Many of these values, both those inherited from ANSI C and those added by C++, have individual entries in the alphabetical reference.

Escape Sequences

Escape sequences allow you to include special characters (such as a newline or tab) in strings. A backslash (\) introduces each escape sequence. Table 9-7 lists the escape sequences supported by C++. Note that you can specify any character in your machine's character set by following the backslash with the octal (base 8) character code, or with an x followed by the hexadecimal character code.

Sequence	Name	Meaning When Printed
\a	alert	Produce an audible alert
\b	backspace	Move character position backwards
\f	form feed	Move to the beginning of a new page
\n	new-line	Move to beginning of next line
\r	carriage return	Move to beginning of current line
\t	horizontal tab	Move to next tabulation position on this line
\v	vertical tab	Move to next vertical tabulation point
\\		Interpret as a single backslash
\'		Interpret as '
\"		Interpret as "
\?		Interpret as ?
\<octal digits>		Specified octal ASCII character
\x<hexadecimal digits>		Specified hexadecimal ASCII character

Table 9-7. Standard character escape sequences

Library Classes and Functions

As noted earlier, C++ compilers inherit a standard function library from ANSI C, often with propietary enhancements. In traditional C, functions are the building blocks of C programs. They are independent collections of declarations and statements you mix and match to create stand-alone applications. Each C or C++ program has at least one function: the *main()* function. The library specified in ANSI C consists mostly of functions (in addition to quite a few macros). For the most part, developing software in C involves writing functions.

In C++, however, the basic building block is not the function but the class: a structure bundling together a set of data and functions that manipulate the data. While a C library consists of functions (and accompanying constants, predefined macros, and so on), a true C++ library consists of one or more classes that are designed to solve particular problems. Most C++ implementations include both an older C library and one or more C++ libraries. Predefined functions and classes are accessed through include files. Table 9-8 lists the header files that are required by the ANSI standard and the most basic ones added by C++ implementations. Many compilers provide additional header files for graphics, calls to operating system functions, and other hardware-dependent matters.

Header File Name	Description
assert.h	Defines the assert macro and NDEBUG symbol. Used for program diagnostics.
complex.h	Defines complex number operations (in most C++ compilers).
ctype.h	Declares character classification and conversion routines.
errno.h	Defines macros for error conditions, EDOM and ERANGE, and the integer variable *errno*.
float.h	Defines symbols for the maximum and minimum values of floating-point numbers.
fstream.h	Defines file-oriented stream classes.
iomanip.h	Defines manipulator functions for C++ streams classes (used for data formatting).
iostream.h	Defines C++ I/O streams classes (pre C++ 2.0 implementations use stream.h instead)
limits.h	Defines symbols for the limiting values of all integer data types.
locale.h	Declares functions necessary for customizing a C program to a particular locale. Defines the *lconv* structure.
math.h	Declares the math functions and the HUGE_VAL constant.
setjmp.h	Defines the *jmp_buf* data type used by the routines *setjmp* and *longjmp*.
signal.h	Defines symbols and routines necessary for handling exceptional conditions.
stdarg.h	Defines the macros that facilitate handling variable-length argument lists.
stddef.h	Defines the standard data types *ptrdiff_t, size_t, wchar_t*, the symbol *NULL*, and the macro offsetof.
stdlib.h	Declares the utility functions such as the string conversion routines, random number generator, memory allocation routines, and process control routines.
string.h	Declares the string manipulation routines.
time.h	Defines data type *time_t*, the *tm* data structure, and declares the *time* functions.

Note: some C++ implementations use the extension .hpp rather than .h for C++ header files.

Table 9-8. Standard header files

The following sections present the library functions in ten categories. For each category two tables—one alphabetical and one organized by task—give you an overview of each set of related functions.

C++ Streams and Files

The C++ and C programming languages have no built-in capability to perform any input and output (I/O). This task is the responsibility of the library accompanying your C++ compiler. Fortunately, all C++ implementations include a set of classes designed to perform a variety of I/O operations. The ANSI standard for C also specifies a set of I/O functions which must be present in a standard-conforming compiler. Table 9-9 lists all the C++ streams I/O routines alphabetically, and Table 9-10 groups them by task. Similarly Table 9-11 lists the traditional C stream I/O functions alphabetically, and Table 9-12 groups them by task.

Notes: the following table does not include functions that are primarily for internal use, or that are involved in low-level programming of streambufs. Many manipulators have alternative member functions. To use general stream functions, include iostream.h or stream.h; to use specialized file functions, include fstream.h;

Name	Class	Description
!	ios	Returns "true" if there has been a stream error; else returns "false."
*	ios	Returns null pointer if error in stream processing, else returns "true" pointer.
>>	istream	Extracts value from input stream into an object.
<<	ostream	Inserts value of object into output stream.
bad	ios	Returns true if badbit or hardfail flag is on.
cerr	ostream_ withassign	Provides standard error stream.
cin	istream_ withassign	Provides standard input stream.
clear	ios	Sets all ios status bits to specified value (clears them by default).
clog	ostream_ withassign	Provides buffered error stream (useful for retreiving error essages).
close	fstream	Closes a file stream.
cout	ostream_ withassign	Provides standard output stream.
dec	<manip.>	Sets conversion base to decimal.
endl	<manip.>	Inserts newline and flushes stream.
ends	<manip.>	Inserts terminal null char. in string.
eof	ios	Returns "true" if at end of file.
fail	ios	Returns true if an operation has set failbit, badbit, or hardfail flag.

Name	Class	Description
filebuf	streambuf	Class that does I/O with file descriptors.
fill	ios	Reports and/or sets fill character.
flags	ios	Reports or sets ios formatting flags.
flush	<manip.>	Flushes an ostream.
fstream	streambuf	Class used for file I/O.
fstreambase	ios	Base class for fstream.
get	istream	Reads single char. or specified chars. from input.
getline	istream	Gets line (including last character) from input.
good	ios	Returns "true" if no ios error flags are on.
hex	<manip.>	Sets conversion base to hexadecimal.
ifstream	fstreamsbase, istream	File stream for input.
ignore	istream	Skips specified number of chars. in input.
ios		Class that contains variables for tracking stream state and for error handling.
iostream	istream, ostream	Class that provides biodirectional I/O using same stream.
istream	ios	Class that manages input from streambufs.
istream withassign	istream_	Provides standard input streams and assignment ops.
oct	<manip.>	Sets conversion base to octal (base 8).
ofstream	fstreambase, ostream	Class that provides file stream for output.
open	fstream	Opens a file stream.
ostream	ios	Manages output stream going to a streambuf.
ostream_ withassign	ostream_	Provides standard streams and assignment ops.
peek	istream	Reads next char. in input without removing it.
precision	ios	Reports and/or sets floating point precision.
put	ostream	Puts char. in output stream.
putback	istream	Puts last character read back into input stream.
rdstate	ios	Returns values of stream state flags.
read	istream	Reads binary data from input stream.
resetiosflags	<manip.>	Clears specified bits in ios format flags.
seekg	istream	Sets read position for file.
seekp	ostream	Sets write position for file.
setbase	<manip.>	Sets conversion base to specified number (0, 8, 10 or 16).

Table 9-9. continued

Name	Class	Description
setf	ios	Reports or sets formatting flags.
setfill	<manip.>	Sets fill character.
setiosflags	<manip.>	Sets specified bits in stream status flags.
setprecision	<manip.>	Sets floating point precision.
setw	<manip.>	Sets character field width.
streambuf		Base class for unformatted streams
tellg	istream	Gives current read location in file.
tellp	ostream	Gives current write location in file.
unsetf	ios	Reports and sets specified formatting flags.
width	ios	Sets width in characters.
write	ostream	Puts multiple characters or bytes in output stream.
ws	<manip.>	Removes white space (blanks, tabs, etc.) from stream.

Notes: <manip.> means function is a manipulator.

Table 9-9. Alphabetical list of C++ stream I/O classes and routines

I/O Task	Routine Names
Create or open a file	open
Close a file	flush, close
Put value from objects into input	<<
Get value from input to object	>>
Formatted read	set format with manipulators or ios member functions then pass stream to read routine
Formatted write	set format with manipulators then write
Set conversion base	dec, oct, hex, setbase
Set or change floating point precision	precision, setprecision
Specify fill character	fill, setfill
Set field width	setw, width
Set or get formatting flags	setf flags
Read a character	get
Read character without removing from input	peek
Skip input characters	ignore
Remove whitespace from input	ws
Write a character	put

I/O Task	Routine Names
Write last character back to input	putback
Read a line	getline
Write a line	write then use endl
Binary read	read
Add end char. to string	ends
Set or get read position	setg, tellg
Set or get write position	setp, tellp
Check EOF condition	eof
Check error conditions	*, !, bad, fail, good, rdstate
Set error flags	setiosflags, resetiosflags

Table 9-10. C++ stream I/O routines classified by task

Name of Routine	Description
clearerr	Clears the error indicator of a stream.
fclose	Closes a stream.
feof	A macro that returns a non-zero value if current position in a stream is at the end of file.
ferror	A macro that returns a non-zero value if an error had occurred during read/write operations on a stream.
fflush	Writes to the file the contents of the buffer associated with a stream
fgetc	Reads a character from a stream.
fgetpos	Returns current position of a stream in an internal format suitable for use by fsetpos.
fgets	Reads a line (up to and including the first newline character) from a stream.
fopen	Opens a named file as a buffered stream (includes options for selecting translation modes and access types).
fprintf	Performs formatted output to a stream.
fputc	Writes a character to a stream.
fputs	Writes a string of characters to a stream.
fread	Reads a specified amount of binary data from a stream.
freopen	Closes a stream and reassigns it to a new file.
fscanf	Performs formatted input from a stream.
fseek	Sets current position to a specific location in the file.
fsetpos	Sets current position of a stream using value returned by an earlier call to fgetpos.

Table 9-11. continued

Name of Routine	Description
ftell	Returns the current position in the file associated with a stream.
fwrite	Writes a specified number of bytes of binary data to a stream.
getc	Reads a character from a stream.
getchar	Reads a character from the stream stdin.
gets	Reads a string up to a newline character from the stream stdin.
printf	Performs formatted output to the stream stdout.
putc	Writes a character to a stream.
putchar	Writes a character to the stream stdout.
puts	Writes a C string to the stream stdout.
remove	Deletes a file specifed by its name.
rename	Changes the name of a file to a new one.
rewind	Sets the current position to the beginning of the file associated with a stream.
scanf	Performs formatted input from the stream stdin.
setbuf	Assigns a fixed-length user-defined buffer to an open stream.
setvbuf	Assigns a variable-length user-defined buffer to an open stream.
sprintf	Performs formatted output to a buffer.
sscanf	Performs formatted input from a buffer.
tmpfile	Creates a temoprary file open for buffered stream I/O.
tmpnam	Generates a temporary file name.
ungetc	Pushes a character back into the buffer associated with a stream.
vfprintf	Version of fprintf that accepts a pointer to a list of arguments and performs formatted output to a stream.
vprintf	Version of printf that accepts a pointer to a list of arguments and performs formatted output to the stream stdout.
vsprintf	Version of sprintf that accepts a pointer to a list of arguments and performs formatted output to a buffer.

Table 9-11. Alphabetical list of ANSI C file I/O

I/O Task	Routine Names
Create or open a file	fopen, freopen
Close a file	fclose
Delete or rename a file	remove, rename
Formatted read	fscanf, scanf
Formatted write	fprintf, printf, vfprintf, vprintf, vsprintf
Read a character	fgetc, fgetchar, getc, getchar
Write a character	fputc, fputchar, putc, putchar
Read a line	fgets, gets
Write a line	fputs, puts
Set read/write position	fseek, fsetpos, rewind
Get read/write position	fgetpos, ftell
Binary read	fread
Binary write	fwrite
Flush buffer	fflush
Check error/eof	clearerr, feof, ferror
Manage temporary files	tmpfile, tmpnam
Control buffering	setbuf, setvbuf
Push character to buffer	ungetc

Table 9-12. File I/O routines in ANSI C classified by task

Process Control and Locale Routines

The process control routines include the signal handling functions that take care of error conditions, and utility functions to terminate a process, communicate with the operating system, and set up numeric and currency formats depending on the locale for which your program is customized. These routines are defined in locale.h, signal.h, setjmp.h, and stdlib.h. Table 9-13 lists these routines alphabetically, and Table 9-14 groups them by task.

Name of Routine	Description
abort	Raises the SIGABRT signal after printing a message to stderr. The normal handler for SIGABRT terminates the process without flushing file buffers.
assert	Prints a diagnostic message and aborts program, if a given logical expression is false.
atexit	Installs a routine to a stack of at least 32 routines that will be called in "last in, first out" order when the process terminates.

Table 9-12. continued

Name of Routine	Description
exit	Calls the functions installed by atexit, flushes all buffers associated with streams that are open for I/O, and finally terminates the process and returns to the operating system.
getenv	Returns the definition of an environment variable from the envrionment of the process.
localeconv	Sets the components of a lconv structure with information about numeric and monetary formatting appropriate for the current locale.
longjmp	Restores the context of a process, thus affecting an unconditional jump to the place where setjmp was called to save that particular context.
perror	Prints an error message using your message and the system message corresponding to the value in the global variable errno.
raise	Generates a signal (an exception).
setjmp	Saves the context of a process in a buffer that can be used by longjmp to jump back.
signal	Installs a function to handle a specific exception or signal.
setlocale	Selects a locale for a specified portion of the program's locale-dependent aspects.
system	Executes an operating system command.

Table 9-13. Alphabetical list of process control and locale routines

Task	Routine Names
Execute an operating system command	system
Terminate a process	abort, exit
Handle errors	assert, perror
Get environment	getenv
Install exception handler and generate an exception	raise, signal
Non-local jump from from one function to another	longjmp, setjmp
Install routines to be called when the process terminates	atexit
Control locale-specific numeric and currency formatting	localeconv, setlocale

Table 9-14. Process control and locale routines by task

Variable Argument List Routines

In writing C++ programs, you encounter built-in functions such as *printf()* that can take a variable number of arguments. Sometimes it is convenient to custom write your own routines that can process a variable number of arguments. Take, for instance, a routine (*findmax()*) that picks the largest element from an array of integers. If the routine can accept a variable number of arguments, you can use such calls as *findmax(1,2,3)* and *findmax(a,b,c,d)* to find the maximum of any number of arguments. A set of macros in ANSI C makes a straightforward task of handling a variable number of arguments. Table 9-15 lists the variable argument handling routines alphabetically—since there are only three of them, no task-oriented table is given.

Name of Macro	Description
va_arg	Gets the next argument from the stack.
va_end	Resets everything so that the function can return normally.
va_start	Initializes the argument pointer to the address of the first argument to the function.

Table 9-15. Alphabetical list of variable argument macros

Memory Allocation Routines

Most computer systems store instructions and data in memory and use a central processing unit (CPU) to repeatedly retrieve instructions from memory and execute them. The operating system, itself a program residing in memory, takes care of loading other programs and executing them. The operating system has its own scheme of managing the available memory for its data and that for other programs as well.

In older programming languages, such as FORTRAN, there is no provision for requesting memory at runtime. All data items and arrays have to be declared before compiling the program. You have to guess beforehand the maximum size of an array and there is no way to exceed the maximum other than recompiling the program. This is inefficient because you are locking in the maximum amount of memory your program will ever need.

In most modern languages, including C++, you can request blocks of memory at runtime and release the blocks when your program no longer needs them. A major advantage of this capability is that you can design your application to exploit all available memory in the system. Like most other capabilities in C, this capability comes in the form of a set of library routines, known as the memory allocation routines. The specific set that comes with ANSI C has four basic memory allocation routines, cataloged in Table 9-16. (Again, due to the limited number of routines in this category, there is no task-oriented table.)

C++ programmers, however, are encouraged to build memory allocation and disposal into class objects via constructors and destructors. This provides a safer and more orderly way to handle memory within the context of a C++ program.

Name of Routine	Description
calloc	Allocates memory for an array of data elements and initializes them to zero.
free	Frees previously allocated memory.
malloc	Allocates a number of bytes and returns a pointer to the first byte of the allocated memory.
realloc	Enlarges or shrinks a previously allocated block of memory. If necessary, this function will move the block in the physical memory of the system.

Table 9-16. Alphabetical list of ANSI C memory allocation routines

Data Conversion Routines

Information management with computers frequently requires crunching numbers. These numbers are internally represented in several forms depending on the type of C variable in which the value is held. It is more convenient to have users enter numbers as strings, however, since strings can be scanned and otherwise checked using a variety of routines. The ANSI C data conversion routines, declared in the header file stdlib.h, allow converting strings to the internal forms needed by numeric variables. These routines are listed alphabetically in Table 9-17 and by task in Table 9-18.

Note that there are a few additional routines in the C library which also provide data conversion facilities. The *sprintf()* and the *sscanf()* functions in the I/O category can respectively convert internal values to strings and strings back to internal representations. The *sscanf()* routine, however, lacks the ability to convert a string to an integer using an arbitrary radix—only decimal, octal, and hexadecimal formats are supported.

Finally, note that C++ programmers can handle many data formatting and conversion tasks through the Streams classes described in Tables 9-9 and 9-10.

Name of Routine	Description
atof	Converts a string to a double precision floating point value.
atoi	Converts a string to an integer.
atol	Converts a string to a long integer.
strtod	Converts a string to a double precision floating point value.
strtol	Converts a string to a long integer.
strtoul	Converts a string to an unsigned long integer.

Table 9-17. Alphabetical list of ANSI C data conversion routines

Task	Routine Names
Convert character string to floating point value	atof, strtod
Convert character string to integer	atoi
Convert character string to long integer	atol, strtol
Convert character string to unsigned long integer	strtoul

Table 9-18. ANSI C data conversion routines by task

Math Routines

In addition to the support for basic floating point operations in the language, the ANSI C library also includes a set of common math functions (such as sine and cosine). Table 9-19 lists the math routines alphabetically, and Table 9-20 groups them by task.

Name of Routine	Description
abs	Returns the absolute value of an integer argument.
acos	Computes the arc cosine of a value between -1 and 1 and returns an angle between 0 and pi radians.
asin	Computes the arc sine of a value between -1 and 1 and returns an angle between -pi/2 and pi/2 radians.
atan	Computes the arc tangent of a value and returns an angle between -pi/2 and pi/2 radians.
atan2	Computes the arc tangent of one argument divided by the other and returns an angle between -pi and pi radians.

Table 9-19. continued

Name of Routine	Description
ceil	Finds the smallest integer larger than or equal to the function's floating point argument.
cos	Evaluates the cosine of an angle in radians.
cosh	Evaluates the hyperbolic cosine of its argument.
div	Divides one integer by another and returns an integer quotient and an integer remainder.
exp	Computes the exponential of a floating point argument.
fabs	Returns the absolute value of a floating point argument.
floor	Finds the largest integer smaller than or equal to the function's floating point argument.
fmod	Computes the floating point remainder after dividing one floating point value by another so that the quotient is the largest possible integer for that division.
frexp	Breaks down a floating point value into a mantissa between 0.5 and 1 and an integer exponent so that the value is equal to the mantissa times two raised to the power of the exponent.
labs	Returns the absolute value of a long integer argument.
ldexp	Computes a floating point value equal to a mantissa times two raised to the power of an integer exponent.
ldiv	Divides one long integer by another and returns a long integer quotient and a long integer remainder.
log	Evaluates the natural logarithm of its floating point argument.
log10	Evaluates the logarithm to the base 10 of its floating-point argument.
modf	Breaks down a floating point value into its integer part and its fractional part.
pow	Computes the value of one argument raised to the power of a second one.
rand	Returns a random integer between 0 and RAND_MAX (defined in stdlib.h).
sin	Evaluates the sine of an angle in radians.
sinh	Evaluates the hyperbolic sine of its argument.
sqrt	Computes the square root of a positive floating point number.
srand	Sets the starting point for the sequence of random numbers generated by rand.
tan	Evaluates the tangent of an angle in radians.
tanh	Evaluates the hyperbolic tangent of its argument.

Table 9-19. Alphabetical list of ANSI math routines

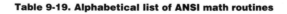

Task	Routine Names
Evaluate trigonometric functions	acos, asin, atan, atan2, cos, sin, tan
Evaluate hyperbolic functions	cosh, sinh, tanh
Evaluate powers and logarithms	exp, frexp, ldexp, log, log10, pow
Compute square root	sqrt
Compute magnitudes and absolute values	abs, fabs
Find integer limits (lower and upper) for floating point numbers	ceil, floor
Break down floating point number into integer and fraction	modf
Find floating point remainder	fmod
Integer arithmetic	abs, div, labs, ldiv
Generate random numbers	rand, srand

Table 9-20. ANSI math routines by task

Character Classification and Conversion Routines

Character classification routines (actually macros) beginning with "is" classify a character by various criteria such as whether it is part of the alphabet, a number, a punctuation mark, and so on. The routines *tolower* and *toupper* convert characters to lower- and uppercase, respectively.

Table 9-21 lists the character classification and conversion routines alphabetically, and Table 9-22 groups them by task.

Name of Routine	Description
isalnum	Tests if a character is alphanumeric.
isalpha	Tests if a character is alphabetic.
iscntrl	Tests if a character belongs to the set of control characters.
isdigit	Tests if a character is a numerical digit.
isgraph	Tests if a character is printable (excluding the space character).
islower	Tests if a character is lowercase.
isprint	Tests if a character is printable (includes space).
ispunct	Tests if a character belongs to the set of punctuation characters.
isspace	Tests if a character belongs to the set of "whitespace" characters.
isupper	Tests if a character is uppercase.

Table 9-21. continued

Name of Routine	Description
isxdigit	Tests if a character is a hexadecimal digit.
tolower	Converts a character to lowercase only if that character is an uppercase letter.
toupper	Converts a character to uppercase only if that character is a lowercase letter.

Table 9 -21. Alphabetical list of character classification and conversion routines

Task	Routine Names
Classify a character	isalnum, isalpha, iscntrl, isdigit, isgraph, islower, isprint, ispunct, isspace, isupper, isxdigit
Convert from uppercase to lowercase	tolower
Convert from lowercase to uppercase	toupper

Table 9-22. Character classification and conversion routines by task

String and Buffer Manipulation Routines

Manipulating text is a major part of many computer applications. The manipulation might involve text editing, word processing, or that part of your application which reads commands typed by the user and interprets them. Typically you read a single line of command into a C++ string and intrepret it. Depending on the syntax of your application's command set, the interpretation will involve chores such as extracting the commands and parameters from the string, comparing the command against entries in a stored table, or copying the parameters into separate strings for later use. Although C++ has no built-in operators for handling strings, the ANSI C standard specifies a set of string manipulation routines that provides all the capablities needed to process strings. Note that "multibyte characters" are new and are not supported by all otherwise ANSI-compliant compilers. They are useful mainly for dealing with special character sets and international alphabets.

As C++ class libraries continue to be developed, more string functions are likely to be "packaged" as operators or other member functions to be used with appropriate string classes.

Table 9-23 lists the string and buffer routines alphabetically, and Table 9-24 groups them by task.

Name of Routine	Description
mblen	Returns the number of bytes that make up a single multibyte character.
mbtowc	Converts a multibyte character to wchar_t type.
mbtowcs	Converts a sequence of multibyte characters into a sequence of codes of wchar_t type.
memchr	Searches for a specific character in a given number of bytes of the buffer.
memcmp	Compares a specified number of bytes of two buffers.
memcpy	Copies a specified number of bytes from one buffer to another (*not for overlapping source and destination*).
memmove	Copies a specified number of bytes from one buffer to another (*handles overlapping source and destination*).
memset	Sets specified number of bytes of a buffer to a given value.
strcat	Appends one string to another.
strchr	Locates the first occurrence of a character in a string.
strcmp	Compares one string to another and differentiates between lowercase and uppercase letters.
strcoll	Compares two strings using a collating sequence specified by the LC_COLLATE category of current locale.
strcpy	Copies one string to another.
strcspn	Returns the position in the string, of the first character that belongs to a given set of characters.
strerror	Returns a string containing the system error message corresponding to an error number.
strlen	Returns the length of a string as the number of bytes in the string excluding the terminating null ('\0').
strncat	Appends a specified number of characters of one string to another.
strncmp	Compares a specified number of characters of two strings while maintaining the distinction between lowercase and uppercase letters.
strncpy	Copies a specified number of characters from one string to another. (Note: resulting string will not automatically have a null character '\0' appended.)
strpbrk	Locates the first occurrence of any character from one string in another.
strrchr	Locates the last occurrence of a character in a string.
strspn	Returns the position in the string of the first character that does not belong to a given set of characters.
strstr	Locates the first occurrence of one string in another.
strtok	Returns the next token in a string with the token delimiters specified in a string.

Table 9-23. continued

Name of Routine	Description
strxfrm	Transforms a string to a new form so that if strcmp is applied to two transformed strings the returned result is the same as that returned when strcoll is applied to the original strings.
wctomb	Converts a character of wchar_t type to a multibyte character.
wcstombs	Converts a sequence of codes of wchar_t type sequence of multibyte characters.

Table 9-23. Alphabetical list of string and buffer manipulation routines

Task	Routine Names
Find length of a string	mblen, strlen
Compare two strings or buffers	memcmp, strcmp, strncmp, strcoll, strxfrm
Copy and append	memcpy, memmove, strcat, strcpy, strncat, strncpy
Search for a character or a substring	memchr, strchr, strcspn, strpbrk, strrchr, strspn, strstr
Extract tokens from a string	strtok
Load the same character into every position in a buffer	memset
Prepare error message in a string	strerror
Convert between multibyte and wide character types	mbtowc, mbstowcs, wctomb, wcstombs

Table 9-24. String and buffer manipulation routines by task

Searching and Sorting Routines

Searching and sorting are commonplace in many applications. All commercial data base programs have these capabilities. If you implement your own data base program tailored to your specific requirements, you will invariably need search and sort capabilities. For example, if your data base contains the names and addresses of the customers of your company, you will often need to search the list for the information about a certain customer. And for mailings, you might want to print labels for all entries in your data base, sorted by the zip code.

If you are developing your data base in C++, the ANSI C standard makes your job easier by providing two library routines for sorting and searching lists in memory, as described in Table 9-25. (See the main alphabetical reference for more details.) Again, since there are only two functions in this group, no "by task" table is provided.

C++ programmers will increasingly be able to take advantage of data manipulation classes (such as lists and containers) that are being provided with C++ compilers or as third party class libraries.

Name of Routine	Description
bsearch	Search for an element in a sorted array.
qsort	Sort an array of elements.

Table 9-25. Alphabetical list of searching and sorting routines

Time and Date Routines

The ANSI C library includes a set of routines for obtaining and displaying date and time information. These routines are declared in the header file *time.h*. The *time* function is at the heart of these routines. It returns the current date and time in an implementation-defined encoded form.

There are library routines to convert this time into a printable string, and otherwise manipulate it. A list of the time and date functions in alphabetical order appears in Table 9-26 while Table 9-27 groups them by task.

Name of Routine	Description
asctime	Converts time from a structure of type *tm* to a string.
clock	Returns the elapsed processor time in number of ticks.
ctime	Converts time from a value of type *time_t* to a string.
difftime	Computes the difference of two values of type *time_t*.
gmtime	Converts time from a value of type *time_t* to a structure of type *tm* which will correspond to the Greenwich Mean Time.
localtime	Converts time from a value of type *time_t* to a structure of type *tm* which will correspond to the local time.
mktime	Converts the local time from a structure of type *tm* into a value of type *time_t*.
strftime	Prepares a string with date and time values from a *tm* structure, formatted according to a specified format.
time	Returns the current date and time encoded as a value of type *time_t*. The encoding is implementation-dependent.

Table 9-26. Alphabetical list of time routines

Task	Routine Names
Get current date and time	time
Convert time from one form to another	asctime, ctime, gmtime, localtime, mktime
Compute elapsed time	clock, difftime

Table 9-27. Time routines by task

CHAPTER 10

► ALPHABETICAL REFERENCE

The reference in this chapter lists every element of the C++ and ANSI C languages—operators, classes, functions, macros, data types, keywords, and so on—in a single alphabetical sequence. You should find this reference to be easy to use, but the following notes will help you get started.

ALPHABETIZATION

The alphabetization of reference entries follows these rules:

➤ Items that have only non-alphabetic characters, such as most of the operators, are placed together in one sequence in ASCII character order before the first "a" entry.

➤ Non-alphabetic characters such as /, #, or _ at the beginning of alphabetic items are disregarded. Thus *#define* is treated as though it were *define*.

➤ Items with underscores inside them are treated as though the underscores spaced the name into separate words. Thus *L_tmpnam* is filed as *L tmpnam* and comes before *LC_ALL* since *LC* comes after *L*.

➤ Case is always disregarded.

FORMAT OF ENTRIES

Each reference entry contains at least some of the following elements—not all entries have all of them.

Name

The name of the item. Below the name is given the type of item (function, macro, keyword, operator, and so on.). For operators the descriptive name of the operator is given below the operator symbol. (For example, *&* (address-of operator) and *&* (reference operator).

Purpose

A brief description of the purpose for which the item is used and the essential details of its behavior.

Syntax

The format needed to use or invoke the item. A full prototype is given for ANSI C functions. The parameters in parentheses following the function name specify the kind of arguments used in calling the function. For example,

```
double cos(double x);
```

indicates that the *cos()* function is given a *double* value *x* and returns a *double* value (in this case the cosine of x).

Because C++ streams functions are often overloaded and can have several prototypes, only the general calling format is given for these functions.

The individual elements in syntax statements are described when not obvious.

Within general syntax statements for operators, keywords, and streams functions the descriptive name for a value is enclosed in angle brackets. For example, the syntax

```
<varname> = <int_value>
```

means that you replace <variable> with an actual variable name, and <int_value> with an actual integer value. Thus the statement

```
Total = 0;
```

satisfies the above syntax.

Any header (include) file needed for use of the item is specified in an *#include* statement.

Example Use

An actual statement or expression using the item. An ellipses *(…)* indicates that other statements that usually occur in that part of the program have been omitted.

Returns

The value or values that can be returned by the item. Not all functions or other items return values.

See Also

Related items—either other items that do similar things or other items that do different things with the same type of data or variable.

MASTER C++ ALPHABETICAL REFERENCE

!
Logical
NOT operator

Purpose

Use the logical *NOT* operator to change a condition to its opposite truth value. *NOT* makes a true condition false and a false condition true.

Syntax
```
!<condition>
```

Example Use
```
!x    /* 1 (true) if x is 0, else 0 (false) */
```

See Also
```
&&, ||
```

!
Stream status
operator

Purpose

Use the *!* operator to determine whether an error has occurred when accessing a C++ stream. This is an overloaded version of the regular "not" operator and is found in the *ios* class.

Syntax
```
#include <iostream.h>
!<stream_object>   invoke for stream accessed for reading and/or writing
```

Example Use
```
ifstream in_file; // declare an input stream
...
if (!in_file) // error in accessing file
    cout << "\nCannot open input file!";
else
    // do stuff with the file
```

Returns

The *!* operator returns a non-zero integer "true" value if the *failbit, badbit,* or *hardfail ios* status flag has been set (indicating an error); otherwise, the operator returns a 0 (false) value. Note: Use the *** operator instead of ! if you want the stream status returned as a pointer value.

See Also
```
istream, ifstream, ios, * (stream status operator), open()
```

!=
Not equal
operator

Purpose
Use the *not equal* operator to test whether two numeric quantities are not equal to each other, or two strings are not the same.

Syntax
```
<expression1> != <expression2>
```

Example Use
```
x!=y /* 1 (true) if x and y are unequal,
     else 0 (false) */
```

See Also
```
==, <, >
```

#
String-izing
preprocessor
operator

Purpose
Use the *string-izing* operator to have the preprocessor make a string out of the item that immediately follows the operator. It does this by putting the value in quotes in the preprocessed source file.

Syntax
```
#<item>
```

Example Use
```
#define value_now(x) printf(#x"=%d\n",x)
value_now(counter);
/* the preprocessor generates this statement:
    printf("counter""= %d\n", counter);
    which is equivalent to:
    printf("counter = %d\n", counter); */
```

See Also
```
## (token-pasting operator), #define
```

##
Token-pasting
preprocessor
operator

Purpose
Use the *token-pasting operator* to join one separate item (token) to another one to form a new token.

Syntax
```
<token1>##<token2>
```

Example Use
```
#define version(x) BCPP##x
/* version(3) results in the token BCPP3 */
```

See Also
```
# (string-izing operator), #define
```

% Modulus operator

Purpose

Use the *modulus operator* to obtain the remainder after one quantity is divided by another.

Syntax
```
<val1> % <val2>
```

Example Use
```
Remainder = 18 % 7; /* assigns 4 to Remainder */
```

See Also
```
/, div, ldiv, mod, modf
```

& Address-of operator

Purpose

Use the *address-of* operator to get the address at which the value of a variable is stored.

Syntax
```
&<varname>
```

Example Use
```
Addr = &x; /* assign address of x to Addr */
```

See Also
```
* (pointer dereferencing operator), & (reference operator),
sizeof
```

& Bitwise AND operator

Purpose

Use the *bitwise AND operator* & to compare two quantities bit by bit. Each bit in the resulting value will be set to 1 if and only if the corresponding bits in the values being compared were both set to 1. Do not confuse & (bitwise AND) with && (logical AND); the latter compares the whole values, not individual bits.

Syntax
```
val1 & val2
```

Example Use
```
Result = 11 & 8; /* 1011 AND 1000 results in 1000 */
```

See Also
```
|, ~, &&, ||
```

&
Reference operator

Purpose

Use the *&* operator to create a reference to a variable. When you create a reference, the reference name and the variable name refer to the same location in memory and thus have the same contents.

Syntax
```
#include <iostream.h>
<typename>& <reference_name> = <varname>
```
typename	*a valid data type*
reference_name	*name to be used as a reference*
varname	*name of the variable to be referred to*

Example Use
```
int counter = 10;
int& current = counter; // current now same as
                        //counter
cout << counter << current; // both are 10
```
Do not confuse a reference (*&* after the type name) with the address-of operator (*&* before a variable name). int& r means "a reference called *r*, but &r means "the address of *r*."

See Also
```
* (pointer), & (address-of operator)
```

&&
Logical AND operator

Purpose

Use the *logical AND operator* to check whether two conditions are both true. The *AND* operator returns a value of 1 (true) only if both of the conditions tested are true (1). Do not confuse && (logical AND) with & (bitwise AND); the latter compares individual bits and sets the bits in the result accordingly.

Syntax
```
val1 && val2
```

Example Use
```
if (Category == CLERICAL && Years_Served >= 10)
/* True only if clerical category and at least 10
   years have been served */
```

See Also
||, !

()
Function
argument list
operator

Purpose

Use parentheses to enclose arguments in function calls and parameter lists in function declarations. An argument is an actual value sent to a function, while a parameter is a formal description of the argument in the function declaration.

Syntax
```
<return_type> <func_name>(<type> <parameter_name>, ...)
                                           function declaration
<func_name>(<argument>, ...)               function call
```

Example Use
```
void *malloc(size_t num_bytes);
    /* declaration of malloc() specifies an argument of type
       size_t called  num_bytes that returns a pointer to
       void*/
malloc(10)   /* call malloc with argument 10 */
```

*
Pointer
dereferencing
operator

Purpose

Use the *pointer dereferencing operator* to get the value stored at the address represented by a pointer.

Syntax
```
*pointer_name    value pointed to by pointer
```

Example Use
```
Val = *p;    /* assigns contents of location whose
                address is stored in pointer p */
```

See Also
```
& (address-of operator), & (C++ reference operator), .*, ->,
->*, []
```

*
Multiplication
operator

Purpose

Use the *multiplication operator* to multiply two values.

Syntax
```
<val1> * <val2>
```

Example Use
```
Product = x * y;   /* assigns product of x and y to Product */
```

See Also
```
+, -, /, %
```

*
Stream status pointer

Purpose

Use the *C++ *stream status pointer operator* to return the error status of a stream as a pointer value. The *(pointer) operator has been overloaded by the *ios* class for this purpose.

Syntax
```
#include <iostream.h>
*<stream_object>
stream_object            a stream accessed for reading and/or writing
```

Example Use
```
if (/.*my_file ==NULL/) handle_error();
// handle error if null pointer returned
```

Returns

The *operator returns a pointer value of 0 (false or *NULL*) if the *failbit, badbit,* or *hardfail ios* flags have been set (indicating an error in accessing the stream); otherwise, a non-null (true) value is returned. Note that this is the opposite logical sense to the *!* operator, which returns "true" if an error occurred and false otherwise.

See Also
```
! (stream status operator), ios, open()
```

+
Addition operator

Purpose

Use the *addition operator* to add two values together.

Syntax
```
<val1> + <val2>
```

Example Use
```
Total = Price + Tax;   /* Adds Price and Tax and assigns to
                             Total */
```

See Also
```
-, *, /, %
```

+
Unary
Plus operator

Purpose

Use the *unary plus operator* to make a value positive.

Syntax
```
+<val>
```

Example Use
```
+x    /* Value of x is positive (new in ANSI C) */
```

See Also
```
- (unary minus operator)
```

++
Increment
operator

Purpose

Use the *increment operator* to add one to the value of a variable. This is often done to increase loop index variables by one each time through the loop. The ultimate effect of $i++$ is the same as that of $i = i + 1;$.

When the increment operator precedes the variable name (for example, $++i$) the value of i is increased by one before any expression containing i is evaluated. When the increment operator follows the variable name (for example, $i++$) the value of i is increased by one *after* the expression containing i is evaluated.

Syntax
```
++val              pre-increment
val++              post-increment
```

Example Use
```
for (i=0, sum=0; i <= limit; sum += i++)
/* i is incremented only after it is added to the sum */
++counter   /* counter is incremented before it is
                used for anything*/
```

See Also
```
+, +=
```

,
Sequential
evaluation
operator

Purpose

Use the *sequential evaluation operator* (a comma) to group together two or more expressions that will be evaluated in succession from left to right. This operator is often used in *for* loops to perform two or more initializations or updates.

Syntax
```
<expression>, <expression> ...
```

Example Use
```
i++, j++;  /* first increment i, then increment j */
```

Note that the order of evaluation within each statement is not affected by the use of the comma to group statements. In particular the rules for pre- and post-increments and decrements described in the entries for ++ and -- are not affected.

See Also
```
for
```

▪ Negation operator

Purpose
Use the *negation operator* to make a quantitiy negative. This operator is sometimes called the unary minus operator. (Do not confuse this operator wtih ~ (the *bitwise negation operator*). The latter negates (reverses) each bit in the specified value, while the - operator simply makes the value as a whole negative.)

Syntax
```
-val        same magnitude as val but negative
```

Example Use
```
x = 10;
y = -x;    /* y = -10 */
```

See Also
```
~ (bitwise negation operator), + (unary plus operator), -
(subtraction operator), ! (logical NOT operator)
```

▪ Subtraction operator

Purpose
Use the *subtraction operator* to subtract one value from another.

Syntax
```
<val1> - <val2>
```

Example Use
```
Diff = X1 - X2   /* subtract X2 from X1 and assign to Diff */
```

See Also
```
- (negation operator), -- (decrement operator)
```

--
Decrement
operator

Purpose

Use the *decrement operator* to subtract one from the value of a variable. This is often done to decrease loop index variables by one each time through the loop. The ultimate effect of *i --* is the same as that of *i = i -1;*.

When the decrement operator precedes the variable name (for example, *-- i*) the value of *i* is decreased by one before any expression containing *i* is evaluated. When the decrement operator follows the variable name (for example, *i--*) the value of *i* is decreased by one *after* the expression containing *i* is evaluated.

Syntax
```
--val          pre-decrement
val--          post-decrement
```

Example Use
```
for (i=MAX_VAL, sum=0; i >= MIN_VAL; sum += i--)
/* i is decremented only after it is added to the sum*/
--counter;/* counter is decremented before it is
            used for anything */
i--, j--;  /* first decrement i, then decrement j*/
```

See Also
```
-, -=
```

->
Object
pointer
member
selection
operator

Purpose

Use the *object pointer member selection operator* to access a particular data member or member function in a class or structure object pointed to by a pointer. The notation *class_pointer -> member* accesses the *member* field of the class or structure object pointed to by *class_pointer*. If you want to access a member of a class or structure directly (not through a pointer) use the notation *object_name.member_name* where *object_name* is a variable of a class or struct type and *member_name* is the name of the member. Note that to set up a pointer to a member of a class or struct itself rather than to a member of an object, use the class pointer member selection operator described in the next entry.

Syntax
```
class_ptr->member_name
```

Example Use

```
class corp_info
{   /*define a class */
    char * name;
    ...
    char* getname() {return name;}
};
corp_info corp;   /* define an object of that type */
corp_info* ptr = &corp;   /* define pointer to the class */
ptr->name = "Turbo C++"; /* assign value to member through
                           pointer */
char* name = ptr->getname(); /* invoke member function
                              through pointer */
```

See Also

.(member selection operator), .* (class member selection
operator), :: (scope resolution operator), struct, class

->*

**Class
pointer
member
selection
operator**

Purpose

Use the *class pointer member selection operator (->*)* to dereference member offset pointers when the class portion of the expression is also a pointer.

Note that member offset pointers are distinctly different from object pointers. Whereas an object pointer points to an object directly in memory, a member offset pointer contains an *offset* to a member relative to an object.

Syntax

```
<type> <class>::* <ptr_name>;          to declare a member offset pointer
<ptr_name> = &<class>::<member>;       to assign it to a member
<object-ptr> ->* <ptr_name>;           to access (dereference) the member
```

The <ptr_name> member offset pointer is set to an offset relative to any object of the same *class* that is the same data or function type as <type>. For example, if <ptr_name> is a member offset pointer to a type *double* member of an object class, then it can be assigned and offset to any type *double* members in that class.

The C++ compiler will assign <ptr_name> with the integer offset to <member> relative to the start of the object in memory, i.e., relative to the *this* pointer for an object. Note that <ptr_name> is not assigned a pointer to a specific object in memory, but it is instead assigned an offset relative to a specific class of objects. This offset is then dereferenced using either the .* operator or the ->* operator as shown in the example.

Note that the notation <object_pointer>->* <member_ptr> where <object_ptr> is a pointer to an object and <member_ptr> is a member offset pointer to a data or function *member* in the same class as <object_ptr>, is equivalent to <object.member>. The ->* operator first dereferences <object_ptr> to the left of the operator and then dereferences the member offset pointer by adding the offset to the first dereference to obtain the second, and final, dereference. Function calls via dereferenced function members must use overriding parentheses around the dereferencing portion of the expression.

```
#include <iostream.h>

struct EXAMPLE {
    int one;
    int two;
    int Total() { return(one + two); } };

void main(void) {
    EXAMPLE Exp;

    /* ExpPtr is a pointer to the Exp EXAMPLE object */
    EXAMPLE *pExp = &Exp;

    /* pExpMem is a member offset pointer to an integer EXAMPLE member. */
    int EXAMPLE::* pExpMem;

    /* pExpMem equals the offset to an EXAMPLE objects 'one' member */
    pExpMem = &EXAMPLE::one;

    /* Dereference the pExp pointer and the member */
    /* offset pointer using the ->* operator. */
    pExp->*pExpMem = 1;

    /* pExpMem equals the offset to an EXAMPLE objects 'two' member */
    pExpMem = &EXAMPLE::two;

    /* Set the 'two' member eqaul to 2 using the .* operator */
    Exp.*pExpMem = 2;

    /* Declare a member offset function pointer called 'pMemFnct' */
    int (EXAMPLE::*pMemFnct)();

    /* Set pMemFnct equal to the offset to the EXAMPLE::Total() function. */
    pMemFnct = &EXAMPLE::Total;

    /* Use the .* and ->* operators with the pMemFnct offset pointer */
    cout << "(Exp.*pMemFnct)()   = " << (Exp.*pMemFnct)() << "\n";
    cout << "(pExp->*pMemFnct)() = " << (pExp->*pMemFnct)() << "\n"; }
```

Member selection operator

Purpose

Use the *member selection operator* to access a member (field) of a class or struct directly. The notation *object_name.member_name* accesses member *member_name* of struct or class object *class_name*. To access a class or structure through a pointer, use the pointer member selection operator (->) instead.

Syntax

```
object_name.member_name
```

Example Use

```
object address                     /* define a stricture*/
{
    char * name
    ...
};
address this_address;/*define a variable of that type*/
this_address.name = "John Q. Public";
/* assign value to member of structure */
```

See Also

```
->, ::, .*, struct, class
```

.*
Pointer Member selection operator

Purpose

Use the *pointer member selection operator* to access a member (field) of a class or struct through a pointer. The notation *pointer_name.*member_name* accesses member *member_name* of struct or class object pointed to by *pointer_name*. Note that the -> and ->* operators provide other ways to access class or structure members through pointers.

Syntax

```
object_name.*member_name
```

Example Use

See the entry for the class member pointer selection operator ->* for examples of the use of the .* operator and a general discussion of the use of member offset pointers.

See Also

```
->, ->*, ::, struct, class
```

/
Division
operator

Purpose

Use the *division operator* to divide one numeric value by another. For integer values the whole-number quotient is returned; for floating-point type values the decimal fraction is returned.

Syntax
```
val1 / val2
```

Example Use
```
quotient = dividend / divisor;   /* Divide dividend by divisor */
```

See Also
```
+, -, *, %
```

/* */
C-style
comment

Purpose

Use the /* */ symbol pair to enclose a non-executable comment in your source code. The comment can be confined to a single line or extend over several lines. Note that while C++ compilers accept the /* */ style of comments, the preferred comment style in C++ introduces comments with the // symbol. Also note that while some C and C++ compilers allow nested comments, nesting is not an ANSI requirement and such code may not be portable.

Syntax
```
/* <text of comment> */            Single-line comment
/* <line of comment text
   ....
   ...                             */  Multiple-line comment
```

Example Use
```
for (day=monday; day <= friday; day++); /* for each
                                         weekday */
   PrintSched (day); /* print that day's calendar */
```

See Also
```
// (C++ comment)
```

//
C++-style
comment

Purpose

Use the // symbol to introduce a *C++-style comment*. All text following // on the line is considered to be a non-executable comment. For multi-line comments each line must begin with //.

Syntax

```
// <text of comment>
```

Example Use

```
// This program has been tested with Borland C++
// and Zortech C++ and runs properly in an MS Windows
// DOS session
class Event { // holds system event info.
```

See Also

```
/* */ (C-style comment)
```

::
Scope
resolution
operator

Purpose

Use the *:: scope resolution operator* to define a class member function (other than an inline one). You can also use this operator in general to refer to a member function or data member of a structure or class that is outside the current scope, or one that is global. For example, you can use the :: operator within a class object to refer to a global data item or function that has the same name as the class's own member data item or function.

Syntax

```
<class_name>::<member_name> or
::<global_name>
class_name      name of a class or structure
member_name     name of a function or data member
global_name     name of a global function or data item
```

Example Use

```
class box {
            int num;
            char* stuff;
public:
            int checknum()
            // access global num rather than class
            // member num
};
int box::checknum() {
    return ::num;
}   // member function defined with :: operator
```

If *box* had a base class called *container* and a member function in *box* wanted to call the function *open* in the base class, the call would look like this:

```
container::open(mode);
```

See Also

```
class, struct, extern
```

<
Less-than
operator

Purpose

Use the *less-than operator* to determine whether a numeric value is less than another numeric value, or whether a character or string comes before another character or string in the collating sequence.

The less-than operator returns 1 (true) if the first value is less than (or comes before) the second one; otherwise, the operator returns 0 (false).

Syntax
```
val1 < val2
```

Example Use
```
if (score > goal) printf("You won!\n");
```

See Also
```
>, =, !=
```

<<
insertion
stream
operator

Purpose

Use the *insertion* or "put-to" *stream operator* to send the value of a constant, literal, or variable to an object of the *ostream* class. Most commonly the value is put to the standard output stream, *cout*. This operator is commonly overloaded to work with user-defined class objects.

Syntax
```
#include <iostream.h>
<output stream> << <value>
output stream     an ostream object
value             a basic data type or overloaded for a user-defined class
```

Example Use
```
cout << total;    /* Puts value of variable total to
                     standard output */
cout << endl;     /* send end of line to output
```

Returns

The insertion operator is left-associative and returns a reference to the *ostream* object for which it is invoked. Thus multiple uses of the operator can be "cascaded" to output several pieces of data, as in

```
cout << "The value of n is " << n << "\n" ;
```

See Also
```
>> (extraction operator), ostream, cout, printf()
```

<<
Left-shift
operator

Purpose

Use the *left-shift operator* to shift all of the bits in a value to the left. Each time you shift the leftmost bit is discarded. A shift of one bit to the left is equivalent to multiplying the value by 2.

Syntax
```
value << <number of times to shift>
```

Example Use
```
x = 2;
x = x << 4; /* x shifted to the left by 4
            bit positions and now equals 32 */
```

See Also
```
>>, &, |
```

<=
Less than
or equal to
operator

Purpose

Use the *less than or equal to operator* to determine whether one numeric value is less than or equal to another. If the first value is less than or equal to the second, the operator returns 1 (true). If the second value is less than the first, the operator returns 0 (false).

Syntax
```
<val1> <= <val2>
```

Example Use
```
if (temperature <= critical_point) printf("Everything's
fine!\n");
```

See Also
```
==, >, >=
```

=
Assignment
operator

Purpose

Use the *assignment operator* to assign a value to a variable. Do not confuse = with ==; the latter operator does not assign a value but rather tests the value for equality.

Syntax
```
<varname> = <value>;        assign value to variable
<var1> = <var2> = <value>;  assign same value to both variables
```

You can combine an arithmetic operator (+, -, *, or /) with the assignment operator. When you do so the indicated arithmetic is performed using the variable and the second value, and the result is assigned to the variable. For example:

```
a += b;     /* add b to a and assign result to a */
a *= 2;     /* multiply a times 2 and make that the
               new value of a */
```

Example Use
```
total = 0;          /* assign 0 to total */
line = word = 1;    /* assign 1 to both line and word*/
counter += value;   /* increase counter by value */
```

See Also
```
=, ++, --
```

==
Equal-to operator

Purpose
Use the *equal-to operator* to determine whether the first value is equal to the second one. For numbers this means that both have the same value; for characters or strings equality means that both characters or strings are the same. The operator returns 1 (true) if the values are equal; otherwise, it returns false (0).

Do not confuse == with = ; the latter does not compare the second value to the first, but rather assigns the second value to the first.

Syntax
```
<val1> == <val2>
```

Example Use
```
if (cust_no == target_no) flag_account(cust_no);
if (choice == 'a') do_choice_a;
```

See Also
```
<=, >=, !=
```

>
Greater-than operator

Purpose
Use the *greater-than operator* to determine whether the first value is greater than the second one. For numbers this means that the first number is larger than the second; for characters or strings it means that the first character or string comes later than the second one in the collating sequence. The > operator returns the value 1 (true) if the first value is greater than (or comes later than) the second; otherwise the operator returns 0 (false).

Syntax
```
val1 > val2
```

Example Use
```
if (line > lines_per page) do_header();
if (choice > 'f') menu_error();
```

See Also

`<, <=, ==, !=`

>> extraction stream operator

Purpose

Use the *extraction* or "get from" *stream operator* to get a value from a stream (an *istream* object) and store it in an object (such as a variable). Typically this operator is used to get input from *cin*. This operator is often overloaded to provide suitable input for user-defined objects.

The extraction operator does much the same job as *sprintf()* does in C, but the parsing and formatting of the input data is transparent rather than having to be specified. This is because once C++ recognizes the type of input the appropriate overloaded version of >> is called to handle the input. By default >> skips whitespace (spaces, tabs, etc.) but this feature can be turned off by clearing the *ios::skipws* flag. Also note that the *ws* manipulator can also be used to "eat" and discard whitespace.

Syntax

```
#include <iostream.h>
<istream object> >> <receiving object>
istream object          an input stream such as cin
receiving object        a variable or class object
```

Example Use

```
cout << "Enter your age, please: ";
cin >> age; // store input value in variable age
```

Returns

The >> operator is left associative and returns a reference to the *istream* object for which it is invoked. This allows the "cascading" of input operations as in

```
cin >> start >> pos;
```

where both *start* and *pos* receive the value from *cin*.

See Also

`<< (insertion operator), istream, cin, ios, ws`

>> Right-shift operator

Purpose

Use the *right-shift operator* to shift all of the bits in a value to the right. Each time you shift the rightmost bit is discarded. A shift of one bit to the right is equivalent to dividing the value by 2.

Syntax
```
<value> >> <times>        Number of times to shift
```

Example Use
```
x = 16;
x = x >> 1; /* x shifted to the right by 1 bit
            position and now equals 8 */
```

See Also
```
<<, &, |
```

[]
Array element reference operator

Purpose

Use the *array element reference operator* to access the indicated element of an array using a numeric subscript. Note that arrays in C++ begin with element number 0; for an element declared to have *n* elements the highest legal subscript is *n − 1*.

Syntax
```
<array_name>[<element_number>]
```

Example Use
```
int total [10];  /* declare array of integer */
total[1] = 25;   /* assign 25 to element 1 of array*/
total[0] = subtotal;      /* assign value of subtotal to
                          first (0) element of the array*/
```

^
Bitwise exclusive OR operator

Purpose

Use the *bitwise exclusive OR operator* to compare two values bit by bit such that the resulting value has a 1 only in positions where the compared bit values differ. Note that with the bitwise exclusive OR operator the result has a 0 in any position where the compared values are either both 1 or both 0. The bitwise OR operator, on the other hand, has a 1 in the resulting position where at least one of the compared bits is a 1.

Syntax
```
<val1> ^ <val2>
```

Example Use
```
bitvals = 6 ^ 10;  /* 0110 ^ 1010; bitvals has value 1100 */
```

See Also
```
|, &, ~
```

|
Bitwise OR
operator

Purpose
Use the *bitwise OR operator* to compare two values bit by bit such that the resulting value has a 1 in positions where one or both of the compared values have a 1. This differs from the bitwise exclusive OR operator in that the latter puts a 1 in the resulting position if one and only one of the compared values has a 1 in that position.

Syntax
```
<val1> | <val2>
```

Example Use
```
bitvals = 6 | 10;  /* 0110 | 1010; bitvals has value 1110 */
```

See Also
```
^, &, ~
```

||
Logical OR
operator

Purpose
Use the *logical OR operator* to determine whether at least one of two conditions is true. The operator returns 1 (true) if one or both of the conditions is true, but returns 0 (false) if both are false.

Syntax
```
<condition1> || <condition2>
```

Example Use
```
if ((temperature > BOILING_POINT) || (pressure >
BURSTING_POINT)) sound_alarm();
```

See Also
```
&&, !
```

~
Bitwise
negation
operator

Purpose
Use the *bitwise negation operator* to reverse each bit position in a value such that ones become zeros and zeros become ones.

Syntax
```
~<bit_value>        reverse each bit in bit_val
```

Example Use
```
bitvals =  40;          /* 00101000 */
newvals = ~bitvals;     /* 11010111 */
```

See Also
&, !

?: Conditional operator

Purpose
Use the *conditional operator* to choose one of two expressions based on the truth of a condition.

Syntax
```
<condition> ? <expression1> : <expression2>
```

If the condition is true then expression1 is evaluated, otherwise expression2 is evaluated. The expressions are often alternative assignments as shown below. This conditional statement is equivalent to

```
if (condition)
    expression1;
else
    expression2;
```

Example Use
```
a > b ? max = a : max = b;
/* max becomes a if a is greater, otherwise max becomes b */
```

See Also
```
if statement
```

\a escape sequence for "alert"

Purpose
Use the *\a escape sequence* to have a string sound an alert (usually a beep) on the system's speaker. The position of the cursor or print head is not changed.

Example Use
```
printf("Do you really want to reformat this disk?\a");
```

See Also
```
printf(), cout, << (insertion stream operator)
```

abort() function

Purpose
Use *abort()* to abnormally exit your program. *abort()* calls *raise(SIGABRT)*. Note that unlike *exit()*, *abort()* will not flush the file buffers or call the routines set up by *atexit()*. However, you can take care of these chores by appropriately setting up the processing for the SIGABRT signal.

Syntax
```
#include <stdlib.h>
void abort(void);
```

Example Use
```
abort();
```

See Also
```
atexit(), exit(), raise(), signal(), SIGABRT
```

abs()
function

Purpose
Use the *abs()* function to get the absolute value of the integer argument *n*.

Syntax
```
#include <stdlib.h>
int abs(int n);
int n;      Integer whose absolute value is returned
```

Example Use
```
x = abs(-5); /* x will be 5 now */
```

Returns
The integer returned by *abs()* is the absolute value of *n*.

See Also
```
fabs(), labs()
```

acos()
function

Purpose
Use the *acos()* function to compute the arccosine of an argument *x* whose value lies in the range –1 to 1. The result is an angle with a value between 0 and pi radians. You can convert an angle from radians to degrees by multiplying it by 57.29578.

Syntax
```
#include <math.h>
double acos(double x);
double x;          Argument whose arccosine is to be computed
```

Example Use
```
angle = acos(0.5); /* angle is pi/3 */
```

Returns
When the value of the argument *x* is in the valid range of –1 to 1, *acos()* returns the arccosine. Otherwise, a domain error occurs.

See Also
```
cos()
```

argc
predefined
value

Purpose

The value *argc*, supported by many operating systems including UNIX and MS-DOS, is used in the call to *main()* that starts the program. *argc* is the number of arguments used on the command line, including the name of the program and any command-line switches, file names, etc. that the user supplied.

Syntax
```
void main (int argc, char **argv);   typical declaration of main()
```

Example Use
```
if (argc < 2)
{
printf("You must supply at least two arguments\n");
exit (EXIT_FAILURE);    /* return to operating system */
};
```

See Also
```
argv, getenv()
```

argv
predefined
value

Purpose

The value *argv*, supported by many operating systems including UNIX and MS-DOS, is used in the call to *main()* that starts the program. *argv* is a pointer to an array of character strings; each string is one of the arguments that the user typed on the command line. *argv[0]* is usually the name of the program itself, and the successive arguments are the option switches, file names, and so on that the user typed.

Syntax
```
void main (int argc, char **argv);   typical declaration of main()
```

Sample Use
```
/* one way for a program to access its arguments */
for (i = 1; i < argc; i++)
    printf("%s", argv[i]);
```

See Also
```
argc, getenv()
```

asctime() function

Purpose

Use the *asctime()* function to convert to a character string the value of a time stored in the structure of type *tm* at the address *time*. The structure *tm* is defined in *time.h* as follows:

```
struct tm
{
  int tm_sec;      /* seconds after the minute - [0,60]  */
  int tm_min;      /* minutes after the hour - [0,59]    */
  int tm_hour;     /* hours since midnight - [0,23]      */
  int tm_mday;     /* day of the month - [1,31]          */
  int tm_mon;      /* months since January - [0,11]      */
  int tm_year;     /* years since 1900                   */
  int tm_wday;     /* days since Sunday - [0,6]          */
  int tm_yday;     /* days since January 1 - [0,365]     */
  int tm_isdst;    /* daylight savings time flag         */
};
```

The string prepared by *asctime()* will be 26 characters long, counting the null character ('\0') at the end, and has the form:

```
Thu Jul 21 19:02:39 1990\n\0
```

As the example shows, a 24-hour clock is used for the time.

Syntax
```
#include <time.h>
char *asctime(tm *time);
tm *time;    Pointer to a structure containing time to be converted to a string
```

Example Use
```
printf("The time is %s\n", asctime(&timedata));
```

Returns

The *asctime()* function returns a pointer to the static data area where the string is stored.

See Also
```
ctime(), gmtime(), localtime(), time(), tm
```

asin() function

Purpose

Use the *asin()* function to compute the arcsine of the argument x provided its value lies in the range -1 to 1. The result is an angle with a value between $-pi/2$ and $pi/2$ radians. You can convert an angle from radians to degrees by multiplying it by 57.29578.

Syntax

```
#include <math.h>
double asin(double x);
double x;    Argument whose arcsine is to be computed
```

Example Use

```
angle = asin(0.707)  /* angle is roughly pi/4 */
```

Returns

For a valid argument *x* with values between −1 and 1, *asin()* returns an angle whose sine is equal to *x*. However, if the argument's value lies outside the acceptable range, a domain error occurs.

See Also

```
sin()
```

asm keyword

Purpose

Use the *asm* keyword to pass instructions from the compiler to an assembler. The implementation of this keyword is compiler-dependant. Typically *asm* is followed by one or more statements in assembly language. The statements are compiled directly into machine code by the supported assembler.

Syntax

```
asm <assembly statement>;
or
asm <assembly statement>; asm <assembly statement>...
or
asm {
    <assembly statement>
    ...
    }
```

You can put *asm* statements one to a line, with *asm* followed by the actual assembly language statement and ending with a semicolon. You can put more than one *asm* statement on the same line, with each statement beginning wtih *asm* and ending with a semicolon. You can also precede a set of lines of assembly language statements with the keyword *asm* and enclose the statements with curly braces (like a regular block of C++ statements.).

Example Use

```
asm mov ax, [sp + 4];    // Example of single-line use

asm {                    // Example of multi-line use
    pop ax               // Get stack top into AX
```

```
inc ax        // increment AX
push ax       // put result back on stack
}
```

Note that you cannot use assembly language comments introduced by semi-colons. Use one of the C++ comment styles instead.

See Also
`/* */ (comment), // (comment), inline`

assert() macro

Purpose
Use the *assert()* macro to print an error message and abort the program if the <expression> is false. The *assert()* macro is typically used to identify program errors during the debugging phase. After the program is debugged, you can disable all occurrences of the *assert()* macro by defining the preprocessor macro NDEBUG.

Syntax
```
#include <assert.h>
void assert(<expression>);
<expression>     C++ statements specifying assertion being tested
```

Example Use
```
assert(arg_value >= 0);
```

See Also
`abort(), NDEBUG`

atan() function

Purpose
Use the *atan()* function to compute the arctangent of the argument *x*. The result will be an angle with a value between –pi/2 and pi/2 radians. You can convert an angle from radians to degrees by multiplying it by 57.29578.

Syntax
```
#include <math.h>
double atan(double x);
double x;          Argument whose arctangent is to be computed
```

Example Use
```
angle = atan(1.0);  /* angle is "pi"/4 */
```

Returns
The *atan()* function returns the angle in the range –pi/2 and pi/2 whose tangent is equal to *x*.

See Also
```
atan2(), tan()
```

atan2() function

Purpose

Use the *atan2()* function to compute the arctangent of the ratio of the arguments *y/x*. The result will be an angle with value between –pi and pi radians. You can convert an angle from radians to degrees by multiplying it by 57.29578. In contrast to *atan()* which takes a single argument, *atan2()* takes two arguments and uses the sign of the two arguments to determine the quadrant (90 degree sector in cartesian coordinates) in which the angle should lie.

Syntax
```
#include <math.h>
double atan2(double y, double x);
double x, y;        Arctangent of y/x will be computed
```

Example Use
```
angle = atan2(y, x);
```

Returns

Provided both arguments *x* and *y* are non-zero, *atan2()* returns an angle whose tangent is equal to *x*. However, if both arguments are zero, a domain error may occur.

See Also
```
atan(), tan()
```

atexit() function

Purpose

Use *atexit()* to set up a stack of up to 32 (this is the minimum number specified by ANSI C) functions that the system will call in a "last-in, first-out" manner when your program terminates normally. Note that the functions passed to *atexit()* can not take any arguments. This feature is useful for setting up house cleaning chores that may be performed upon program termination.

Syntax
```
#include <stdlib.h>
int atexit(void (*func)(void));
void (*func)(void);        Pointer to function to be called
```

Example Use
```
atexit(cleanup_all);
```

Returns

The *atexit()* function returns a zero if successful. Otherwise, it returns a non-zero value.

See Also
```
exit()
```

atof() function

Purpose

Use the *atof()* function to convert the argument *string* into a double value. A call to *atof()* is equivalent to the call *strtod(string, (char **)NULL)*.

Syntax
```
#include <stdlib.h>
double atof(const char *string);
const char *string;     String to be converted
```

Example Use
```
dbl_value = atof(input_string);
```

Returns

The *atof()* function returns the double precision value after conversion.

See Also
```
atoi(), atol(), strtod(), NULL
```

atoi() function

Purpose

Use the *atoi()* function to convert the argument *string* into an *int* value. A call to *atoi()* is equivalent to the call *(int)strtol(string, (char **)NULL, 10)*.

Syntax
```
#include <stdlib.h>
int atoi(const char *string);
const char *string;     String to be converted
```

Example Use
```
int_value = atoi(input_string);
```

Returns

The *atoi()* function returns the integer value as an *int* variable.

See Also
```
atof(), atol(), strtol(), strtoul(), NULL
```

**atol()
function**

Purpose

Use the *atol()* function to convert the argument *string* into a *long* integer value. A call to *atol()* is equivalent to the call *strol (string, (char**) NULL, 10)*.

Syntax
```
#include <stdlib.h>
int atol (const char*string);
const char* string;     String to be converted
```

Example Use
```
long_value = atol(input_string);
```

Returns

The *atol()* function returns the converted value as a long variable.

See Also
```
atof(), atoi(), strtol(), strtoul(), NULL
```

**auto
keyword**

Purpose

Use the *auto* storage class specifier to declare temporary variables. These variables are created upon entering a block statement and destoyed upon exit. Local variables of a function have the *auto* storage class by default.

Syntax
```
auto <type> <varname>;
```

Example Use
```
/* the variables i, limit, and sum are created only when the if
statement is true—when the user presses a C */
#include <stdio.h>
main()
{
    int c;
    c = getchar();
    if(c == 'C')
    {
        auto int i, limit, sum;
        printf("Sum from 1 to ?");
        scanf(" %d",&limit);
        /* Compute sum from 1 to limit */
        for(i=0, sum=0; i <= limit; sum += i, i++);
        printf("\nSum from 1 to %d = %d\n", limit, sum);
    }
}
```

See Also
```
extern, register, static
```

\b escape sequence for backspace

Purpose

Use the \b escape sequence to move the cursor or print head back one space. Other effects depend on the hardware in use.

Example Use
```
/* backs up to start of last word printed */
for (pos = 1; pos < len(word); pos++)
    putc('\b');
```

See Also
```
printf(), cout, << (put-to stream operator), \r, \n
```

bad() function

Purpose

Use the *bad() ios* member function to determine if an invalid operation was attempted involving a stream, or an unrecoverable error occurred.

Syntax
```
#include <fstream.h>
<stream_name>.bad()
stream_name      stream to be accessed
```

Example Use
```
#include <fstream.h>
ifstream testfile; // declare an input file
if (testfile.bad()) cout << "Serious file error\n";
```

Returns

The *bad()* function returns a non-zero ("true") integer value if the *badbit* or *hardfail ios* flag bit has been set for the stream.

See Also
```
ios, istream, fail(), good(), rdstate(), setiosflags(),
resetiosflags()
```

break keyword

Purpose

Use the *break* keyword to exit the innermost *do, while,* or *for* loop. It is also used to exit from a *switch* statement.

Syntax
```
break;
```

Example Use

```
/* add the numbers from 1 to 10 in an endless loop.
   Use break to exit the loop  */
sum = 0;
i = 0;
while(1)
{
    sum += i;
    i++;
    if(i > 10) break;
}
```

See Also

```
case, continue, do, for, switch, while
```

bsearch() function

Purpose

Use the *bsearch()* function to search a sorted array beginning at the address *base* and comprising *num* elements, each of size *width* bytes. The argument *key* points to the value being sought. Note that you can use the *qsort()* routine to sort the array before calling *bsearch()*.

Syntax

```
#include <stdlib.h>
void *bsearch(const void *key, const void *base, size_t num,
size_t width, int (*compare)(const void *elem1, const void
*elem2));
```

`const void *key;`	*Pointer to element value being searched for*
`const void *base;`	*Pointer to beginning of array being searched*
`size_t     num;`	*Number of elements in array*
`size_t     width;`	*Size of each element in bytes*
`int (*compare)(const void *elem1, const void *elem2);`	*Pointer to a function that compares two elements* e l e m 1 *and* e l e m 2 *each of type const void **

Example Use

```
int mycompare(const void *, const void *);
result = (char **) bsearch((const void *)keyword,
                   (const void *)envp,
                   (size_t)count,
                   (size_t)sizeof(char *),
                   mycompare);
```

Returns

The *bsearch()* function returns a pointer to the first occurrence of the value *key* in the array. If the value is not found, *bsearch()* returns a NULL.

See Also

```
qsort(), NULL, size_t
```

BUFSIZ predefined value

Purpose

The *BUFSIZ* predefined value gives the size of the buffer used by *setbuf()*. It is defined in *limits.h*.

See Also
```
FOPEN_MAX
```

calloc() function

Purpose

Use *calloc()* to allocate memory for an array of *num_elems* elements each of size *elem_size* bytes. All bytes of the allocated array will be initialized to zero. Note that C++ objects should be allocated with the *new* operator.

Syntax
```
#include <stdlib.h>
void *calloc(size_t num_elems, size_t elem_size);
size_t    num_elems;          Number of elements
size_t    elem_size;          Size of each element in bytes
```

Example Use
```
p_int = (int *) calloc(100, sizeof(int));
```

Returns

The return value from *calloc()* is a pointer to *void*, representing the address of the allocated memory. If the memory allocation is unsuccessful because of insufficient space or bad values of the arguments, a *NULL* is returned.

See Also
```
free(), malloc(), realloc(), NULL, size_t
```

case keyword

Purpose

Use the *case* keyword to label cases in a *switch* statement. If the switch variable has the specified value the statements associated with the case are executed. A *break* statement is used at the end of the statements for each case in order to prevent the next case from being executed, unless that behavior is intended.

Syntax
```
case <value> : <statement; ... >
```

Example Use
```
case 'A':  do_choice_A();
           break;
```

See Also
```
default, switch
```

catch keyword

Purpose

Use the *catch* keyword to define an exception handler. An exception handler is a block of code designed to deal with a particular error (exception) usually involving an invalid index, argument, or data value. Note that the C++ exception-handling features are not yet widely implemented, and are not covered in *Master C++*.

Syntax

```
catch (<Exception class>) {
    // Code to handle exceptions
    // that were tested by exception class
}
exception class  contains functions for checking execeptions
```

Typically for exceptions involving a particular class you define a nested class (subclass) with functions or operators that check values for validity. When some other part of the program wants to use the class being safeguarded with error checking, a block of code begun with the keyword *try* peforms some manipulation of the data. During the processing of a *try* block construct, if an error is detected by your program, you can write a statement to *throw* the exception to a matching *catch* exception handler defined immediately following the *try* block. A *catch* block must immediately follow either a *try* block or another *catch* block.

Example Use

```
class Counter {
    int total;
public:
    class Range { }; // exception class
    int show_total() {
            if (total >= 0 && total <= MAX_TOT)
                return total; // total is in
                              // range
            throw Range(); // if executed, means
                           // that it was out of
                           //     range
    }
}
// Elsewhere in the program...
try {       // Enclose function that will work with data
    check_total(total-n);
}
catch (Counter::Range) {
            // handler for Counter::Range exception
            // check_total() must have gotten an invalid
            // total in Counter::show_total()
            // Handle the exception here
    ...
    ...
}
```

See Also
`throw, try`

ceil()
function

Purpose

Use the *ceil()* function to find the "ceiling" of a *double* argument *x*. The "ceiling" is the smallest integral value that is equal to or that just exceeds *x*. This can be used in rounding a *double* value *up* to the next integer.

Syntax
```
#include <math.h>
double ceil(double x);
double x;            Variable whose "ceiling" is to be returned
```

Example Use
```
x_ceiling = ceil(4.1);  /* x_ceiling is 5.0 */
```

Returns

The return value is the "ceiling" of *x* expressed as a *double*.

See Also
`floor()`

cerr
stream

Purpose

Use the *cerr* stream to receive error messages. *cerr* is the standard error stream, corresponding to *stderr* in the ANSI C library. By default, *cerr* is assigned to the screen, but it can be redirected.

Syntax
```
#include <iostream.h>
cerr << <message or value>
```

Example Use
```
if (pressure > red_line)
    cerr << "Gonna blow!" << endl;
```

See Also
`<< (insertion operator), cin, clog, cout`

char
keyword

Purpose

Use the *char* type specifier to declare character variables and arrays. A character variable actually stores the character's ASCII code number in the machine's character set. A *signed char* has a range between −128 and 127, while a regular *char* (occasionally called *unsigned char*) has a range of 0 through 255.

Syntax
```
char <varname>;
```

Example Use
```
/* declare a character, a pointer to a char, and an array of
    characters */
    char c, *p_c, string[80];
```

See Also
```
double, float, int, long, short, signed, unsigned
```

CHAR_BIT predefined value

Purpose

The *CHAR_BIT* predefined value gives the maximum number of bits in *char*. It is defined in *limits.h*.

See Also
```
CHAR_MAX, CHAR_MIN
```

CHAR_MAX predefined value

Purpose

The *CHAR_MAX* predefined value gives the maximum value of a *char*. It is defined in *limits.h*.

See Also
```
CHAR_MIN, CHAR_BIT
```

CHAR_MIN predefined value

Purpose

The *CHAR_MIN* predefined value gives the minimum value of a *char*. It is defined in *limits.h*.

See Also
```
CHAR_MAX, CHAR_BIT
```

cin stream

Purpose

Use the *cin* stream as an input source for your program. *cin* is the standard input stream, corresponding to *stdin* in the ANSI C library. By defaulti *cin* is assigned to the console (keyboard), but it can be redirected. Typically the extraction stream operator >> is used to get data from *cin* and store it in an object. In C++ 2.0 *cin* has predefined operators for handling the following data types: *short, int, long, float, double, long double, char,* and *char* *.

Syntax
```
cin >> <receiving variable>
```

Example Use
```
int age;
...
cin >> age // Get user's age from keyboard
```

Returns
cin passes the incoming data via the >> (extraction) operator to the receiving variable.

See Also
```
cerr, clog, cout, >> (extraction operator), sprintf()
```

class keyword

Purpose
Use the *class* keyword to begin the definition of a class. A class is the specification for an object to be manipulated by the program. A class can contain declarations of values (data members) and ways of working with the values (function members). A class can be derived from one or more "parent" classes. The keywords *private, public,* and *protected* control access from the rest of the program to the data and functions included in the class.

Syntax
```
class <class_name> : <derivation> <base_class> ...{
                            How derived and base class (optional)
member declaration          One or more data members and/or member functions
...
}
```

Begin the class definition with the keyword *class,* followed by the name of the class, which will be the name of the data type for objects of the class. (You can have an unnamed class, but this is usually not useful.) If the class is derived from one or more base classes, follow the class name with a colon and the name(s) of the base classes, separated by commas. If desired, the name of any base class can be preceded by the keyword *public, private,* or *protected* to specify the access the class will have to members of the base class. (See the entries for these keywords for more information.)

The rest of the body of the class definition consists of declarations of the data members and/or member functions of the class. These follow the usual rules for declarations, and again the keywords *public, private,* and *protected* can be used to specify the degree of access to the items in the following declarations.

A class can be nested inside another class definition. If this is done the contents of the nested class are accessible only within the enclosing class.

The structure and syntax of a *class* is the same as that of a *struct* except that access to a *class* is private by default while access to a *struct* is public by default.

Example Use
```
class planet : public sky_object {
private    // restricted data
           float mass;
           float radius;
           float density;
           Point position;
           planet (stats_array[]);     // constructor
           ~planet ();                 // destructor
           Point calc_position();
           public          // functions for outside access
           Mag calc_magnitude(Point view);
}
```

See Also
```
private, protected, public, struct, typedef, union
```

clear() function

Purpose
Use the *clear() ios* member function to set the values of the error bits of a stream according to the integer value you supply. (If you specify 0 or do not give an argument, all error bits will be cleared.) A typical use is to set an error flag if a problem is encountered or to clear the error bits after a problem has been dealt with.

Syntax
```
#include <iostream.h>
<stream_name>.clear(intval);
stream_name      name of stream to be affected
intval           integer value for setting bits
```

Example Use
```
ifstream my_input;
... // some stream operations
my_input.clear(0) // clears all error bits
my_input.clear(ios::failbit|my_input.rdstate());
```

The second call to *clear()* above uses the | (logical OR) operator to "or" the flag values returned by *rdstate()* with the current value of *failbit*; the result is to set *failbit* without affecting the other flags for the stream.

See Also
```
ios, rdstate(), fail()
```

clearerr() function

Purpose
Use *clearerr()* to reset the error and end-of-file indicators of the ANSI C stream specified by the stream pointer *stream*. (Note that *ios* member functions such as *clear()* are used to set or clear error bits for C++ streams.)

Syntax
```
#include <stdio.h>
void clearerr(FILE *stream);
FILE *stream;       Pointer to stream whose error flag is being cleared
```

Example Use
```
clearerr(outfile);
```

See Also
```
ferror(), feof(), FILE
```

CLK_TCK predefined value

Purpose
The *CLK_TCK* predefined value gives the number of clock ticks per second returned by the *clock()* function. It is defined in *time.h*.

See Also
```
clock()
```

clock() function

Purpose
Use *clock()* to obtain the amount of processor time used by the current process in "number of ticks." The constant CLK_TCK, defined in *time.h* is the number of ticks per second, so the value returned by *clock* should be divided by CLK_TCK to get the elapsed processor time in seconds.

Syntax
```
#include <time.h>
clock_t clock(void);
```

Example Use
```
ticks_now = clock();
```

Returns

If the processor time is available to *clock()*, it returns the current time in ticks, cast as a value of type *clock_t* which is defined in *time.h*. Otherwise, it returns the value –1, cast as *clock_t*.

See Also

```
difftime(), time(), CLK_TCK, clock_t
```

clock_t predefined data type

Purpose

The *clock_t* data type is capable of holding the value of the time returned by the *clock* function. It is defined in *time.h*.

See Also

```
time_t, tm
```

clog stream

Purpose

Use the predefined *clog* C++ stream to hold output to "standard error." While this output goes by default to the screen, it can be reassigned to another destination (such as a disk file). *clog* is the same as *cerr* except that *clog* is fully buffered.

Syntax

```
#include <iostream.h>
```

Example Use

```
clog << "Error number " << errno << "has occurred." << endl;
```

See Also

```
cerr, cout, ostream, errno
```

close() function

Purpose

Use the *close() ios* member function to properly close a C++ file and the associated stream. Any data in the buffer will be flushed before the file is closed.

Syntax

```
#include <fstream.h>
<filename>.close()
filename    name of file to close
```

Example Use

```
ofstream output_file;    // declare an output file
// open file and write data to it
output_file.close();    // close the file
```

See Also
```
open(), flush(), fclose() (ANSI C streams)
```

const keyword

Purpose

Use the *const* type qualifier to indicate that the variable that follows may not be modified by the program. (You can, however, initialize the constant at the time of declaration, as shown in the following examples). You can not later assign a value to a *const*, increment it, or decrement it. Declaring constants can protect key values from change, accommodate data in read-only memory, or improve optimization in some compilers by assuring the compiler that a value will not be changed later. *const* guarantees only that you the programmer will not change the value later; the value may in some cases be changed by the operation of the hardware. You can declare such a hardware-dependent value to be *const volatile*.

Use of *const* is preferable to using *#define* with a numeric literal, because the compiler doesn't provide type-checking in the latter case.

Syntax
```
const <name> = <value>
```

Example Use
```
const short x = 32;        /* x is constant */
const int *p_i = 2048;     /* value pointed to by p_i is
                              constant */
int *const p_c_i = &total; /* pointer p_c_i is constant*/
```

See Also
```
volatile, #define
```

continue keyword

Purpose

Use the *continue* keyword to skip execution of the body of a loop. It is equivalent to executing a *goto* to the end of the loop. After skipping the rest of the body of the loop, control returns to the loop condition, which is checked as usual. The *continue* statement affects the innermost loop in which it appears.

Syntax
```
continue;
```

Example Use
```
/* The statement sum += i; will be skipped when i is 5,giving
the sum of the numbers from 1 to 10, excluding 5 */
```

```
for(i=0, sum=0; i <= 10, i++)
{
    if(i == 5) continue;
    sum += i;
}
```

See Also
```
for, if, while
```

cos() function

Purpose

Use the *cos()* function to compute the cosine of *double* argument *x*, which must be expressed in radians. You can convert an angle from degrees to radians by dividing it by 57.29578.

Syntax
```
#include <math.h>
double cos(double x);
double x;              Angle in radians whose cosine is to be computed
```

Example Use
```
cos_angle = cos(ang_radian);
```

Returns

The *cos()* function returns the cosine of *x*. If the value of *x* is large in magnitude, the result may be very imprecise.

See Also
```
acos(), sin()
```

cosh() function

Purpose

Use the *cosh()* function to compute the hyperbolic cosine of *x*.

Syntax
```
#include <math.h>
double cosh(double x);
double x;              Variable whose hyperbolic cosine is to be computed
```

Example Use
```
result = cosh(x);
```

Returns

Normally, *cosh()* returns the hyperbolic cosine of *x*. If the value of the result is too large (a *double* variable can be as large as 10^{308}), a range error will occur.

See Also
```
sinh()
```

**cout
stream**

Purpose
Use the *cout* C++ stream to output data. *cout* corresponds to the *stdout* (standard output) stream in ANSI C. By default *cout* is assigned to the screen, but it can be redirected. Typically the *insertion stream* operator << is used to put the value of a variable, literal, or constant to the output stream. In C++ 2.0 *cout* has predefined operators for the following data types: *short, int, long, float, double, long double, char,* and *char* * plus (new with 2.0) *void* * (for pointer values).

Syntax
```
#include <iostream.h>
cout << <data>
data          numeric or string constant, literal, variable, or user-defined class object
```

Example Use
```
cout << "Welcome to Master C++\n"; // string output
cout << total; // output value of variable total
```

See Also
```
ostream, << (stream extraction operator)
```

**_ _cplusplus
predefined
macro**

Purpose
Use the _ _*cplusplus* macro when you need to compile or link something depending on whether the program being compiled is a C program or a C++ program. Most compilers automatically define _ _*cplusplus* if C++ compilation has been set.

Syntax
```
<test> _ _cplusplus      test is #ifdef, #ifndef, etc.
```

Example Use
```
#ifndef _ _cplusplus /* not compiling C++ */
    #error C++ must be used for this program!
#endif
```

Returns
The state of _ _*cplusplus* is communicated by whether it is defined or not: if it is defined the compiler mode is C++.

See Also
```
_ _STDC_ _
```

**ctime()
function**

Purpose
Use the *ctime()* function to convert to a character string the value of time

stored in the variable of type *time_t* at the address *timer*. Calling *ctime()* is equivalent to the call *asctime(localtime(timer))*.

Syntax
```
#include <time.h>
char *ctime(const time_t *timer);
const time_t  *timer;        Pointer to calendar time
```

Example Use
```
printf("Current time = %s\n", ctime(&bintime));
```

Returns
The *ctime()* function returns the pointer to the string.

See Also
```
asctime(), time(), time_t
```

_ _DATE_ _ predefined macro

Purpose
Use the _ _DATE_ _ predefined macro to display the date of translation of the source file by the preprocessor. This macro inserts a string constant into the file of the form "MMM DD YYYY" (such as "Jun 15 1990").

Example Use
```
printf("Compiled on: ");
printf(_ _DATE_ _);
```

See Also
```
FILE, TIME, LINE, STDC_ _
```

DBL_DIG predefined value

Purpose
The *DBL_DIG* predefined value gives the number of significant decimal digits in a *double* value. It is defined in *float.h*.

See Also
```
DBL_EPSILON, DBL_MANT_DIG, DBL_MIN, DBL_MIN_10_EXP,
DBL_MIN_EXP, DBL_MAX, DBL_MAX_10_EXP, DBL_MAX_EXP
```

DBL_EPSILON predefined value

Purpose
The *DBL_EPSILON* predefined value gives the smallest positive *double* value x such that $1+x \mathrel{!}= 1$. It is defined in *float.h*.

See Also
```
DBL_DIG, DBL_MANT_DIG, DBL_MIN, DBL_MIN_10_EXP,
DBL_MIN_EXP, DBL_MAX, DBL_MAX_10_EXP, DBL_MAX_EXP
```

DBL_MANT_DIG predefined value

Purpose

The *DBL_MANT_DIG* predefined value gives the number of base *FLT_RADIX* digits in the mantissa of a *double*. It is defined in *float.h*.

See Also

DBL_DIG, DBL_EPSILON, DBL_MIN, DBL_MIN_10_EXP, DBL_MIN_EXP, DBL_MAX, DBL_MAX_10_EXP, DBL_MAX_EXP

DBL_MAX predefined value

Purpose

The *DBL_MAX* predefined value gives the maximum representable finite value that can be stored in a *double*. It is defined in *float.h*.

See Also

DBL_DIG, DBL_MANT_DIG, DBL_EPSILON, DBL_MIN, DBL_MIN_10_EXP, DBL_MIN_EXP, DBL_MAX_10_EXP, DBL_MAX_EXP

DBL_MAX_10_EXP predefined value

Purpose

The *DBL_MAX_10_EXP* predefined value gives the maximum integer such that 10 raised to that power is representable in a *double*.

See Also

DBL_DIG, DBL_MANT_DIG, DBL_EPSILON, DBL_MIN, DBL_MIN_10_EXP, DBL_MIN_EXP, DBL_MAX, DBL_MAX_EXP

DBL_MAX_EXP predefined value

Purpose

The *DBL_MAX_EXP* predefined value gives the maximum integer such that FLT_RADIX raised to that power is representable in a *double*. It is defined in *float.h*.

See Also

DBL_DIG, DBL_MANT_DIG, DBL_EPSILON, DBL_MIN, DBL_MIN_10_EXP, DBL_MIN_EXP, DBL_MAX, DBL_MAX_10_EXP

DBL_MIN predefined value

Purpose

The *DBL_MIN* predefined value gives the minimum positive floating-point number that can be stored in a *double*. It is defined in *float.h*.

See Also

DBL_DIG, DBL_MANT_DIG, DBL_EPSILON, DBL_MIN_10_EXP, DBL_MIN_EXP, DBL_MAX, DBL_MAX_10_EXP, DBL_MAX_EXP

DBL_MIN_10_EXP predefined value

Purpose

The *DBL_MIN_10_EXP* predefined value gives the minimum negative integer such that 10 raised to that power is representable in a *double*. It is defined in *float.h*.

See Also
```
DBL_DIG, DBL_MANT_DIG, DBL_EPSILON, DBL_MIN,
DBL_MIN_EXP, DBL_MAX, DBL_MAX_10_EXP, DBL_MAX_EXP
```

DBL_MIN_EXP predefined value

Purpose

The *DBL_MIN_EXP* predefined value gives the minimum negative integer such that FLT_RADIX raised to that power minus 1 is representable in a *double*.

See Also
```
DBL_DIG, DBL_MANT_DIG, DBL_EPSILON, DBL_MIN,
DBL_MIN_10_EXP, DBL_MAX, DBL_MAX_10_EXP, DBL_MAX_EXP
```

dec manipulator

Purpose

Use the *dec* C++ stream manipulator to set the conversion base format flag for a stream to decimal. The conversion base is used to control the base used in inputting or displaying numbers using the specified stream.

Syntax
```
#include <iostream.h>
ostream << dec;    set base to decimal for output stream
istream >> dec;    set basse to decimal for input stream
```

Example Use
```
int num = &H20; // set num to hex 20
cout << dec << num; // outputs value 32 decimal
```
dec is equivalent to *setbase(10)*

See Also
```
hex, oct, setbase()
```

default keyword

Purpose

Use *default* as the label in a *switch* statement to mark code that will be executed when none of the *case* labels match the *switch* expression.

Syntax
```
default: <statement; ..>
```

Example Use
```
default: printf("Unknown command!\n");
```

See Also
```
case, switch
```

#define preprocessor definition operator

Purpose

Use the *#define* operator to define a symbol or a macro. A definition such as *#define PI 3.14159* simply tells the preprocessor to replace each occurrence of *PI* in the source code with the numeric literal *3.14159*. A macro is a more flexible definition with one or more parameters that control what is actually put into the source code. For example, *#define SQUARE(x) ((x)*(x))* allows you to use a statement such as *SQUARE(2)* your code; the result of this statement is to place *((2)*(2))* or 4 in the code. You can redefine a macro with the same expression as often as you want. (Note that ANSI C and C++ prefer the use of the *const* keyword to simple defined values because a *const* is automatically guarded against its value being changed by the program. C++ practice prefers the use of inline functions to macros because the former provide full argument checking.

Example Use
```
ZOOM(v, r)  ((v)*(r))
ZOOM(4, 8) /* puts 4 * 8 or 32 in the code */
```

See Also
```
# (string-izing operator), ## (token-pasting operator)
```

defined preprocessor condition

Purpose

Use the *defined* preprocessor condition to determine whether a preprocessor symbol or macro is defined in the current program. Typically this is used to control conditional compilation.

Syntax
```
defined (symbol)        true if symbol is defined
!defined (symbol)       true if symbol is not defined
```

Note that *#ifdef* is an alternate form of *#if defined* and *#ifndef* is an alternate form of *#if !defined.*

Example Use
```
#if defined (NON_STANDARD)
   #include "ourdefs.h"
#endif
```

delete operator

Purpose

Use the *delete* operator to deallocate (free up) the memory being used by an object. You can use the delete operator with any standard data type as well as using it in a destructor to free up an object of a class. delete is not usually needed for simple data types that go out of scope but it *is* needed when a pointer goes out of scope, because with pointers the object pointed to is not automatically deallocated.

When you delete a class object the object's destructor is automatically called. You can overload the delete operator to provide special memory management for an object.

Note that delete should be used only to free memory that was originally allocated with the new operator, and should not be used with objects that had been created by ANSI C functions of the *malloc()* family. C++ *does* guarantee that deleting a 0 (null) pointer will be harmless. You cannot delete using a pointer to *const* since a constant cannot be altered.

Syntax

```
delete <pointer> or
delete <[elements]> <cast expression>     to delete an array of objects
pointer               pointer to object to be deallocated
[elements]            number of array elements
```

Example Use

```
delete this_object;        // delete a single object
delete [255] flags         // delete each of 255 elements of
    // flags (which could be a simple array or
    // an array of class objects)
```

Note that C++ 2.0 specifies that you can use empty brackets ([]) to delete all elements of an array. Not all compilers currently support this specification, however.

See Also

```
new, malloc() functions (for ANSI C)
```

difftime() function

Purpose

Use the *difftime()* function to compute the difference between two time values *time2* and *time1*, both of type *time_t*.

Syntax

```
#include <time.h>
double difftime(time_t time2, time_t time1);
time_t  time2;          Value of time from which time1 will be subtracted
time_t  time1;          Value of time to be subtracted from time2
```

Example Use
```
seconds_used = difftime(oldtime, newtime);
```

Returns
The *difftime()* function returns the elapsed time, *time2–time1*, in seconds as a double precision number.

See Also
```
clock(), time(), time_t
```

div()
function

Purpose
Use the *div()* function to divide the first integer *numer* by the second one *denom* and obtain the resulting quotient and remainder packed in a structure of type *div_t*. The structure of type *div_t* is defined in *stdlib.h* as

```
typedef struct
{
    int quot;   /* The quotient  */
    int rem;    /* The remainder */
} div_t;
```

Syntax
```
#include <stdlib.h>
div_t div(int numer, int denom);
int numer;          Numerator
int denom;          Denominator
```

Example Use
```
result = div(32, 5);
/* result.quot = 6 and result.rem = 2 */
```

Returns
The *div()* function returns a structure of type *div_t* containing the quotient and remainder of the division.

See Also
```
ldiv(), div_t
```

div_t
predefined
data type

Purpose
The *div_t* data type can hold the value returned by the *div* function. It is defined in *stdlib.h*.

See Also
```
div()
```

**do
keyword**

Purpose

Use the *do* keyword with *while* to form iterative loops where the statement or statements in the body are executed until the expression evaluates to 0 (false). The expression is evaluated after each execution of the loop body. Note that a *do...while* statement is always executed at least once. Since the entire *do...while* structure counts as a statement it must end with a semicolon.

Syntax
```
do
{
    statement;
    ...
}
while(condition);
```

*if there is only one statement in the body the loop can be written:
do statement while (condition);*

Example Use
```
do
{
    sum += i;
    i++;
}
while(i >= 10);
```

See Also
```
for, if, while
```

**double
keyword**

Purpose

Use the *double* type specifier to declare double precision floating-point variables and arrays. In most implementations the *double* type is stored in twice as many bytes as *float*, though this is not required by the ANSI standard.

Syntax
```
double <varname>;
```

Example Use
```
/* declare a double, a pointer to a
   double, and an array of doubles */
   double d, *p_d, dvars[80];
```

See Also
```
char, float, int, long, short, signed, unsigned
```

EDOM predefined value

Purpose
The *EDOM* constant indicates an invalid argument (or "domain") error. It is defined in *errno.h*.

See Also
ERANGE

#elif preprocessor else-if operator

Purpose
Use the *#elif* operator to specify an alternate branch for conditional compilation.

Syntax
See *#if*

Example Use
See *#if*

See Also
#if, #else, #endif

else keyword

Purpose
Use the *else* keyword as part of an *if* statement when you want to specify statements to be executed if the condition is false (0). When *if...else* statements are "nested" a particular *else* is always associated with the first preceding *if* that does not have an *else*.

Syntax
```
if (condition)
    statement_1;
else
    statement_2;
```
where *statement_1* is executed if the *expression* is not equal to zero, otherwise *statement_2* is executed.

Example Use
See *if* for an example.

See Also
if, default, #else (preprocessor else operator)

#else preprocessor operator

Purpose
Use the *#else* operator to specify an alternate branch for conditional compilation.

Syntax
See *#if*

Example Use
See *#if*

See Also
`#if, #elif, #endif`

#endif preprocessor operator

Purpose
Use the *#endif* preprocessor operator to mark the end of an *#if* preprocessor directive.

Syntax
See *#if*

Example Use
See *#if*

See Also
`#if, #else, #elif`

endl manipulator

Purpose
Use the *endl* manipulator to send a newline character to a C++output stream. This action also flushes the line (sends any pending characters in the line to the stream).

Syntax
```
#include <iostream.h>
<output_stream> << endl;
output stream     stream for output (usually cout)
```

Example Use
```
cout << "This is a line." << endl;
```

The above is equvialent to:

```
cout << "This is a line." << "\n";
```

but it is a bit easier to write.

Returns
As with all manipulators, *endl* returns a reference to the stream object, allowing cascading of output.

See Also
```
ends, flush, "\n" (escape sequence for newline)
```

ends manipulator

Purpose
Use the *ends* manipulator to insert the string terminating null character (ASCII 0) and flush pending characters. You can use this to create an "official" C/C++ string from a series of characters.

Syntax
```
#include <iostream.h>
<output_stream> << ends;
output stream     stream for output
```

Example Use
```
ofstream names; // set up an output stream
for (int str = 1; str <= numstrs; str++)
        names << phrases[str] << ends;
```

Each phrase in the char array *phrases* is sent to the output and followed by a string terminator. The result is a file of strings.

Returns
As with all manipulators, *ends* returns a reference to the stream object, allowing cascading of output.

See Also
```
endl
```

enum keyword

Purpose
Use the *enum* keyword to define a set of related values, often values that are considered to be in a particular order. This is an integral data type that can take its values from a list of enumerated constants.

Syntax
```
enum identifier { enumerated_list };    declare an enumerated type
                                        and a list of values
enum identifier var1, var2;       declare two variables to be of this type
```

Example Use
```
/* make traffic_signal the name of an enumerated type, with
   the values red, yellow, and green */
enum traffic_signal {red = 10, yellow = 20, green = 30};
/* declare signal_1 to be a variable of the traffic_signal
   type and p_signal to be a pointer to data of the
   traffic_signal type */
enum traffic_signal signal_1, *p_signal;
```

See Also
```
typedef
```

EOF predefined value

Purpose
The *EOF* integer constant indicates "end-of-file." It usually has a value of –1, and is defined in *stdio.h*.

Example Use
```
while (datafile.get(ch) != EOF)
        cout << ch;
```

See Also
```
eof() (C++ member function)
```

eof() function

Purpose
Use the *eof() ios* member function with a C++ input stream (*istream*) to determine whether you have reached the end of the file.

Syntax
```
#include <iostream.h>
int eof()
<input_stream>.eof()
```

Example Use
```
while (!cin.eof())
{
// process the file
}
```

The expression *!cin.eof()* becomes false when *eof()* returns a "true" value indicating end of file. The *while* loop is then exited, ending processing of the file.

Returns
The *eof()* function returns a non-zero (true) value if the end of the file has been reached (as indicated by the *eofbit ios* status bit having been set). Otherwise, *eof()* returns a zero (false).

See Also
```
ios, bad(), fail(), ! and * (stream status operators)
```

errno predefined value

Purpose
The *errno* predefined variable is a code indicating the last error that has occurred. It is defined in *errno.h* and the values are dependant on the compiler

and operating system. Some commonly encountered values under MS-DOS are:

Constant	Value	Meaning
ENOENT	2	No such file or directory
ENOPATH	3	Path not found
EMFILE	4	Too many open files
EACCES	5	Permission denied
EBADF	6	Bad file number
EINVDRV	15	Invalid drive specified
ECURDIR	16	Attempted to remove current directory
ENMFILE	18	No more files
EEXIST	35	File already exists

See Also
```
perror(), cerr, clog
```

#error preprocessor operator

Purpose
Use the *#error* preprocessor operator to produce a diagnostic message during compilation.

Syntax
```
#error <message text>
```

Example Use
```
#if defined(WRONG_OPTION)
    #error Recompile with correct option
#endif
```

See Also
```
#if, #else, #elif, #endif, defined
```

exit() function

Purpose
Use the *exit( )* function to terminate your program normally by flushing file buffers, closing files, and invoking functions set up with *atexit()*. A value of 0 or EXIT_SUCCESS for *status* means normal exit, whereas the value of EXIT_FAILURE is used to indicate errors.

Syntax
```
#include <stdlib.h>
void exit(int status);
int status;              Exit status code
```

Example Use
```
exit(EXIT_SUCCESS);
```

See Also
```
abort(), atexit(), EXIT_FAILURE, EXIT_SUCCESS
```

EXIT_FAILURE predefined value

Purpose

The *EXIT_FAILURE* status code can be used with *exit()* to indicate that the program ended with an error. It is defined in *stddef.h*.

See Also
```
EXIT_SUCCESS
```

EXIT_SUCCESS predefined value

Purpose

The *EXIT_SUCCESS* status code can be used with *exit()* to indicate that the program executed successfully. It is defined in *stddef.h*.

See Also
```
EXIT_FAILURE
```

exp() function

Purpose

Use the *exp()* function to compute the exponential of the *double* variable *x*. The exponential of a variable *x* is e^x where *e* is the base of natural logarithms is $(e - 2.7182818)$.

Syntax
```
#include <math.h>
double exp(double x);
double x;          Variable whose exponential is to be computed
```

Example Use
```
y = exp(x);
```

Returns

Normally, *exp* returns the exponential of *x*. If the value of the result is too large, a range error occurs.

See Also
```
log
```

extern keyword

Purpose

Use the *extern* keyword to tell the compiler that a variable or a function is defined in another module (a separate file) and that you want to use it in the current module. The data item or function must be declared in one of the program modules without the *static* or the *extern* qualifier.

Syntax
```
extern <type> <varname>;
```

Example Use
```
/* In the example below the variables current_state and
state_table are shared between FILE 1 and FILE 2.They are
defined in FILE 1, and.declared to be extern in FILE 2 */

/* FILE1 */
int current_state, state_table[MAXSTATE][MAXSYMB];

/* following is reference to variable declared in file2 */
extern void next_state(int in_symbol);
main()
{
  int in_symbol;
  ...
  current_state = 0;
  next_state(in_symbol);
  ...
}

/* FILE2 */
void next_state(int in_symbol)
{
  /* following declaration is referenced in file1 */
extern int current_state,state_table[MAXSTATE] [MAXSYMB];
if ( current_state == 0 ) ...
  ...
  current_state = state_table[current_state]
  [in_symbol];
  ...
}
```

See Also
```
static
```

\f escape sequence for form feed

Purpose
Use the \f (form feed) escape sequence to start a new page on the printer. On most systems the form feed displays as a single character rather than affecting the screen display.

Example Use
```
printf("%s", footer);
printf('\f'); /* start a new page */
printf("%s", header);
```

See Also
```
printf(), cout, form), << (insertion stream operator)
```

fabs()
function

Purpose

Use the *fabs()* function to obtain the absolute value of its argument, which must be a double value.

Syntax
```
#include <math.h>
double fabs(double x);
double x;              Variable whose absolute value is to be returned
```

Example Use
```
y = fabs(-5.15); /* y will be 5.15 */
```

Returns

The return value is of type *double* with a positive value which is the absolute value of *x*.

See Also
```
abs()
```

fail()
function

Purpose

Use the *fail()* *ios* member function to check whether a C++ file stream access has encountered an error.

Syntax
```
#include <iostream.h>
<input_stream>.fail();
```

Example Use
```
istream input; // input stream
...
if (input.fail()) handle_error();
// deal with error if encountered
```

Returns

The *fail()* function returns a a nonzero (true) value if the *ios failbit, badbit,* or *hardfail* status bit has been set, indicating an error. Otherwise *fail()* returns a 0 (false).

See Also
```
ios, bad(), eof(), ! and * (stream status operators)
```

fclose() function

Purpose

Use the *fclose()* function to close the ANSI C stream specified by *stream*. If the stream was open for writing, the contents of the buffer associated with the stream is written to the file ("flushed") before the file is closed. If it was open for reading, any unread data in the buffer are discarded. Note that you should use the member function *close()* to close a C++ file stream.

Syntax
```
#include <stdio.h>
int fclose(FILE *stream);
FILE *stream;          Pointer to stream to be closed
```

Example Use
```
fclose(infile);
```

Returns

fclose() returns 0 if the stream was successfully closed; otherwise, it returns EOF.

See Also
```
fopen(), fflush(), EOF, FILE
```

feof() function

Purpose

Use the *feof()* function to determine whether *stream*'s end-of-file indicator is set. When you get an error return from a read operation, you can call *feof()* to determine if the error occurred because you tried to read past the end-of-file. Note: You should use *eof()* or another *ios* status function to check for end of file on a C++ stream.

Syntax
```
#include <stdio.h>
int feof(FILE *stream);
FILE *stream;      Pointer to FILE data structure associated with the stream
                   whose status is being checked
```

Example Use
```
if (feof(infile) != 0) printf("File ended\n");
```

Returns

feof() returns a non-zero if and only if the end-of-file indicator is set for *stream*.

See Also
```
clearerr(), ferror(), rewind(), FILE; ios (for C++ streams)
```

ferror()
function

Purpose

Use *ferror()* to determine if the error indicator is set for the specified *stream*. Note that you should use *ios* member functions to check for errors in C++ streams.

Syntax

```
#include <stdio.h>
int ferror(FILE *stream);
FILE *stream;          Pointer to FILE data structure associated
                       with the stream whose status is being checked
```

Example Use

```
if (ferror(infile) != 0) printf("Error detected\n");
```

Returns

ferror() returns a non-zero value if and only if the error indicator is set for *stream*.

See Also

```
clearerr(), feof(), FILE; ios (for C++ streams)
```

fflush()
function

Purpose

Use the *fflush()* function to flush the current contents of the buffer associated with the ANSI C stream specified by *stream*. If the file is open for write operations, the "flushing" involves writing the contents of the buffer to the file. Otherwise, the buffer is cleared. If *stream* is NULL, the flushing action is performed on all open streams. Note that this function is used with C streams, not C++ streams, for which the *flush()* manipulator can be used.

Syntax

```
#include <stdio.h>
int fflush(FILE *stream);
FILE *stream;    Pointer to stream whose buffer is being flushed
```

Example Use

```
fflush(stdin);
```

Returns

If the flushing is successful, *fflush* returns a 0. In case of an error, it returns the constant EOF defined in *stdio.h*.

See Also

```
fopen(), fclose(), setbuf(), setvbuf(), EOF, FILE, NULL
```

fgetc()
function

Purpose

Use *fgetc* to read a single character from the ANSI C stream specifed by the pointer *stream*. The character is read from the current position in the stream. After reading the character, the current position is advanced to the next character. Note: This function is used with C streams, not C++ streams.

Syntax
```
#include <stdio.h>
int fgetc(FILE *stream);
FILE *stream;      Pointer to stream from which a character is to be read
```

Example Use
```
char_read = fgetc(infile);
```

Returns

If there are no errors, *fgetc()* returns the character read, as an *unsigned char* converted to an *int*. Otherwise, it returns the constant *EOF*. You should call *ferror()* and *feof()* to determine if there really was an error or the file simply reached its end.

See Also
```
getc(), getchar(), fputc(), putc(), putchar(), EOF, FILE,
stdin
```

fgetpos()
function

Purpose

Use the *fgetpos()* function to get and save the current position indicator of the stream specified by the argument *stream* in the *fpos_t* data object *current_pos*. This value can be used only by the companion function *fsetpos()* to reposition the stream to its position at the time of the call to *fgetpos()*. Note: This function is used with C streams, not with C++ streams, for which the functions *tellp()* and *tellg()* can be used for this purpose.

Syntax
```
#include <stdio.h>
int fgetpos(FILE *stream, fpos_t *current_pos);
FILE *stream;          Pointer to stream whose current position is requested
fpos_t *current_pos;   Pointer to variable where file's current position is returned
```

Example Use
```
fgetpos(infile, &curpos);
```

Returns

If successful, *fgetpos()* returns a 0. In case of error, it returns a non-zero value and sets the global variable *errno* to an implementation-defined error constant.

See Also
```
fsetpos(), errno, fpos_t
```

fgets() function

Purpose

Use the *fgets()* function to read a line from the ANSI C stream specified by *stream*. The line is read into the character array *string* until a newline ('\n') character is encountered, an end-of-file condition occurs, or the number of characters read reaches one less than the value given in the argument *maxchar*. A null character is written to *string* immediately after the last character. Note that the equivalent function for C++ file streams is *getline()*.

Syntax
```
#include <stdio.h>
char *fgets(char *string, int maxchar, FILE *stream);
char *string;      Pointer to buffer where characters will be stored
int maxchar;       Maximum number of characters that can be stored
FILE *stream;      Pointer to stream from which a line is read
```

Example Use
```
fgets(buffer, 80, infile);
```

Returns

If there are no errors, *fgets()* returns the argument *string*. Otherwise, it returns a *NULL*. You can call *ferror()* and *feof()* to determine whether the error is a genuine one or it occurred because the file reached its end.

See Also
```
gets(), fputs(), puts(), FILE, NULL
```

FILE predefined data type

Purpose

The *FILE* data type contains the information needed to perform standard C file I/O. It is defined in *stdio.h*. Note that in C++ the stream functions defined in *iostream.h* are preferred.

See Also
```
EOF, FILENAME_MAX
```

_ _FILE_ _ predefined macro

Purpose

Use the _ _FILE_ _ predefined macro to display the name of the source file being translated by the preprocessor.

Example Use
```
printf("Now preprocessing: ");
printf(__FILE__);
```

See Also
```
__DATE__, __TIME__, __LINE__, __STDC__
```

filebuf class

Purpose

The *filebuf* class is derived from the *streambuf* class and adds data structures and member functions needed to adapt the general stream buffer mechanism to files. *filebuf* is defined in *fstream.h*.

See Also
```
streambuf, ios, iostream.h, fstream.h
```

FILENAME_MAX predefined value

Purpose

The *FILENAME_MAX* predefined value gives the maximum length of a file name string, and is dependent on the operating system in use. It is defined in *stdio.h*.

See Also
```
FILE
```

fill() function

Purpose

Use the *fill() ios* member function to set the character that will be used to fill leading spaces in numeric quantities. By default the fill character is a space.

Syntax
```
#include <iostream.h>
fill();              returns fill character
fill(<char>);        to set fill character and return old fill character
```

Example Use
```
char fchar = fill(); // store old fill char. in fchar
fill('*'); // set fill char to *
int check_amount = 1000;
cout.width(8); // set number width to 8
cout << check_amount; // displays ****1000
```

The way a number is padded is also affected by the settings of *ios* format flags such as *ios::width*, which is set to 8 by the *width()* manipulator above. The *ios::adjustfield* flag determines where numbers will be padded by specifying their justification; *ios::left* can also be used for left justification (padding to right) or *ios::right* for right justification (padding to left).

The *setfill()* function can also be used to specify a fill character. This function takes an *int* or *char const* value.

Returns

If *fill()* is called without an argument it returns the current fill character. If it is called with an argument it sets the fill character to that argument and also returns the previous fill character. Thus in the above example we also could have written:

```
char fchar = fill ('*');
```

See Also

```
ios (formatting flags), width(), setfill()
```

flags()
function

Purpose

Use the *flags() ios* member function to return and/or set the *ios* formatting flags for a C++ stream. The *ios* formating flags are listed in the entry for *ios*. Typically you set flags by providing a value of type *long* that provides a *mask value* that sets one or more flags while leaving the remaining ones untouched.

Syntax

```
<stream_name>.flags();            to get current flags
<stream.name>.flags(<longval>);   to set flags and return previous flag values
```

Example Use

```
long old_flags = cout.flags(); // get current flags
cout.flags(old_flags ^ ios::dec | ios::hex | ios::showbase);
```

In using *flags()* all conflicting flags have to be accounted for. Above, we first save the old flags by getting them from a call to *flags()* with no argument. The next call to *flags()* uses the bitwise exclusive or operator (^) to clear the flag for decimal output. This is then *or*ed with the flags for hex output and for displaying the base, to provide the desired output.

As a practical matter the *setf()* and *unsetf()* functions are easier and more convenient to use because they allow you to specify just the flag you want to set or clear and take care of the "bit-twiddling" for you. The *setiosflags()* and *resetiosflags()* functions provide yet another way to set or clear *ios* format flags.

Returns

When called without an argument *flags()* returns the current *long* value containing the flag settings. When called with a *long* argument (normally a logical expression using the predefined *ios* mask values as shown above), *flags()* returns the *previous long* flag value.

See Also
```
ios (formatting flags), setf(), unsetf(), setiosflags(),
resetiosflags()
```

float keyword

Purpose

Use the *float* data type specifier to declare single precision floating-point variables and arrays.

Syntax
```
float <varname>;
```

Example Use
```
/* declare a float, a pointer to a
    float, and an array of float */
float f, *p_f, fvars[100];
```

See Also
```
char, double, int, long, short, signed, unsigned
```

floor() function

Purpose

Use the *floor()* function to get the "floor" of a *double* argument *x*. The "floor" is the largest integral value that is less than or equal to *x*. This can be used in rounding a *double down* to the preceding integer.

Syntax
```
#include <math.h>
double floor(double x);
double x;       Variable whose "floor" is to be returned
```

Example Use
```
x = floor(4.15);  /* x will be 4.0 */
```

Returns

The return value is the "floor" of *x* expressed as a *double*.

See Also
```
ceil()
```

**FLT_DIG
predefined
value**

Purpose

The *FLT_DIG* predefined value gives the number of significant decimal digits in a *float* value. It is defined in *float.h*.

See Also

```
FLT_EPSILON, FLT_MANT_DIG, FLT_MIN, FLT_MIN_10_EXP,
FLT_MIN_EXP, FLT_MAX, FLT_MAX_10_EXP, FLT_MAX_EXP, FLT_RADIX
```

**FLT_EPSILON
predefined
value**

Purpose

The *FLT_EPSILON* predefined value gives the smallest positive *float* value x such that $1+x != 1$. It is defined in *float.h*.

See Also

```
FLT_DIG, FLT_MANT_DIG, FLT_MIN, FLT_MIN_10_EXP,
FLT_MIN_EXP, FLT_MAX, FLT_MAX_10_EXP, FLT_MAX_EXP, FLT_RADIX
```

**FIT_MANT_DIG
predefined
value**

Purpose

The *FLT_MANT_DIG* predefined value gives the number of base *FLT_RADIX* digits in the mantissa of a *float*. It is defined in *float.h*.

See Also

```
FLT_DIG, FLT_EPSILON, FLT_MIN, FLT_MIN_10_EXP,
FLT_MIN_10, FLT_MAX, FLT_MAX_10_EXP, FLT_MAX_EXP, FLT_RADIX
```

**FLT_MAX
predefined
value**

Purpose

The *FLT_MAX* predefined value gives the maximum representable finite value that can be stored in a *float*. It is defined in *float.h*.

See Also

```
FLT_DIG, FLT_MANT_DIG, FLT_EPSILON, FLT_MIN, FLT_MIN_10_EXP,
FLT_MIN_10, FLT_MAX_10_EXP, FLT_MAX_EXP, FLT_RADIX
```

**FLT_MAX_10_EXP
predefined
value**

Purpose

The *FLT_MAX_10_EXP* predefined value gives the maximum integer such that 10 raised to that power is representable in a *float*. It is defined in *float.h*.

See Also

```
FLT_DIG, FLT_MANT_DIG, FLT_EPSILON, FLT_MIN, FLT_MIN_10_EXP,
FLT_MIN_EXP, FLT_MAX, FLT_MAX_EXP, FLT_RADIX
```

**FLT_MAX_EXP
predefined
value**

Purpose

The *FLT_MAX_EXP* predefined value gives the maximum integer such that
FLT_RADIX raised to that power is representable in a *float*. It is defined in
float.h.

See Also

FLT_DIG, FLT_MANT_DIG, FLT_EPSILON, FLT_MIN, FLT_MIN_10_EXP,
FLT_MIN_EXP, FLT_MAX, FLT_MAX_10_EXP, FLT_RADIX

**FLT_MIN
predefined
value**

Purpose

The *FLT_MIN* predefined value gives the minimum positive floating-point
number that can be stored in a *float*. It is defined in *float.h*.

See Also

FLT_DIG, FLT_MANT_DIG, FLT_EPSILON, FLT_MIN_10_EXP,
FLT_MIN_EXP, FLT_MAX, FLT_MAX_10_EXP, FLT_MAX_EXP, FLT_RADIX

**FLT_MIN_10_EXP
predefined
value**

Purpose

The *FLT_MIN_10_EXP* predefined value gives the minimum negative
integer such that 10 raised to that power is representable in a *float*. It is defined
in *float.h*.

See Also

FLT_DIG, FLT_MANT_DIG, FLT_EPSILON, FLT_MIN,
FLT_MIN_EXP, FLT_MAX, FLT_MAX_10_EXP, FLT_MAX_EXP, FLT_RADIX

**FLT_MIN_EXP
predefined
value**

Purpose

The *FLT_MIN_EXP* predefined value gives the minimum negative integer
such that FLT_RADIX raised to that power minus 1 is representable in a *float*.
It is defined in *float.h*.

See Also

FLT_DIG, FLT_MANT_DIG, FLT_EPSILON, FLT_MIN, FLT_MIN_10_EXP,
FLT_MAX, FLT_MAX_10_EXP, FLT_MAX_EXP, FLT_RADIX

**FLT_RADIX
predefined
value**

Purpose

The *FLT_RADIX* predefined value gives the radix of the exponent used for
numeric representation (usually 2 for binary exponent). It is defined in *float.h*.

See Also
```
FLT_DIG, FLT_MANT_DIG, FLT_EPSILON, FLT_MIN, FLT_MIN_EXP,
FLT_MIN_10_EXP, FLT_MAX, FLT_MAX_10_EXP, FLT_MAX_EXP
```

FLT_ROUNDS predefined value

Purpose

The *FLT_ROUNDS* predefined value gives a constant that indicates how floating-point values are rounded. The possible values are −1 (indeterminate), 0 (towards 0), 1 (to nearest representable value), 2 (towards positive infinity), and 3 (towards negative infinity). It is defined in *float.h*.

See Also
```
FLT_DIG, FLT_MANT_DIG, FLT_EPSILON, FLT_MIN, FLT_MIN_EXP,
FLT_MIN_10_EXP, FLT_MAX, FLT_MAX_10_EXP, FLT_MAX_EXP,
FLT_RADIX
```

flush manipulator

Purpose

Use the *flush* C++ stream manipulator to flush an output stream (that is, send any data waiting in the stream buffer to the file).

Syntax
```
#include <iostream.h>
<output_stream> << flush;
```

Example Use
```
cout << flush;  // send remaining data to output
```

Returns

As with all manipulators, *flush* returns a reference to the stream so that it can be "cascaded" with other output.

See Also
```
endl, ends, close()
```

fmod() function

Purpose

Use the *fmod()* function to compute the floating-point remainder after dividing the floating-point number x by y and ensuring that the quotient is the largest possible integral value. If this quotient is n, then *fmod()* returns the value r computed from the expression r = x − n*y. The entire operation is equivalent to:

```
        double n, r;
        ...
        ...
        n = floor(x/y);
        r = x - n*y;
```

Syntax
```
#include <math.h>
double fmod(double x, double y);
double x, y;              The remainder after the division x/y is returned
```

Example Use
```
rem = fmod(24.95, 5.5); /* rem will be 2.95 */
```

Returns
When y is zero, *fmod()* returns a zero. Otherwise, it returns the remainder as described above.

See Also
```
floor()
```

fopen()
function

Purpose
Use the *fopen()* function to open the file whose name is in the string *filename* and associate a stream with it. The argument *access_mode* contains one of the following strings

Access_mode	Intrepretation
"r"	Open a text file for reading. Fail if file does not exist.
"w"	If file exists, open and truncate it to zero length. Otherwise, create the file and open it for writing in the text mode.
"a"	Open text file for appending—writing at the end of file. Create file if it does not already exist.
"rb"	Same as "r" — but binary mode.
"wb"	Same as "w" — but binary mode.
"ab"	Same as "a" — but binary mode.
"r+"	Open text file for updating—reading as well as writing.
"w+"	If file exists, open it and truncate it to zero length. Otherwise, create it and open it for updating.
"a+"	Open text file for appending. Create file if it does not already exist.
"r+b" or "rb+"	Open binary file for updating.
"w+b" or "wb+"	If file exists, truncate to zero length; else create a binary file for update operations.
"a+b" or "ab+"	Open or create binary file for appending.

Note that the *fopen()* function is used with C file streams, not C++ streams. Use the *ios* member function *open()* to open a C++ file stream.

Syntax
```
#include <stdio.h>
FILE *fopen(const char *filename, const char *access_mode);
const char *filename;          Name of file to be opened
const char *access_mode;       A character string denoting whether file is
                               being opened for read, write, or append
```

Example Use
```
input_file = fopen("data.in", "rb");
```

Returns
If the file is successfully opened, *fopen()* returns a pointer to the FILE data structure that controls the stream. The FILE structure is allocated elsewhere and you do not have to allocate it. In case of an error, *fopen*() returns NULL.

See Also
```
fclose(), freopen(), setbuf(), setvbuf(), FILE, NULL
```

FOPEN_MAX predefined value

Purpose
The *FOPEN_MAX* predefined value gives the maximum number of files that can be open simultaneously. This value is dependent on the operating system. It is defined in *stdio.h*.

See Also
```
BUFSIZ, FILENAME_MAX
```

for keyword

Purpose
Use the *for* keyword to create a loop that will be executed a specified number of times. Usually an index variable is set to a starting value and progressively varied each time the body of the loop is executed. The index variable is compared to a specified condition before each execution of the loop body. When the condition is satisfied (evaluates as 1 or true), the body of the loop is not executed and control resumes with the statement following the end of the loop.

Syntax
```
for (initialization; condition; varying) statement;
```
where the *initialization* is evaluated once at the beginning of the loop, and the *varying statement* is executed until the *condition* evaluates to 0 (false).

The statement for varying the loop index is evaluated after each execution of *statement*.

Example Use
```
/* add the numbers from 1 to limit, all inside
   the loop specifications */

for(i=0, sum=0; i <= limit; sum += i, i++);
   printf("\nSum from 1 to %d = %d\n", limit, sum);
```
Notice that there can be more than one statement in each part of the loop specification, with successive statements in a group being separated with commas. Here the initialization is *i = 0, sum = 0;* and the varying statements are *sum += i, i ++*.

A *for* loop does not need to have a statement in the body; if the *printf()* statement in the preceding example were omitted the loop would still function correctly and accumulate the sum.

See Also
```
break, continue, if, switch, , (sequential evaluation operator)
```

**form()
function**

Purpose
The *form()* function was provided in C++ 1.2 as a general-purpose formatting facility. It accepted essentially the same specifiers as the *sprintf()* C library function. Since *form()* is no longer supported in C++ 2.X, the expanded range of overloaded versions of the extraction and insertion operators and manipulators should be used to construct the desired format.

See Also
```
<< and >> operators, cout, cin, get(), getline(), read(),
readline(), setf(), unset(), sprintf()
```

**fpos_t
predefined
value**

Purpose
The *fpos_t* data type contains information enabling the specification of each unique position in a file. It is defined in *stdio.h*.

See Also
```
fseek(), ftell()
```

**fprintf()
function**

Purpose
Use the *fprintf()* function to format and write character strings and values of variables to the stream specified by the argument *stream*. See reference entry

for *printf()* for a description of the argument *format_string*. Note that this function is used with C streams, not C++ streams, which use *ios* member functions such as *write()* or the insertion operator <<.

Syntax

```
#include <stdio.h>
int fprintf(FILE *stream, const char * format_string,...);
FILE *stream;                    Pointer to output stream
const char *format_string;       A character string which describes the
                                 format to be used
...          A variable number of arguments depending on the
             number of items being printed
```

Example Use

```
fprintf(resultfile, "The result is %f\n", result);
```

Returns

The *fprintf()* function returns the number of characters it has printed. In case of error, it returns a negative value.

See Also

```
printf(), vfprintf(), vprintf(), sprintf(), vsprintf(), FILE;
<<, write() (C++ streams)
```

fputc() function

Purpose

Use *fputc()* to write the single character *c* to the stream specified by *stream*. Note that this function is used with C streams, not C++ streams, which use *ios* member functions such as *put()*.

Syntax

```
#include <stdio.h>
int fputc(int c, FILE *stream);
int c;            Character to be written
FILE *stream;     Pointer to output stream
```

Example Use

```
fputc('X', p_datafile);
```

Returns

If there are no errors, *fputc()* returns the character written. Otherwise, it returns the constant *EOF*. You should call *ferror()* to determine if there really was an error or if the integer argument *c* just happened to be equal to EOF.

See Also

```
fgetc(), getc(), getchar(), putc(), puts(), EOF, FILE; put()
(C++ streams)
```

fputs()
function

Purpose

Use the *fputs()* function to write the C string given by *string* to the stream specified by *stream*. Note that this function is used with C streams, not C++ streams, which can use the insertion operator << for this purpose.

Syntax
```
#include <stdio.h>
int fputs(const char *string, FILE *stream);
const char *string;        Null ('\0') terminated character string to be output
FILE *stream;              Pointer to stream to which the string is output
```

Example Use
```
fputs("Sample Input Data", p_datafile);
```

Returns

The *fputs()* function returns a non-negative value if all goes well. In case of error, it returns the constant EOF.

See Also
```
fgets(), gets(), puts(), EOF, FILE; << (C++ streams)
```

fread()
function

Purpose

Use the *fread()* function to read the number of data items specified by *count*, each of the size given by the argument *size*, from the current position in *stream*. The current position of *stream* is updated after the read. Note that this function is used with C streams, not C++ streams.

Syntax
```
#include <stdio.h>
size_t fread(void *buffer, size_t size, size_t count,
                         FILE *stream);
void *buffer;      Pointer to buffer where fread will store the bytes it reads
size_t size;       Size in bytes of each data item
size_t count;      Maximum number of items to be read
FILE *stream;      Pointer to stream from which data items are to be read
```

Example Use
```
numread = fread(buffer, sizeof(char), 80, infile);
```

Returns

The *fread()* function returns the number of items it successfully read. If the return value is less than you expected, you can call *ferror()* and *feof()* to determine if a read error had occurred or if end-of-file has been reached.

See Also
```
fopen(), fwrite(), fclose(), FILE, size_t
```

free()
function

Purpose

Use the *free()* function to deallocate (return to the pool of free memory) a block of memory which was allocated earlier by *malloc()*, *calloc()*, or *realloc()*. The address of the block is specified by the argument *mem_address,* which is a pointer to the starting byte of the block. A *NULL* pointer argument is ignored by *free()*. Note that C++ objects are normally deallocated via their class destructor and the delete operator.

Syntax
```
#include <stdlib.h>
void free(void *mem_address);
void *mem_address;        Pointer to block of memory to be released
```

Example Use
```
free(buffer);
```

See Also
```
calloc(), malloc(), realloc(), NULL; delete (C++ objects)
```

freeopen()
function

Purpose

Use the *freopen()* function to close *stream* and open another file whose name is in the string *filename* and attach *stream* to it. For example, you can use *freopen*() to redirect I/O from the pre-opened file *stdout* to a file of your choice. See *fopen()* for a description of the argument *access_mode*. The error indicator of *stream* will be cleared after the reopening. Note that this function is used for C streams, not C++ streams.

Syntax
```
#include <stdio.h>
FILE *freopen(const char *filename, const char
*access_mode, FILE *stream);
const char *filename;    Name of file to be reopened including drive
                         and directory specification
const char *access_mode;    A character string denoting whether file is being
                            reopened for read, write, or append
FILE *stream;            Pointer to stream to be reopened
```

Example Use
```
freopen("output.txt", "w", stdout);
/* Redirect stdout to a file */
```

Returns

If all goes well, *freopen()* returns a pointer to the newly opened file. This returned pointer will be the same as the argument *stream*. In case of error, a NULL is returned.

See Also
```
fopen(), fclose(), FILE(), NULL, stdout
```

frexp()
function

Purpose
Use the *frexp()* function to break down the floating-point number *x* into a mantissa *m* whose absolute value lies between 0.5 and 1.0, and an integer exponent *n*, so that $x = m\,2^n$. The integer exponent *n* is stored by *frexp()* in the location whose address is given in the argument *expptr*. If *x* is zero, the exponent will also be zero.

Syntax
```
#include <math.h>
double frexp(double x, int *expptr);
double x;          Floating-point argument to be decomposed
int *expptr;       Pointer to an integer where the exponent will be returned
```

Example Use
```
mantissa-= frexp(5.1, &exponent);
/* mantissa will be 0.6375, exponent = 3 */
```

Returns
Normally *frexp()* returns the mantissa *m* computed as described above. When *x* is zero, *frexp()* returns a zero as the mantissa.

See Also
```
1dexp(), modf()
```

fscanf()
function

Purpose
Use the *fscanf()* function to read characters from *stream*, convert them to values according to format specifications embedded in the argument *format_string,* and finally store the values into variables whose addresses are provided in the variable length argument list. See *scanf()* for more details on the argument *format_string*. Note that this function is normally used with C streams. Use *ios* member functions such as *getline()* with C++ streams.

Syntax
```
#include <stdio.h>
int fscanf(FILE *stream, const char* format_string,...);
FILE *stream;              Pointer to the stream from which reading will occur
const char *format_string;     A character string which describes the
                               format to be used
```
Variable number of arguments representing addresses of variables whose values are being read

Example Use
```
fscanf(infile, "Date: %d/%d/%d", &month, &day,&year);
```

Returns

The *fscanf()* function returns the number of input items that were successfully read, converted, and saved in variables. The count does not include items that were read and ignored. If an end-of-file is encountered during read, the return value will be equal to the constant EOF (defined in *stdio.h*).

See Also
```
scanf(), sscanf(), eof(), FILE, getline() (C++ streams)
```

fseek()
function

Purpose

Use the *fseek()* function to reposition *stream* to the location specified by *offset* with respect to the argument *origin*. The valid values of *origin* are the following constants:

Origin	Interpretation of Constant
SEEK_SET	Beginning of file
SEEK_CUR	Current position in the file
SEEK_END	End of file

Note that the *fseek()* function is used with C streams, not C++ streams. For C++ streams use *ios* member functions *seekg()* (to set read position) or *seekp* (to set write position).

Syntax
```
#include <stdio.h>
int fseek(FILE *stream, long offset, int origin);
FILE *stream;      Pointer to stream whose current position is to be set
long offset;       Offset of new position (in bytes) from origin
int origin;        A constant indicating the position from which to offset
```

Example Use
```
fseek(infile, 0L, SEEK_SET); /* Go to the beginning*/
```

Returns

fseek() returns a non-zero value only if it fails to position the stream.

See Also
```
fgetpos(), fsetpos(), ftell(), FILE, SEEK_SET, SEEK_CUR,
SEEK_END; seekg(), seekp() (for C++ streams)
```

fsetpos() function

Purpose

Use the *fsetpos()* function to set the position where reading or writing will take place in *stream*. The new position is specified in a *fpos_t* data object whose address is in *current_pos*. For file position, you should use a value obtained by an earlier call to *fgetpos()*. Note that this function is used with C streams, not C++ strteams. Use *seekg()* to set the read position for a C++ stream, or *seekp()* to set the write position.

Syntax

```
#include <stdio.h>
int fsetpos(FILE *stream, const fpos_t *current_pos);
FILE *stream;               Pointer to stream whose current position is to be set
const fpos_t *current_pos;   Pointer to location containing new
                             value of file position
```

Example Use

```
fsetpos(infile, &curpos);
```

Returns

If successful, *fsetpos()* clears the end of file indicator of *stream*, and returns zero. Otherwise, the return value will be non-zero and the global variable *errno* will be set to an implementation-defined error constant.

See Also

```
fgetpos(), FILE, errno, fpos_t; setg(), setp() (C++ streams)
```

fstream class

Purpose

Use the *fstream* class to declare a stream object for use with a file. The *fstream* class is derived from the *fstreambase* and *iostream* classes. See the *ios* and *open()* entries for more information on opening files, and the *istream* and *ostream* entries for more information on input and output files.

Syntax

```
#include <fstream.h>
fstream <object_name> ; or
fstream <handle_no>; or
fstream <object_name>, <"filename">, <ios::mode>,
<filebuf::mode>;
object_name    name of stream object in program
handle_no      integer handle number (e.g., for DOS)
"filename"     filename acceptable to operating system
ios::open_mode read, write, etc. mode (see ios entry) (optional; default is ios::in)
filebuf::mode  file protection mode (always filebuf::openprot in current DOS
               implementations; check for others)
```

If you declare an *fstream* with just the object name, you must use the *fstream::open()* function to open the file before use. The use of a file handle number assumes that this handle has already been set up with the operating system. Since there is currently only one file protection mode in *filebuf* and the constructor defaults to it, you normally don't have to use this parameter at all.

Example Use
```
fstream test_input; // create object, must open file
                    // before use
fstream(5);         // use file handle 5 in operating
                    // system
fstream(input, "datafile"); // create object "input" // and
associate it with "datafile" on disk
fstream(datafeed, "specdev", ios::binary); //
// declare object "datastream", associate it with
// actual file "specdev", and open in explicit binary
// mode
```

See Also
```
iostream.h, ios, fstream.h, fstreambase, istream, ostream
```

fstreambase class

Purpose
The *fstreambase* is, as the name suggests, the base class for *fstream*, providing file-related facilities and declared in *fstream.h*. *fstreambase* is derived from the more general *ios* class. In turn the input file (*ifstream*) is derived from *fstreambase* and *istream*, and the output file (*ofstream*) classes are dervied from *fstreambase* and *ostream*.

Syntax
```
#include <fstream.h>
```

See Also
```
ios, filebuf, fstream, ifstream, ofstream
```

fstream.h header file

Purpose
Use the *fstream.h* header file to include the file-related classes such as *ifstream* and *ofstream* and member functions such as *close()* and *open()*. Since the *fstream.h* header file includes the directive *#include <iostream.h>* you need not include *iostream.h* separately in order to use the general *ios* formatting and stream state functions.

Syntax
```
#include <fstream.h>
```

See Also
```
iostream.h, stream.h, iomanip.h, filebuf
```

ftell() function

Purpose

Use the *ftell()* function to obtain the current position of *stream*. The position is expressed as a byte offset from the beginning of the file. Note that this function is used with C streams, not C++ streams. Use *tellg()* to obtain the current read position in a C++ stream, or *tellp()* to get the write position.

Syntax
```
#include <stdio.h>
ftell(FILE *stream);
FILE *stream;        Pointer to stream whose current position is to be returned
```

Example Use
```
curpos = ftell(infile));
```

Returns

If successful, *ftell()* returns a long integer containing the number of bytes the current position of *stream* is offset from the beginning of the file. In case of error, *ftell()* returns −1L. Also, the global variable *errno* is set to an implementation-defined constant.

See Also
```
fgetpos(), fseek(), fsetpos(), FILE, errno; tellg(), tellp()
(C++ streams)
```

fwrite() function

Purpose

Use the *fwrite()* function to write the number of data items specified by *count*, each of the size given by *size*, from *buffer* to the current position in *stream*. The current position of *stream* is updated after the write. Note that this function is used with C streams, not C++ streams. Use the *write() ios* member function to write binary data to a C++ stream.

Syntax
```
#include <stdio.h>
size_t fwrite(const void *buffer, size_t size, size_t
                      count, FILE *stream);
const void *buffer;        Pointer to buffer in memory from where fwrite will
                           get the bytes it writes
```

```
size_t size;        Size in bytes of each data item
size_t count;       Maximum number of items to be written
FILE *stream;       Pointer to stream to which the data items are to be written
```

Example Use
```
numwrite = fwrite(buffer, sizeof(char), 80, outfile);
```

Returns
The *fwrite()* function returns the number of items it actually wrote. If the return value is less than what you expect, an error may have occurred. Use *ferror()* to verify this.

See Also
```
fopen(), fread(), fclose(), FILE, size_t; write() (C++ streams)
```

**get()
function**

Purpose
Use the *get() ios* member function with an *istream* object in C++ to get a single character or a series of characters from a stream.

Syntax
```
#include <iostream.h>
<stream>.get (char* string, int numchars, char term_char =
'\n');              for string input
char * string      string in which characters are to be stored
int numchars       maximum number of characters to read
char term_char     character at which to stop reading (default is newline)

<stream>.get(char onechar&);   for binary or single-character input
char onechar       single-char or binary value
<stream>.get();    for single-char or binary input; returns integer
```

As usual all forms are called by referencing the stream object (for example, *cin.get(C);*. The first form of *get()* shown above reads up to a newline or until one less than the number of characters specified have been read. (You can specify a character other than newline as input terminator; in any case the terminating character is not included in the string, but the string *is* ended with a null character.)

The second form of *get()* reads any single character (even whitespace) or a *char*-sized binary value. The third form works like the second, but returns the integer equivalent of the character rather than a reference to the *istream*. (In Borland/Turbo C++, this version, when used with *cin*, waits until you have pressed ENTER after typing a character. It also treats CTRL-C as a system break.)

Example Use

```
char * name;        // string to hold name
cout << "Enter your name and press enter ";
cin.get (name, 40); // read up to 40 chars.
                    // or newline
cin.get (name, 20, '\t'); // read up to 20
        // characters or a tab
char choice;
cin.get(choice); // get single character
```

Returns

The *get()* function returns a reference to the *istream* object, except for the *int get()* version, which returns the *int* value of the character input.

See Also

```
read(), getline(), peek()
```

getc() macro

Purpose

Using the *getc()* macro to read a single character from *stream*. *getc()* is identical to *fgetc()*, except that it is implemented as a macro. This means you should not provide it an argument that may cause any side effects. Note: Use this macro for C streams; use the *get() ios* member function for C++ streams.

Syntax

```
#include <stdio.h>
int getc(FILE *stream);
FILE *stream;    Pointer to stream from which a character is to read
```

Example Use

```
in_char = getc(p_txtfile);
```

Returns

The *getc()* macro returns the character read as an integer value. A return value of *EOF* indicates an error.

See Also

```
fgetc(), fputc(), getchar(), putc(), putchar(), EOF, FILE;
get() (C++ streams)
```

getchar macro

Purpose

Use the *getchar()* macro to read a single character from the pre-opened file *stdin* which is normally connected to your keyboard input. Note that *getchar()* is identical to *getc()* with *stream* set to *stdin*. (Use the *ios* member function *get()* to read a single character from a C++ stream.)

Syntax
```
#include <stdio.h>
int getchar(void);
```

Example Use
```
c = getchar();
```

Returns

The *getchar()* macro returns the character read from *stdin* as an integer value. In case of any error the return value is equal to the constant EOF.

See Also
```
fgetc(), fputc(), getc(), putc(), putchar(), EOF, stdin; get()
(C++ streams)
```

getenv() function

Purpose

Use *getenv()* to get the definition of the environment variable *varname* from the environment of the process.

Syntax
```
#include <stdlib.h>
char *getenv(const char *varname);
const char *varname;     Name of environment variable to look for
```

Example Use
```
current_path = getenv("PATH");
```

Returns

If *varname* is found, *getenv* returns a pointer to the string value of *varname*. If *varname* is undefined, *getenv()* will return a *NULL*. Predefined environment variables vary with the operating system in use.

See Also
```
argc, argv
```

getline() function

Purpose

Use the *getline() ios* member function to get a line of input. You can specify the total number of characters to be read and/or the character at which to terminate input. *getline()* produces the same effect with a string as *get()* except that *getline() does* include the terminating character (usually a newline) before appending the string terminating null character. Note that your string object must allow for the extra character, as shown below.

Syntax
```
#include <iostream.h>
<stream>.getline(char* string, int numchars, char term_char =
'\n');
char* string        string to receive input
numchars            maximum chars to input
term_char           character at which to terminate input
```

Example Use
```
char command[80]; // array to hold command
cin.getline(command, 79); // command up to 79 chars.
          // must make room for terminating character
```

Returns

The *getline()* function returns a reference to the *istream* object.

See Also
```
get(), read()
```

gets()
function

Purpose

Use *gets()* to read a line from the standard input file *stdin* into the string *buffer*. The reading continues until *gets* encounters a newline character or end-of-file. At this point, it replaces the newline character with a null character ('\0') and creates a C-style string. You must allocate room for the buffer in which the characters will be stored. Note that *fgets()* performs similarly, but unlike *gets()*, it retains the newline character in the final string. Also note that *gets()* should not be used with C++ streams; use the *ios* member function *getline()* instead.

Syntax
```
#include <stdio.h>
char *gets(char *buffer);
char *buffer;              Buffer where string will be stored
```

Example Use
```
gets(command_line);
```

Returns

If successful, *gets()* returns *buffer*. Otherwise, it returns a NULL.

See Also
```
fgets(), fputs(), puts(), NULL, stdin; getline() (C++ streams)
```

gmtime()
function

Purpose

Use the *gmtime()* function to break down a time value of type *time_t* stored at the location *time* into year, month, day, hour, minutes, seconds, and several other fields that it saves in a structure of type *tm* maintained internally. The structure *tm* is defined in *time.h* and shown in the entry for *asctime()*. The fields setting up *gmtime* will correspond to Greenwich Mean Time (GMT).

Syntax
```
#include <time.h>
struct tm *gmtime(const time_t *time);
const time_t *time;          Pointer to calendar time
```

Example Use
```
t_gmt = gmtime(&bintime);
```

Returns

The *gmtime()* function returns a pointer to the *tm* structure where the converted time is stored. If GMT is not available, it returns a NULL.

See Also
```
asctime(), localtime(), time(), NULL, time_t, tm
```

good() function

Purpose

Use the *good() ios* member function to check whether any error has occurred involving a stream.

Syntax
```
<stream_name>.good()
```

Example Use
```
while (cin.good()) {
// process the input
}
```

Returns

The *good()* function returns a non-zero (true) value if no *ios* error bits have been set for the stream. If one or more error bits have been set, *good()* returns a 0 (false).

See Also
```
ios, bad(), fail()
```

goto keyword

Purpose

Use the *goto* keyword to jump unconditionally to a label in the current function. The label ends in a colon. If the *goto* is executed, control jumps to the code following the specified label.

Use of *goto* is not recommended for most applications because it makes it hard to follow the flow of execution in the program.

Syntax
```
goto <label>;
```

Example Use
```
if (system_price > 6000.0) goto TooExpensive;
    ...
TooExpensive:
    seek_alternative();
```

hex manipulator

Purpose
Use the *hex* C++ stream manipulator to set the conversion format flag for a stream to hexadecimal (base 16). The conversion format controls the base in which numbers will be output to or input from the stream. Note: *hex* is equivalent to *setbase(16)*.

Syntax
```
#include <iostream.h>
ostream << hex;          set base to hexadecimal for output stream
istream >> hex;          set base to hexadecimal for input stream
```

Example Use
```
int n = 255;
cout << hex << n; // outputs 'ff'
```

Returns
The *hex* manipulator returns a reference to the stream. This allows the manipulator to both change the stream state and pass a value along a chain of input or output.

See Also
```
dec, oct, setbase()
```

HUGE_VAL predefined value

Purpose
The value *HUGE_VAL* is a predefined *double* expression that evaluates to a very large value (for use as a return value by math functions when the computed result is too large). It is defined in *math.h*.

See Also
```
INT_MAX, DBL_MAX, FLT_MAX
```

if
keyword

Purpose

Use *if* to execute code only when certain conditions hold true. You can use *if* alone or with *else* to specify multiple alternatives.

Syntax

```
if (<condition>)
    <statement; ...>
or
if (<condition>)
    <statement_1>
else
    <statement_2>;
```

The statement following the *if* is executed if *condition* is true (not equal to 0). When an *else* is present, statement_2 is executed if *condition* is false (equal to 0).

Example Use

```
if (x <= y)  smaller = x;
else smaller = y;
...
```

If *x* is less than or equal to *y*, then *smaller* is assigned the value *x*. Otherwise, (else) *smaller* is assigned the value *y*.

See Also

```
else
```

#if
preprocessor
conditional
directive

Purpose

Use the *#if* preprocessor directive to control which parts of your code will be compiled under which conditions.

Syntax

```
#if <condition>
    <directive1>
#elif <condition2>
    <directive2>
...
#else
    <default_directive>
#endif
```

If *condition1* is true, *directive1* is executed by the preprocessor; otherwise, if *condition2* is true, *directive2* is executed. If neither *condition1* nor *condition2* is true, then *default_directive* is executed. You can have no *#elif* or more than one of them; you can omit *#else* but not have more than one *#else*.

Example Use
```
#if !defined(FILE_1_INCLUDED)
    #include <file1.h>
#elif defined(INCLUDE_FILE_2)
    #include <file2.h>
#else
    #include <file3.h>
#endif
```

See Also
```
defined (preprocessor condition), #include
```

#ifdef preprocessor operator

Purpose
Use the *#ifdef* preprocessor operator to determine whether a preprocessor symbol or macro is defined in the current program. The *#ifdef* operator is equivalent to *#if defined*.

Syntax
```
#ifdef (<SYMBOL>)
```

Example Use
```
#ifdef (NON_STANDARD)
    #include "ourdefs.h"
#endif
```

See Also
```
defined (preprocessor operator), #ifndef
```

#ifndef preprocessor operator

Purpose
Use the *#ifndef* preprocessor operator to determine whether a preprocessor symbol or macro is not defined in the current program. *#ifndef* is equivalent to *#if !defined*.

Syntax
```
#ifndef (<SYMBOL>)
```

Example Use
```
#ifndef (COPROCESSOR)
    #include "emulate.h"
#endif
```

See Also
```
defined (preprocessor operator), #idef
```

ifstream class

Purpose

Use the *ifstream* class to declare an input stream object. The *ifstream* class is derived from the *istream* class and adds file-related functions and the extraction (>>) operator. See the *ios* and *open()* entries for more information on opening files. The input file *cin* is predefined for standard input (by default, the keyboard).

Syntax
```
#include <fstream.h>
ifstream <object_name> ; or
ifstream <handle_no>; or
ifstream <object_name>, <"filename">, <ios::mode>,
<filebuf::mode>;
```
`object_name`	*name of stream object in program*
`handle_no`	*integer handle number (e.g., for DOS)*
`"filename"`	*file name acceptable to operating system*
`ios::open_mode`	*read, write, etc. mode (see ios entry) (optional; default is ios::in)*
`filebuf::mode`	*file protection mode (always filebuf::openprot in current DOS implementations; check for others)*

If you declare an *ifstream* with just the object name, you must use the *ifstream::open()* function to open the file before use. The use of a file handle number assumes that this handle has already been set up with the operating system. Since there is currently only one file protection mode in *filebuf* and the constructor defaults to it, you normally don't have to use this parameter at all.

Example Use
```
ifstream test_input; // create object, must open file
                     // before use
ifstream(5);        // use file handle 5 in operating
                    // system
ifstream(input, "datafile"); // create object "input"
// and associate it with "datafile" on disk
ifstream(datafeed, "specdev", ios::binary);
// declare object "datastream", associate it with
// actual file "specdev", and open in explicit binary
// mode
```

See Also
```
iostream.h, ios, fstream.h, fstreambase, istream, ostream
```

ignore function

Purpose

Use the *ignore()* function wtih an *istream* (C++ input stream) to skip over (ignore) the specified number of input characters. This is a binary mode operation that treats whitespace (tabs, form feeds, etc.) as just another character value.

Syntax
```
#include <iostream.h>
<istream>.ignore(int numchars = 1, int delim = EOF);
numchars    number of characters to skip over
delim       delimiter character indicating end of file (default is standard EOF value)
```

Example Use
```
ifstream infile ("data.txt, ios::in); // set up file
infile.ignore(80, CR); // skip 20 chars. but stop at
                       // a CR if found
```

The above example supposes that a file "data.txt" has a first line that you want to skip, and that the line is not longer than 80 characters. If the line is shorter, skipping will stop when the carriage return character is encountered. (We assume CR is a constant with the value 13.)

Returns

The *ignore()* function returns a reference to the *istream*, allowing its operation to be combined with other input operations.

See Also
```
istream, cin, >> (extraction operator), get(), getline()
```

#include preprocessor directive

Purpose

Use the *#include* preprocessor directive to have the preprocessor read a header file (sometimes called an "include file") into the source code. The contents of the included file will be compiled along with the original source file.

Syntax
```
#include <filename>   /* read file from default directory */
#include "filename"   /* read file from same directory as
                          source code—details vary
                          with implementation */
```

Example Use
```
#include <stdio.h>
```

inline keyword

Purpose

Use the *inline* keyword to have a function's code inserted in the object file each time the function is called. Use of inline functions increases the size of the object program, but can speed up the program by removing the overhead involved in function calls. The effects of using an inline function are similar to those of using macros, but an inline function is safer to use as it is a true function with a prototype and full data type-checking is peformed.

Syntax

```
inline <type> <func_name> (<arg>..._) {<function
definition>;} // standalone inline function

<type> <func_name> (<arg>...) {function definition;}
// implicit inline function defined in a class
```

type	*return type of function*
func_name	*name of the function*
arg	*function argument(s) (optional)*
function definition	*statement(s) implementing the function*

There are two ways to use inline functions. You can declare a standalone function (one that is not a member of a class) as inline by preceding its declaration with the *inline* keyword and following the declaration with the function's definition code enclosed in curly braces ({}). Standalone inline functions must be declared *and* defined before any call is made to the function.

You can also declare a class member function to be *implicitly* inline. You do this by including the function's definition in curly braces ({}) immediately following the function's declaration. (The only difference from an explicit inline declaration is that the keyword *inline* is omitted.)

The inline function mechanism is really suitable only for very short, simple functions usually consisting of a single line of code. The degree to which functions declared *inline* are actually placed inline is compiler-dependant.

Example Use

```
inline int triple (int num) { return num * 3;} //standalone
class runner
{
...
public
int triple (int bases) { return bases * 3;}
...
} // implicit in member function
```

See Also
#define, register

int keyword

Purpose

Use the *int* type specifier to declare integer variables and arrays. The size qualifiers *short* and *long* should be used to declare an integer of desired size. The size of an *int* is implementation-dependent.

Syntax
int <varname>;

Example Use
int i, x[100];

See Also
char, double, float, long, short, signed, unsigned

INT_MAX predefined value

Purpose

The predefined value *INT_MAX* is the maximum value of an *int*. It is defined in *limits.h*.

See Also
HUGE_VAL, DBL_MAX, FLT_MAX

INT_MIN predefined value

Purpose

The predefined value *INT_MIN* is the minimum value of an *int*. It is defined in *limits.h*.

See Also
DBL_MIN, FLT_MIN

_IOFBF predefined value

Purpose

The predefined value *_IOFBF* indicates "full buffering" when used with *setvbuf()*. It is defined in *stdio.h*.

See Also
_IOLBF, _IONBF, setvbuf()

_IOLBF predefined value

Purpose

The predefined value _IOLBF indicates "line buffering" when used with *setvbuf()*. It is defined in *stdio.h*.

See Also
```
_IOFBF, _IONBF, setvbuf()
```

iomanip.h header file

Purpose

Include the *iomanip.h* header file in your program when you want to use stream manipulator functions that take parameters (arguments). The manipulator functions that require *iomanip.h* are *setbase()*, *resetiosflags()*, *setiosflags()*, *setfill()*, *setprecision()*, and *setw()*.

Syntax
```
#include <iomanip.h>
```

Example Use
```
#include <iostream.h>    // for general stream functions
#include <iomanip.h>     // for manipulators that take
                         // parameters

cout << setw(8);         // set output width to 8
cout << 100;             // display '100' in 8 char.
                         // field
```

See Also
```
iostream.h, fstream.h, ios, setbase(), resetiosflags(),
setiosflags(), setfill(), setprecision(), setw(), << (inser-
tion operator), >> (extraction operator), cin, cout
```

_IONBF predefined value

Purpose

The predefined value _IONBF indicates "line buffering" when used with *setvbuf()*. It is defined in *stdio.h*.

See Also
```
IOFBF, _IOLBF, setvbf()
```

ios class

Purpose

The *ios* class provides the basic interface to a *streambuf* and includes a variety of status flags. The member functions of *ios* are usually not used directly. Rather, the stream is accessed through the appropriate class derived from *ios*:

istream (for input from a streram) and *ostream* (for output to a stream), and *fstream* and its derivatives for streams related to disk files.

Formatting Status Flags

ios provides all input and output streams with the following flags, which have the indicated effects when set:

Flag	Effect When Set
Flags for Positioning Output	
skipws	skip whitespace (space, tab, etc.) chars. on input
left	padding before value
right	padding after value (default)
internal	padding after sign or base indicator
Base for Numeric Output	
dec	convert numeric values to decimal (base 10) (default)
oct	convert numeric values to octal (base 8)
hex	convert numeric values to hexadecimal (base 16)
showbase	include base indicator in output (off by default)
uppercase	show base, exponent indicators in uppercase (off by default)
Sign and Decimal Format	
showpos	show '+' for positive numbers (off by default)
showpoint	always show decimal point in floating-point output (off by default)
scientic	use scientific notation (for example, 1.2345E4) (off by default)
fixed	use standard decimal notation (for example, 123.45) (default)
Flushing Stream After Output (Insertion)	
unitbuf	flush all streams after insertion
stdio	flush stdout, stderr after insertion

IOS File Stream Opening Modes

The *ios* class also provides a set of modes that determine how a file stream will be opened:

Mode	Effect
in	open for input (default for *ifstream* objects)
out	open for output (default for *ofstream* objects)
app	open for append, start writing at end of file
ate	open and position at end of file
trunc	create file; if file already exists, truncate to length 0
nocreate	open file if file already exists, otherwise fail
noreplace	if truncation requested, fail rather than truncate if file exists
binary	open in explicit binary mode

The file opening modes given above are used with the *ios open()* member function and are similar to those used with the standard C function *fopen()*. As with the formatting flags, the file opening modes can be combined using the bitwise or (|) operator.

File Positioning Specifiers

ios provides three enumerated values that specify how the current read and/ or write position for the file will be set:

Position	Effect
beg	seek relative to file beginning
cur	seek relative to the current position
end	seek relative to the end of file

These specifiers are used with the *seekg()* and *seekp()* functions for positioning the file's read and write positions, respectively. See the entries for *seekg()* and *seekp()* for details.

Stream Error Status Values

ios provides five flags that are set automatically depending on the result of an attempt to access a file stream:

Flag	Set When
goodbit	no errors encounterd with stream
eofbit	end of file was reached
failbit	error encountered and *failbit, badbit,* or *hardfail* was set
badbit	last operation was invalid (not defined or not allowed)
hardfail	an irrevocable error occured

The above flags are actually masks that test appropriate bits in a status value called *state*. The flags are not generally used directly: the functions *good()*, *eof()*, *fail()*, and *bad()* test the indicated bits conveniently. Once an error has ocurred no further operations with that stream will succeed until the error bit(s) are cleared: this is usually done with the *clear()* function.

Syntax
```
#include iostream.h
ios::<flagname>              to refer to an ios flag
ios::<flagname>|ios::<flagname>|  ...   to combine flags
```

See the entries for *flags()*, *setf()* , *setiosflags()*, and *resetiosflags()* for examples of setting the *ios* formatting flags. See the entry for *open()* for syntax using the file opening mode flags. See the entries for *seekg()* and *seekp()* for use of the file position specifiers. For the stream error status flags see the entries for *rdstate()* and *clear()* as well as specific bit-testing functions such as *eof()* and *failbit()*.

Note that you can set an integer value to the bitwise *or* of several flags, for example:

```
const int io_opts = ios::left | ios::showpoint | ios::fixed;
```

These options specify that values will be left-adjusted, fixed-point, with the decimal point always shown. This technique can also be used for the other type of *ios* flags.

Example Use
```
// set some ios format flags
cout.flags(ios::hex | ios::showbase); // base 16 with
                                      // base indicator
setf(ios::left, ios::adjustfield);    // pad output to
                                      // left
// use ios file open specifiers
fstream my_input;
myfile.open("input.txt",ios::in,filebuf::openprot);
...
// set file read position
seekg(1, ios::end);       // set read point to char. just
                          // before end of file
// test for EOF using stream status values
if (cin.ios::state & ios::eofbit)
   return (MyEOFValue);
...
```

See Also
```
istream, ostream, iostream, iostream.h, stream.h, fstream,
fstreambase, fstream.h, iomanip.h (as well as other entries
mentioned in the text)
```

iostream class

Purpose

The *iostream* class is used for I/O operations in which a stream is used "bidirectionally"—that is, for both input and output. The *iostream* class is derived from the *istream* and *ostream* classes (which are in turn derived from the *ios* class).

Syntax
```
#include <iostream.h>
```

See Also
```
ios, istream, ostream, stream.h, iostream.h, fstream,
fstreambase, fstream.h, istream, ostream, iomanip.h
```

iostream.h header file

Purpose

Use the *iostream.h* header file to include C++ stream I/O in your program. *iostream.h* contains the basic classes for streams in C++ version 2.0 or later. Older compilers that support version 1.0 or 1.2 only use the file *stream.h* instead.

Syntax
```
#include <iostream.h>    For C++ 2.0 or later stream I/O
```

See Also
```
fstream, fstreambase, fstream.h, istream, ostream, iomanip.h
```

isalnum(), isalpha(), iscntrl(), isdigit(), isgraph(), islower(), isprint(), ispunct(), isspace(), isupper(), isxdigit()

Purpose

Use this group of macros to check for specific properties of the character *c* such as whether it is a control character, a digit, lowercase, printable, and so on. The table below shows the test performed by each of the functions. Note that some compilers may implement these tests as functions rather than as macros.

Macro Name	Tests For
isalnum()	alphanumeric character
isalpha()	character in alphabet
iscntrl()	control character
isdigit()	decimal digit
isgraph()	printable character excluding the space
islower()	lowercase letter
isprint()	printable character including space
ispunct()	punctuation character
isspace()	"whitespace" character (in "C" locale these are space, form feed '\f', newline '\n', carriage return '\r', horizontal tab '\t', and vertical tab '\v')
isupper()	uppercase letter
isxdigit()	hexadecimal digit

Syntax

```
#include <ctype.h>
int isalnum(int c);
int isalpha(int c);
int iscntrl(int c);
int isdigit(int c);
int isgraph(int c);
int islower(int c);
int isprint(int c);
int ispunct(int c);
int isspace(int c);
int isupper(int c);
int isxdigit(int c);
int c;          Character to be tested
```

Example Use

```
if(isprint(c) != 0) printf("%c is printable\n", c);
if(isdigit(c) != 0) printf("%c is a digit\n", c);
if(iscntrl(c) != 0) printf("%d is a control char\n"",c);
```

Returns

Each macro returns a non-zero value if the *c* satisfies the criterion for that function. Otherwise, it returns a zero.

See Also

```
int, char
```

istream class

Purpose

Use the member functions of the *istream* class for both unformatted and formatted input from a stream (such as from *cin*, the standard input stream, to obtain keyboard input). The *istream* class is derived from the base class *ios*, from which it gets its interface to a *streambuf*. In turn the class *istream_withassign* is derived from *istream* in order to provide the four standard streams (*cin, cout, cerr,* and *clog*). Note that in C++ 2.X streams connected to disk files must be handled using an *fstream* object such as an *ifstream* or *ofstream*.

Syntax
```
#include <iostream.h>
```

See Also
```
cin, >> (extraction operator), iostream.h, stream.h, fstream,
fstreambase, fstream.h, ostream, iomanip.h
```

jmp_buf predefined data type

Purpose
The *jmp_buf* array type is capable of holding information necessary to restore a calling environment. It is defined in *setjmp.h*.

See Also
```
longjmp(), setjmp()
```

L_tmpnam predefined value

Purpose
The predefined value *L_tmpnam* is the size of a char array large enough to hold temporary file names generated by *tmpnam()*. It is defined in *stdio.h*.

See Also
```
tmpnam(), FILENAME_MAX
```

LC_ALL predefined value

Purpose
The predefined constant *LC_ALL* indicates the program's entire locale (aspects that depend on country-specific formats). It is defined in *locale.h*.

See Also
```
LC_COLLATE, LC_CTYPE, LC_MONETARY, LC_NUMERIC, LC_TIME
```

labs() function

Purpose
Use the *labs()* function to get the absolute value of the long integer n.

Syntax
```
#include <stdlib.h>
long labs(long n);
long n;    Long integer whose absolute value is returned
```

Example Use
```
lresult = labs(-65540L); /* result will be 65540 */
```

Returns

The long integer returned by *labs()* is the absolute value of *n*.

See Also
```
abs(), fabs()
```

LC_COLLATE predefined value

Purpose

The predefined constant *LC_COLLATE* affects the behavior of *strcoll()* and *strxfrm()*. It is defined in *locale.h*.

See Also
```
LC_ALL, LC_CTYPE, LC_MONETARY, LC_NUMERIC, LC_TIME,
strcoll(), strxfrm()
```

LC_CTYPE predefined value

Purpose

The predefined constant *LC_CTYPE* affects the behavior of all locale-aware character handling routines. It is defined in *locale.h*.

See Also
```
LC_ALL, LC_COLLATE, LC_MONETARY, LC_NUMERIC, LC_TIME,
```

LC_MONETARY predefined value

Purpose

The predefined constant *LC_MONETARY* affects monetary formatting information returned by *localeconv*. It is defined in *locale.h*.

See Also
```
LC_ALL, LC_COLLATE, LC_CTYPE, LC_NUMERIC, LC_TIME,
localeconv()
```

LC_NUMERIC predefined value

Purpose

The predefined constant *LC_NUMERIC* affects the locale-specific decimal point formatting information returned by *localeconv*. It is defined in *locale.h*.

See Also
```
LC_ALL, LC_COLLATE, LC_CTYPE, LC_TIME, LC_MONETARY,
localeconv()
```

LC_TIME predefined value

Purpose

The predefined constant *LC_TIME* affects the behavior of the *strftime()* function. It is defined in *locale.h*.

See Also

`LC_ALL, LC_COLLATE, LC_CTYPE, LC_NUMERIC,LC_MONETARY, strftime()`

lconv predefined data type

Purpose

The *lconv* struct holds strings to be used in formatting numeric and monetary values for a specified locale. It is defined in *locale.h*.

See Also

`localeconv(), LC_NUMERIC, LC_MONETARY`

LDBL_DIG predefined value

Purpose

The predefined value *LDBL_DIG* is the number of significant decimal digits in a *long double* value. It is defined in *float.h*.

See Also

`LDBL_EPSILON, LDBL_MANT_DIG, LDBL_MIN, LDBL_MIN_10_EXP, LDBL_MIN_EXP, LDBL_MAX, LDBL_MAX_10_EXP, LDBL_MAX_EXP, LDBL_RADIX`

LDBL_EPSILON predefined value

Purpose

The *LDBL_EPSILON* predefined value gives the smallest positive *long double* value x such that $1+x\ != 1$. It is defined in *float.h*.

See Also

`LDBL_DIG, LDBL_MANT_DIG, LDBL_MIN, LDBL_MIN_10_EXP, LDBL_MIN_EXP, LDBL_MAX, LDBL_MAX_10_EXP,LDBL_MAX_EXP, LDBL_RADIX`

LDBL_MANT_DIG predefined value

Purpose

The *LDBL_MANT_DIG* predefined value gives the number of base IDBL_RADIX digits in the mantissa of a *long double*. It is defined in *float.h*.

See Also
```
LDBL_DIG, LDBL_EPSILON, LDBL_MIN, LDBL_MIN_10_EXP,
LDBL_MIN_10, LDBL_MAX, LDBL_MAX_10_EXP, LDBL_MAX_EXP,
LDBL_RADIX
```

LDBL_MAX predefined value

Purpose

The *LDBL_MAX* predefined value gives the maximum representable finite value that can be stored in a *long double*. It is defined in *float.h*.

See Also
```
LDBL_DIG, LDBL_MANT_DIG, LDBL_EPSILON, LDBL_MIN,
LDBL_MIN_10_EXP, LDBL_MIN_EXP LDBL_MAX_10_EXP, LDBL_MAX_EXP,
LDBL_RADIX
```

LDBL_MAX_10_EXP predefined value

Purpose

The *LDBL_MAX_10_EXP* predefined value gives the maximum integer such that 10 raised to that power is representable in a *long double*.

See Also
```
LDBL_DIG, LDBL_MANT_DIG, LDBL_EPSILON, LDBL_MIN,
LDBL_MIN_10_EXP, LDBL_MIN_EXP, LDBL_MAX, LDBL_MAX_EXP,
LDBL_RADIX
```

LDBL_MAX_EXP predefined value

Purpose

The *LDBL_MAX_EXP* predefined value gives the maximum integer such that LDBL_RADIX raised to that power is representable in a *long double*. It is defined in *float.h*.

See Also
```
LDBL_DIG, LDBL_MANT_DIG, LDBL_EPSILON, LDBL_MIN,
LDBL_MIN_10_EXP, LDBL_MIN_EXP, LDBL_MAX, LDBL_MAX_10_EXP,
LDBL_RADIX
```

LDBL_MIN predefined value

Purpose

The *LDBL_MIN* predefined value gives the minimum positive long floating-point number that can be stored in a *long double*. It is defined in *float.h*.

See Also
```
LDBL_DIG, LDBL_MANT_DIG, LDBL_EPSILON, LDBL_MIN_10_EXP,
LDBL_MIN_EXP, LDBL_MAX, LDBL_MAX_10_EXP, LDBL_MAX_EXP,
LDBL_RADIX
```

LDBL_MIN_10_EXP
predefined
value

Purpose

The *LDBL_MIN_10_EXP* predefined value gives the minimum negative integer such that 10 raised to that power is representable in a *long double*. It is defined in *float.h*.

See Also
```
LDBL_DIG, LDBL_MANT_DIG, LDBL_EPSILON, LDBL_MIN,
LDBL_MIN_EXP, LDBL_MAX, LDBL_MAX_10_EXP, LDBL_MAX_EXP,
LDBL_RADIX
```

LDBL_MIN_EXP
predefined
value

Purpose

The *LDBL_MIN_EXP* predefined value gives the minimum negative integer such that LDBL_RADIX raised to that power minus 1 is representable in a *long double*. It is defined in *float.h*.

See Also
```
LDBL_DIG, LDBL_MANT_DIG, LDBL_EPSILON, LDBL_MIN,
LDBL_MIN_10_EXP, LDBL_MAX, LDBL_MAX_10_EXP,
LDBL_MAX_EXP, LDBL_RADIX
```

ldexp()
function

Purpose

Use the *ldexp()* function to compute and obtain the floating-point number equal to x times 2^{exp}.

Syntax
```
#include <math.h>
double ldexp(double x, int exp);
double x;          Floating-point value of the mantissa
int exp;           Integer exponent
```

Example Use
```
value = ldexp(0.6375, 3); /* value will be 5.1 */
```

Returns

Normally *ldexp()* returns the value computed as described above. When the result is too large a range error may occur.

See Also
```
frexp(), modf()
```

ldiv()
function

Purpose

Use the *ldiv()* function to divide the long integer *numer* by another long integer *denom* and obtain the resulting quotient and remainder packed in a structure of type *ldiv_t*. The structure type *ldiv_t* is defined in *stdlib.h* as:

```
typedef struct
{
    long quot;  /* The quotient */
    long rem;   /* The remainder */
} ldiv_t;
```

Syntax
```
#include <stdlib.h>
ldiv_t ldiv(long numer, long denom);
long numer;                 Numerator
long denom;                 Denominator
```

Example Use
```
lresult = ldiv(65540L, 65536L);
/* lresult.quot = 1, lresult.rem = 4 */
```

Returns

The *ldiv()* function returns a structure of type *ldiv_t* containing the quotient and remainder of the division.

See Also
```
div(), ldiv_t
```

ldiv_t predefined data type

Purpose

The *ldiv_t* data type can hold the value returned by *ldiv()*. It is defined in *stdlib.h*.

See Also
```
ldiv, div_t
```

#line preprocessor line numbering directive

Purpose

Use the *#line* preprocessor to set the current line number for this location in the source code. This can be used as a debugging aid.

_ _LINE_ _ predefined macro

Purpose

Use the _ _*LINE*_ _ predefined macro to display or check the number of the line currently being translated by the preprocessor.

Example Use
```
printf("%d",_ _LINE_ _);
```

See Also
```
_ _DATE_ _, _ _TIME_ _, _ _FILE_ _,_ _STDC_ _
```

localeconv() function

Purpose

Use the *localeconv()* function to obtain detailed information on formatting monetary and numeric values according to the rules of the current locale. Note that many compilers support only the "C" locale at this time. The table below lists the categories of locale information that may be available.

Locale Category	Parts of Program Affected
LC_ALL	The entire program's locale-specific parts (all categories shown below)
LC_COLLATE	Behavior of the routines *strcoll* and *strxfrm*
LC_CTYPE	Behavior of the character handling functions and multibyte functions
LC_MONETARY	Monetary formatting information returned by the *localeconv* function
LC_NUMERIC	Decimal point character for the formatted output routines (for example, *printf()* and the data conversion functions, and the non-monetary formatting information returned by the *localeconv()* function
LC_TIME	Behavior of the *strftime()* function

Syntax
```
#include <locale.h>
struct lconv *localeconv(void);
```

Example Use
```
p_lconv = localeconv();
```

Returns

The *localeconv()* function returns a pointer to a statically allocated *lconv* structure whose fields are filled in with formatting information appropriate for the current locale. Use *setlocale()* to set the current locale. The *lconv* structure is declared in *locale.h* as follows:

```
struct lconv
{
    char *decimal_point; /* Decimal point character for non-
        monetary quantities */
    char *thousands_sep;    /* Separator for groups of digits to
        the left of decimal point for non-monetary quantities */
    char *grouping;  /* Size of each group of digits in non-
        monetary quantities */
    char *int_curr_symbol;       /* International currency
        symbol for the current locale */
    char *currency_symbol;       /* Local currency symbol for
        the current locale */
    char *mon_decimal_point; /* Decimal point character for
        monetary quantities */
    char *mon_thousands_sep; /* Separator for groups of digits
        to the left of decimal point for monetary quantities */
    char *mon_grouping;   /* Size of each group of digits in
        monetary quantities */
    char *positive_sign; /* String denoting sign for non-
        negative monetary quantities */
    char *negative_sign; /* String denoting sign for negative
        monetary quantities */
    char int_frac_digits;/* Number of digits to the right of
        decimal point for internationally formatted monetary
        quantities*/
    char frac_digits;     /* Number of digits to the right of
        decimal point in formatted monetary quantities */
    char p_cs_precedes; /* 1 = currency_symbol precedes, 0 =
        succeeds positive value */
    char p_sep_by_space; /* 1 = space, 0 = no space between
        currency_symbol and positive formatted values */
    char n_cs_precedes;  /* 1 = currency_symbol precedes, 0 =
        succeeds negative value */
    char n_sep_by_space; /* 1 = space, 0 = no space between
        currency_symbol and negative formatted values */
    char p_sign_posn;    /* Position of positive_sign in
        positive monetary quantities */
    char n_sign_posn;    /* Position of negative_sign in
        negative monetary quantities */
};
```

See Also

```
setlocale(), lconv()
```

localtime()
function

Purpose

Use the *localtime()* function to break down the value of time of type *time_t* stored at the location *time* into year, month, day, hour, minutes, seconds and several other fields that it saves in a structure of type *tm* maintained internally. The structure *tm* is defined in *time.h* and is shown in the reference pages on *asctime()*. The fields set up by *localtime()* will correspond to the local time.

Syntax
```
#include <time.h>
struct tm *localtime (const time_t *time);
const time_t *time;      Pointer to stored calendar time
```

Example Use
```
t_local = localtime(&bintime);
```

Returns
The *localtime()* function returns a pointer to the *tm* structure where the converted time is stored.

See Also
```
asctime(), gmtime(), time(), time_t, tm
```

log() and log10() functions

Purpose
Use the *log()* and *log10()* functions, respectively, to compute the natural logarithm and logarithm to the base 10 of the positive *double* variable *x*.

Syntax
```
#include <math.h>
double log(double x);
double log10(double x);
double x;             Variable whose logarithm is to be computed
```

Example Use
```
y = log(2);      /* y = 0.693147 */
a = log10(2);    /* a = 0.30103  */
```

Returns
For positive *x*, *log()* and *log10()* return the logarithm of *x*. If *x* is negative, a domain error occurs. If *x* is zero, a range error occurs.

See Also
```
exp(), pow()
```

long keyword

Purpose
Use the *long* type specifier as a size qualifier for *int* and *unsigned int* variables. Note that *long* alone means *signed long int*. A *long* qualifier indicates that the integer data type is at least 32 bits, and is often twice as long as an *int*.

Example Use

```
long filepos; unsigned long timer_tick;
```

See Also

```
char, double, float, int, short, signed, unsigned
```

LONG_MAX predefined value

Purpose

The *LONG_MAX* predefined value is the maximum value of a *long int*. It is defined in *limits.h*.

See Also

```
LONG_MIN
```

LONG_MIN predefined value

Purpose

The *LONG_MIN* predefined value is the minimum value of a *long int*. It is defined in *limits.h*.

See Also

```
LONG_MAX
```

longjmp() function

Purpose

Use the *longjmp()* function to restore the calling environment to that contained in the *jmp_buf* array *env*. This environment must have been saved by an earlier call to *setjmp()*. *longjmp()* restores all local variables (except the ones declared *volatile*) to their previous states and returns as if from the last call to *setjmp()* with the return value *retval*. Since *longjmp()* jumps to the return address of the last matching call to *setjmp*, you must make sure that the call to *longjmp()* occurs before the function where you had called *setjmp()* has returned.

Syntax

```
#include <setjmp.h>
void longjmp(jmp_buf env, int retval);
jmp_buf env;    Array data type where the calling environment is stored
int retval;    Value that will appear to be returned by the earlier call to setjmp
```

Example Use

```
longjmp(stack_env, 1);
```

See Also

```
setjmp(), jmp_buf()
```

malloc()
function

Purpose

Use the *malloc()* function to allocate a specified number of bytes. Note that you should use the *new* operator instead of a *malloc()* type function to allocate space for a C++ object.

Syntax
```
#include <stdlib.h>
void *malloc(size_t num_bytes);
size_t num_bytes;            Number of bytes needed
```

Example Use
```
buffer = (char *)malloc(100*sizeof(char));
```

Returns

The *malloc()* function returns a pointer which is the starting address of the memory allocated. If the memory allocation is unsuccessful because of insufficient space or bad values of the arguments, a *NULL* is returned.

See Also
```
free(), calloc(), realloc(), NULL, size_t
```

MB_CUR_MAX
predefined
value

Purpose

The *MB_CUR_MAX* predefined value is the minimum value of a multibyte character for the current locale. It is defined in *stdlib.h*, and is always less than *MB_LEN_MAX*.

See Also
```
MB_LEN_MAX
```

MB_LEN_MAX
predefined
value

Purpose

The *MB_LEN_MAX* predefined value is the maximum number of bytes in a multibyte character. It is defined in *limits.h*.

See Also
```
MB_CUR_MAX
```

mblen()
function

Purpose

Use the *mblen()* function to obtain the number of bytes that makes up a single multibyte character. Note that some otherwise ANSI-compliant compilers do not support multibyte characters.

Syntax

```
#include <stdlib.h>
int mblen(const char *s, size_t n);
const char *s;    Pointer to multibyte character whose length is to be determined
size_t n;         Maximum number of bytes expected to comprise a multibyte
                  character (MB_CUR_MAX is a good choice for this argument)
```

Example Use

```
mbsize = mblen(p_mbchar, MB_CUR_MAX);
```

Returns

If *s* is NULL, *mblen()* returns a 0 or a non-zero depending on whether multibyte encodings have state dependencies or not. If *s* is not NULL, *mblen()* returns the number of bytes that comprise the multibyte character provided the next *n* or fewer characters form a valid multibyte character. Otherwise, it returns –1.

See Also

```
mbtowc(), mbstowcs(), wctomb(), wcstombs(), MB_CUR_MAX,
NULL, size_t
```

mbtowc() function

Purpose

Use the *mbtowc()* function to convert a multibyte character at *s* to *wchar_t* type and store the result in the array *pwchar*. If *pwchar* is NULL, *mbtowc* will not save the resulting wide character. Also, *mbtowc()* will check at most *n* characters in *s* when trying to locate a valid multibyte character. Note that some otherwise ANSI-compliant compilers do not support multibyte characters.

Syntax

```
#include <stdlib.h>
int mbtowc(wchar_t *pwchar, const char *s, size_t n);
wchar_t *pwchar;  Pointer to array where the wide character equivalent of
                  multibyte character will be stored
const char *s;    Pointer to multibyte character to be converted to wide character
                  format
size_t n;         Maximum number of bytes expected to comprise a multibyte
                  character (MB_CUR_MAX is a good choice for this argument)
```

Example Use

```
mdc_size = mbtowc(pwc, mbchar, MB_CUR_MAX);
```

Returns

If *s* is NULL, *mbtowc()* will return a 0 or a non-zero depending on whether multibyte encodings have state dependencies or not. If *s* not NULL, *mbtowc()* returns the number of bytes that comprise the multibyte character provided the next *n* or fewer characters form a valid multibyte character. Otherwise, it returns –1.

See Also
```
mblen(), mbstowcs(), wctomb(), wcstombs(), MB_CUR_MAX, NULL,
size_t, wchar_t
```

mbstowcs() function

Purpose
Use the *mbstowcs()* function to convert a sequence of multibyte characters in *mbs* into a sequence of codes of *wchar_t* type and store at most *n* such codes in the array *pwcs*. Note that some otherwise ANSI-compliant compilers do not support multibyte characters.

Syntax
```
#include <stdlib.h>
size_t mbstowcs(wchar_t *pwcs, const char *mbs, size_t n);
wchar_t *pwcs;      Pointer to array where wide character results will be stored
const char *mbs;    Pointer to array of multibyte characters being converted to wide
                    character
size_t   n;         Maximum number of wide characers to be stored in pwcs
```

Example Use
```
mbstowcs(wc_array, mb_array, 10);
```

Returns
If successful, *mbstowcs()* returns the number of wide characters it stored in *pwcs*. If it encountered less than *n* multibyte characters, it returns -1 cast as *size_t*.

See Also
```
mblen(), mbtowc(), wctomb(), wcstombs(), size_t, wchar_t
```

memchr() function

Purpose
Use the *memchr()* function to search through the first *count* bytes in the buffer at the address *buffer* and find the first occurrence of the character *c*.

Syntax
```
#include <string.h>
void *memchr(const void *buffer, int c, size_tcount);
const void *buffer;    Pointer to buffer in which search takes place
int c;                 Character to look for
size_t  count;         Maximum number of bytes to be examined
```

Example Use
```
/* Look for the first occurrence of 'I' in a 100 byte buffer */
first_i = memchr(start_address, 'I'', 100);
```

Returns
If *memchr()* finds the character *c*, it will return a pointer to this character in *buffer*. Otherwise, *memchr()* returns a *NULL*.

See Also
```
memcmp(), strchr(), NULL, size_t
```

memcmp() function

Purpose
Use the *memcmp()* function to compare the first *count* bytes of the two buffers *buffer1*, *buffer2*.

Syntax
```
#include <string.h>
int memcmp(const void *buffer1, const void *buffer2,
size_t count);
const void *buffer1;        Pointer to first buffer
const void *buffer2;        Pointer to second buffer
size_t count;               Number of bytes to be compared
```

Example Use
```
if (memcmp(buffer1, buffer2, sizeof(buffer1)) == 0)
printf("The buffers are identical\n");
```

Returns
The *memcmp()* function returns an integer less than, equal to, or greater than zero according to whether the string *buffer1* is less than, equal to, or greater than the string *buffer2*.

See Also
```
strcoll(), strcmp(), strncmp(), size_t
```

memcpy() function

Purpose
Use the *memcpy()* function to copy *count* bytes from the buffer at address *source* to another buffer at *dest*. The behavior of *memcpy()* is undefined if the source and destination buffers overlap. (If this situation is anticipated, use *memmove()* instead.)

Syntax
```
#include <string.h>
void *memcpy(void *dest, const void *source, size_t count);
```

```
void *dest;              Pointer to buffer to which data will be copied
const void *source;      Pointer to buffer from which data will be copied
size_t  count;           Maximum number of bytes to be copied
```

Example Use
```
memcpy(dest, src, 80);   /* Copy 80 bytes from dest to src */
```

Returns
The *memcpy()* function returns a pointer to the destination buffer *dest*.

See Also
```
memmove(), strcpy(), strncpy(), size_t
```

memmove() function

Purpose
Use the *memmove()* function to copy *count* bytes from the buffer at address *source* to another buffer at *dest*. Parts of the source and destination buffers may overlap. (If you can guarantee that there's no overlap, *memcpy()* is faster.)

Syntax
```
#include <string.h>
void *memmove(void *dest, const void *source, size_t count);
void *dest;              Pointer to buffer to which data will be copied
const void *source;      Pointer to buffer from which data will be copied
size_t  count;           Maximum number of bytes to be copied
```

Example Use
```
memmove(dest, src, sizeof(src));
```

Returns
The *memmove()* function returns a pointer to the destination buffer *dest*.

See Also
```
memcpy(), strcpy(), strncpy(), size_t
```

memset() function

Purpose
Use the *memset()* function to set the first *count* bytes in the *buffer* to the character *c*.

Syntax
```
#include <string.h>
void *memset(void *buffer, int c, size_t count);
void *buffer;       Pointer to memory where bytes are to be set
int c;              Each byte in buffer will be set to this character
size_t count;       Maximum number of bytes to be set
```

Example Use
```
memset(big_buffer, '\0', 2048);
```

Returns
The *memset()* function returns the argument *buffer*.

See Also
```
memcpy(), memmove(), strcpy(), strncpy(), size_t
```

mktime() function

Purpose
Use the *mktime()* function to convert the local time currently in the structure of type *tm* at the address *timeptr* to a value of type *time_t*. Essentially, the local time given in the form of year, month, day, etc. will be converted to the number of seconds elapsed since 00:00:00 hours GMT, January 1, 1970. This is the same format in which *time* returns the current time and is the format used in the argument to the functions *ctime*, *difftime*, and *localtime*. Two fields in the structure of type *tm* are ignored by *mktime*. These are the fields *tm_wday* and *tm_yday*, denoting respectively the day of the week and the day of the year. The *mktime()* function will set the fields in the *tm* structure to appropriate values before returning.

Syntax
```
#include <time.h>
time_t mktime(struct tm *timeptr);
struct tm *timeptr;        Pointer to structure of type tm where local time is stored
```

Example Use
```
bintime = mktime(&timebuf);
```

Returns
If successful, *mktime()* will return the current contents of *timeptr* encoded as a value of type *time_t*. If the local time in *timeptr* can not be handled by *mktime()*, the return value will be a –1 cast to the type *time_t*.

See Also
```
asctime(), time(), time_t, tm
```

modf() function

Purpose
Use the *modf()* function to separate the floating-point number *x* into its fractional part and its integral part. The integer part is returned as a floating-point value in the location whose address is given in the argument *intptr*.

Syntax

```
#include <math.h>
double modf(double x, double *intptr);
double x;        Floating-point value to be decomposed
double *intptr;  Integral part of x is returned here
```

Example Use

```
fraction = modf(24.95, &int_part);
/* fraction is .95 */
/* int_part points to value 24 */
```

Returns

The *modf()* function returns the signed fractional part of *x*.

See Also

```
frexp(), ldexp()
```

\n escape sequence for newline

Purpose

Use the *\n* (newline) escape sequence to move the cursor or print head to the beginning of the next line. (The difference between *\r* (carriage return) and *\n* is that a carriage return moves the cursor or print head to the beginning of the *current* line.)

With C++ streams you can use the *endl* manipulator to send a newline to the output.

Example Use

```
printf("This string is on one line\n");
printf("and this one goes on the next line.");
```

See Also

```
printf(), \r, endl()
```

NDEBUG predefined value

Purpose

The *NDEBUG* value by default is not defined. If it is defined, *assert()* will be ignored. This allows you to globally deactivate debugging code.

See Also

```
assert()
```

new operator

Purpose

Use the *new* operator to allocate memory for a user-defined object. new offers a service similar to that provided by the *malloc()* family of functions in the standard C library, but with superior management through use of the class hierarchy. new is often used in class constructors and for creating dynamic arrays (arrays whose size is determined at runtime). Note that memory allocated with new must be deallocated (freed) using delete.

Syuntax

```
<type>* <ptr_name> = new <type_name>          single object
<type>* <ptr_name> = new <array_name> <[elements]...>   array
```

type*	*pointer to a valid data type*
ptr_name	*name of pointer to be returned*
type_name	*type of object or variable to be created*
array_name	*name of array to be created*
elements	*number of array elements (repeat if array has more than one dimension)*

Example Use

```
int* next_block = new int;      // allodate integer-zied
                                // object
* scores = new int [players][games]; // allocate two-
                                // dimensional integer array
```

Returns

The address of the newly allocated object is stored in the supplied pointer (you can use a previously-defined pointer if you wish). If insufficient memory is available for the new object a null (0) pointer is returned.

See Also

```
delete, malloc(), free()
```

NULL predefined pointer

Purpose

The value *NULL* indicates an implementation-defined null pointer constant. It is defined in *locale.h, stddef.h, stdio.h, stdlib.h, string.h*, and *time.h*. This is more accurate than casting a pointer to a value of 0, which looks like an address, while *NULL* means "doesn't point to anything at all."

See Also

```
* (pointer reference operator)
```

oct manipulator

Purpose

Use the *oct* C++ stream manipulator to have numeric values output in octal (base 8) notation. The effect of *oct* is equivalent to a call to *setbase(8)*.

Syntax

```
<output_stream> << oct;
```

Example Use
```
cout << 32 << oct; // outputs 40
```

Returns
The *oct* manipulator returns a reference to the stream object with which it is used. This allows *oct* to be used as part of a "cascade" of output as shown above.

See Also
```
dec, hex, setbase()
```

offsetof predefined macro

Purpose
The predefined *offsetof* macro has the form *offsetof(structure_type, member)* and returns a *size_t* value that is the offset in bytes, of the *member* from the beginning of a structure. It can be used to manipulate structure directly. It is defined in *stddef.h*.

See Also
```
struct, union, . (member access operator),
-> (pointer member access operator)
```

ofstream class

Purpose
Use an object of the *ofstream* class for an output file (typically a disk file). You can open the *ofstream* as you declare it or use the *open()* function later. *ofstream* inherits the insertion operator (>>) from *ostream*, making it easy to send data of any defined type to the file. See the entry for *fstream* for details.

Syntax
```
#include <fstream.h>
ofstream <object_name> ; or
ofstream <handle_no>; or
ofstream <object_name>, <"filename">, <ios::mode>,
<filebuf::mode>;
object_name      name of stream object in program
handle_no        integer handle number (e.g., for DOS)
"filename"       file name acceptable to operating system
ios::open_mode   read, write, etc. mode (see ios entry)
                 (optional; default is ios::out)
filebuf::mode    file protection mode (always filebuf::openprot in current DOS
                 implementations; check for others
```

If you declare an *ofstream* with just the object name, you must use the *ofstream::open()* function to open the file before use. The use of a file handle number assumes that this handle has already been set up with the operating system. Since there is currently only one file protection mode in *filebuf* and the constructor defaults to it, you normally don't have to use this parameter at all.

Example Use

```
ofstream results; // create object, must open file
                  // before use
ofstream(3);      // use file handle 3 in operating
                  // system
ofstream(output, "datafile"); // create object "output"
// and associate it with "datafile" on disk
ofstream(datafeed, "specdev", ios::binary);
// creates output file "datafeed," associates it with
// device "specdev" and opens in explicit binary
// mode.
```

See Also

```
fstream, ostream, istream, ifstream, cout, << (insertion
operator), open()
```

open()
function

Purpose

Use the *ios* member function *open()* to open a C++ file stream for input or output. *open()* is used with a previously declared stream object (usually an *ifstream* for input or an *ofstream* for output).

Syntax

```
#include <fstream.h>
<stream_name>.open(<filename>,<open_mode>,<protection_mode>;
stream_name       Name of stream to be used for file
filename          actual file name used by operating system
open_mode         how file is to be accessed (see ios entry for list of file modes)
protection_mode   degree of file protection (defined in fstream class)
```

Most compilers have only the value *filebuf::openprot* for the protection_mode, so this parameter can be omitted.

Example Use

```
ofstream my_output; // declare an output file
ofstream.open("datafile", ios::out); // open for
// output
```

Note that you can declare and open a file in one statement by using the constructor for *fstream* with one of its derivative classes, for example:

```
ofstream my_output("datafile",ios::out) // equivalent
// to above two statements
```

See Also
```
ios, fstream, ifstream, ofstream
```

ostream class

Purpose

The *ostream* class is used for output to a C++ stream such as *cout*, the standard output stream that is usually assigned to the screen. The *ostream* class is derived from the *ios* class. The *ostream_withassign* class is in turn derived from *ostream* to provide the four predefined standard streams (*cin, cout, cerr,* and *clog*) and stream assignment operators.

Syntax
```
#include <iostream.h>
ostream <stream_name>;
```

See Also
```
ios, istream, iostream.h, stream.h, cout, << (insertion
operator), iomanip.h
```

peek function

Purpose

Use the *peek() ios* member function to get the value of the next character in the input stream without removing it from the stream. This allows you to test the validity of the input without processing it.

Syntax
```
#include <iostream.h>
char_var = <stream>.peek();
char_var          character variable to receive peeked value
```

Example Use
```
char ch;
while ((ch = cin.peek()) != '*') {
     cin.get(ch);
     cout << ch;
     }
// echoes characters typed until "*" is
// entered (due to buffering, doesn't
// respond until <Enter> is pressed)
```

Returns

The *peek()* function returns a copy of the *char* value found in the input.

See Also
```
get(), getline(), cin, >> (insertion operator)
```

perror()
function

Purpose

Use the *perror()* function to construct an error message by concatenating your message provided in the argument *string* with that from the system message corresponding to the current value in the global variable *errno*, and print the message to *stderr*.

Syntax
```
#include <stdio.h>
void perror(const char *string);
const char *string;      Your part of the message
```

Example Use
```
perror("Error closing file");
```

See Also
```
matherr(), errno, stderr
```

pow()
function

Purpose

The *pow()* function computes the value of x raised to the power y. Neither x nor y may be zero and when x is negative, y must be an integer.

Syntax
```
#include <math.h>
double pow(double x, double y);
double x, y;            x raised to the power y will be computed
```

Example Use
```
x = pow(2.0, 3.0); /* x will be 8.0 */
```

Returns

When both x and y are non-zero positive numbers, *pow* returns the value x raised to the power y. If x is non-zero and y is zero, the return value is 1.

See Also
```
log(), log10(), sqrt()
```

#pragma
preprocessor
directive

Purpose

Use the *#pragma* directive to instruct the compiler in some way. Details are implementation-dependant. Typically pragmas control the kinds of optimization to be performed, whether the intrinsic form of functions should be compiled, and other characteristics of the compiler.

Syntax
```
#pragma <pragma_name (arguments...)>
```

Example Use
```
#pragma loop_opt(on)   /* turns on loop optimization for
Microsoft C Compiler 5.1 or later */
```

printf() function

Purpose

Use *printf()* to write character strings and values of variables, formatted in a specified manner, to the standard output file *stdout()*, normally the screen. The value of each argument is formatted according to the codes embedded in the string *format_string*. The formatting command for each variable consists of a percent sign ('%') followed by a single letter denoting the type of variable being printed. The complete format specification is of the following form:

```
%[Flags][Width].[Precision][Size][Type]
```

The table below summarizes each component of the format string. The subsequent tables explain the *Flag* and the *Type* fields, respectively.

Field	Explanation
Flags (Optional)	One or more of the characters '-', '+', '#' or a blank space to specify justification, appearance of plus/minus signs and of the decimal point in the values printed (see below).
Width (Optional)	A number to indicate how many characters, at a minimum, must be used to print the value.
Precision (Optional)	Another number specifying how many characters, at most, can be used in printing the value. When printing integer variables, this is the minimum number of digits used.
Size (Optional)	This is a character that modifies the *Type* field which comes next. One of the characters 'h', 'l' or 'L' appears in this field. This field is used to differentiate between short and long integers, and between *float* and *double*. Shown below is a summary of this field:

Prefix	When to Use
h	Use when printing integers using *Type* d, i, o, x or X to indicate that the argument is a short integer. Also, use with *Type* u to indicate that the variable being printed is a short unsigned integer.

Prefix	When to Use
l	Use when printing integers or unsigned integers with a *Type* field of d, i, o, u, x, or X to specify that the variable to be printed is a long integer.
L	Use when the floating-point variable being printed is a long double and the *Type* specifier is one of e, E, f, g, or G.
Type (Required)	A letter to indicate the type of variable being printed. The following table lists the possible characters and their meanings.

Flag	Meaning
–	Left-justify output value within the field.
+	If the output value is numeric, print a '+' or a '–' according to the sign of the value.
space	Positive numerical values are prefixed with blank spaces. This flag is ignored if the '+' flag also appears.
#	When used in printing variables of type o, x, or X (i.e, octal or hexadecimal), non-zero output values are prefixed with 0, 0x, or 0X, respectively. When the *Type* field in the format specification is e, E, f, g, or G, this flag forces the printing of a decimal point. For a g or a G in the *Type* field, all trailing zeros will be printed.
0	For d, i, o, u, x, X, e, f, g, or G *Type* leading zeros will be printed. This flag is ignored if the – flag also appears.

Specifier	Data Type	Resulting Output Format
c	char	Single character.
d	int	Signed decimal integer as a sequence of digits with or without a sign depending on the Flags used. *printf ("%d", 95)*; prints *95*.
e	double or float	Signed value in the scientific format. For example, *–1.234567e+002*.
E	double or float	Signed value in the scientific format, exponent letter capitalized, the above example will print *–1.234567E+002* if the *%E* format is used.

Specifier	Data Type	Resulting Output Format
f	double or float	Signed value in the format, *(sign)(digits).(digits)*, the example for *Type e* will print *−123.456700* if the *%f* format is used. The number of digits that come before the decimal point depends on the magnitude of the variable, and the number of digits that come after the decimal point depends on the *Precision* field in the format specification. The default precision is 6. Thus a *%f* format alone always produces six digits after the decimal point, but a *%.3f* will print the value *−123.457* which is *−123.4567* rounded off to three decimal places.
g	double or float	Signed value printed using one of *e* or *f* format. The format that generates the most compact output for the given *Precision* and value is selected. The *e* format is used only when the exponent is less than −4 or when it is greater than the value of the *Precision* field. Printing the value *−123.4567* using a *%g* format will result in *−123.457* because the *g* format rounds off the number.
G	double or float	Signed value printed using the *g* format, but with the letter *G* in place of *e* whenever exponents are printed.
i	int	Signed decimal integer as a sequence of digits with or without a sign depending on the Flags field.
n	pointer to int	This is not really a printing format. The argument corresponding to this format is a *pointer to an integer*. Before returning, the *printf()* function will store in this integer the total number of characters it has printed thus far to the output file or to the file's buffer.
o	unsigned	Octal digits without any sign.
p	pointer to void	The address is printed in an implementation-defined format.
u	unsigned	Unsigned decimal integer as a sequence of digits.
x	unsigned	Hexadecimal digits using lowercase letter, *abcdef*.

Specifier	Data Type	Resulting Output Format
X	unsigned	Hexadecimal digits using uppercase letters, *ABCDEF*.
%	—	Prints *a* %.

We recommend that C++ programmers use the streams formatting facilities instead of *printf()* for output formatting. The multiple overloaded versions of operator << for the basic data types produce reasonable default formatting, and a selection of manipulators and flags are available for tailoring the format of output.

Syntax
```
#include <stdio.h>
int printf(const char *format_string,...);
const char *format_string;    A character string which describes the
                              format to be used. A variable number of
                              arguments depending on the number of
                              items being printed
```

Example Use
```
printf("The product of %d and %d is %d\n", x, y, x*y);
```

Returns
The *printf()* function returns the number of characters it has printed. In case of error, it returns a negative value.

See Also
```
fprintf(), sprintf(), vfprintf(), vprintf(), vsprintf(),
stdout, cout, << (insertion operator), ios, flags(),
setflags()
```

private keyword

Purpose
Use the *private* keyword to restrict access to the data or member functions of a class. *private* class members can only be used by member functions of the same class. By default, members of a class are *private* unless they follow the keywords *public* or *protected*. (In a *struct*, access is *public* by default.)

You can also use the keyword *private* to restrict access to a base class by a derived class. When this is done, the *public* and *protected* members of the base class become *private* members of the derived class (and thus cannot be accessed from outside it). The *private* members of the base class are not inherited at all.

Syntax

```
class <classname> {
<member>...
}               members private by default

class <classname> {
...
private
<member>
...
}               members explicitly private

class <derived_class> private <base_class>
...             private derivation from base class
```

Example Use

```
class point {
int X, Y;
long color; // these members are private
public:
point()     // public members start here
...
};

class checking : private account {
...
}; // private derivation from "account" class
```

See Also

`class`, `struct`, `public`, `protected`

protected keyword

Purpose

Use the *protected* keyword to provide limited access to a class's member functions or to a base class from a derived class. Members in the *protected* section of a class can be accessed only by the class's member functions. When a class is derived from a class with a *protected* section, members of the derived class can access the *protected* members of the base class, but cannot access *private* members.

Syntax

```
class <classname< {
...
protected:
members...            these members are protected
...
};
class <derived_class> : protected <base_class> [
...
};                   derived can access protected members of base, but not private members
```

Example Use

```
class acct_data {
char name [40];
...
protected
long acct_number;
...
};  // acct_number is protected

class cust_data : protected acct_data {
...
};  // cust_data can access acct_number in
    // acct_data
```

See Also

```
private, protected, class, struct
```

ptrdiff_t predefined data type

Purpose

The *ptrdiff_t* data type is a signed integral type that can hold the result of subtracting one pointer from another. It is defined in *stddef.h*.

See Also

```
* (pointer-to)
```

public keyword

Purpose

Use the *public* keyword to allow access to class members from outside the class, or to allow derived classes access to all but private members of the base class. *public* is the least restrictive access to a C++ object, and should be used carefully. Typically a class's data members are made *private* (absent a strong reason to do otherwise), and a group of *public* member functions are used to provide access to the data from outside the class. Put another way, the *public* part of a class defines its interface to the outside world. By default all members of a *struct* are *public*, but all members of a class are *private*.

Syntax

```
class <classname> {
...
public:
members...          these members are public
...
};

class <derived_class> : public <base_class> {
...
}             derived class can access all but private members of the base class
```

Note that when a class has *public* derivation any *public* members of the base class are also *public* in the derived class, and thus can be accessed there by the rest of the program. *protected* members of the base class remain *protected* in the derived class, while *private* members of the base class are not inherited.

Example Use
```
class grab_bag {

int internal_status;
public:
container contents;
...
}; // "contents" publically accessible

class purse : public grab_bag {
...
}; users of "purse" can access "contents"
```

See Also
```
private, protected, class, struct
```

put() function

Purpose
Use the *ios* member function *put()* to insert a character (or a character-sized binary value) into a C++ output stream.

Syntax
```
#include <iostream.h>
<output_stream>.put(<charvar>);
output_stream     an ostream object (or derivative)
charvar           a variable of type char
```

Example Use
```
char chout;
cout.put(chout);
```

Returns
The *put()* function returns a reference to the output stream.

See Also
```
cout, << (insertion operator); putc(), putchar() (for ANSI C
streams)
```

putback() function

Purpose
Use the *fstream* member function *putback()* to "push" a character back into a C++ input file stream. This can be done if it is decided that the program should not process the character and should return it so it is available for

another part of the program to use. (See the entry for *peek()* for an alternative way to accomplish this procedure).

Syntax
```
#include <fstream.h>
<output_stream>.putback(charvar);
charvar            a variable of type char
```

Example Use
```
ifstream input;
char inchar;
...
input.get(inchar);
// check the character
// can't process, so put it back
input.putback(inchar);
...
```

Returns
The *putback()* function returns a reference to the *istream* object from which the character was obtained.

See Also
```
istream, cin, >> (insertion operator), peek()
```

putc() predefined macro

Purpose
Use the *putc* macro to write a single character *c* to an ANSI C stream. *putc()* is equivalent to *fputc()*, except that it is implemented as a macro. (For C++ streams the *ios* member function *put()* should be used for single-character output.)

Syntax
```
#include <stdio.h>
int putc(int c, FILE *stream);
int  c;             Character to be written
FILE *stream;       Pointer to stream to which the character is written
```

Example Use
```
putc('*', outfile);
```

Returns
The *putc()* macro returns the character written. A return value of *EOF* indicates an error. The *ferror* function should be called to determine if there was an error.

See Also
```
fgetc(), fputc(), getc(), getchar(), putchar(), EOF, FILE,
put() (C++ streams)
```

putchar() predefined macro

Purpose

Use the *putchar()* macro to write the character *c* to the pre-opened stream *stdout* which is initially connected to your display. *putchar()* is equivalent to *putc* with the second argument set to *stdout*. (For C++ streams the *ios* member function *put()* should be used with *cout* for single-character output to the standard output stream.)

Syntax
```
#include <stdio.h>
int putchar(int c);
int c;                  Character to be written
```

Example Use
```
putchar('?');
```

Returns

The *putchar()* macro returns the character written to *stdout*. In case of any error the return value is equal to the constant EOF.

See Also
```
fgetc(), fputc(), getc(), getchar(), putc(), EOF, stdout;
cout, put() (C++ streams)
```

puts() function

Purpose

Use the *puts()* function to output the null-terminated string *string* to the standard output stream *stdout*. The terminating null character ('\0') is replaced by a newline ('\n') in the output. (You can output a string to the C++ standard output stream by using the *ios* member function *write* with the *cout* stream.)

Syntax
```
#include <stdio.h>
int puts(const char *string);
const char   *string;           Null-terminated string to be output
```

Example Use
```
puts("Do you really want to quit?");
```

Returns

If successful, *puts()* returns a non-negative value. Otherwise, it returns EOF to indicate error.

See Also
```
fgets(), fputs(), gets(), EOF, stdout; cout, <<, write() (for
C++ streams)
```

qsort() function

Purpose

Use the *qsort()* function to sort an array beginning at the address *base* and comprising *num* elements, each of size *width* bytes. During the sort, *qsort()* compares pairs of elements from the array by calling a routine whose address you provide in the argument *compare*. This function should accept two arguments *elem1* and *elem2*, each a pointer to an element in the array. Internally your comparison routine can call upon *strcmp()* or other appropriate functions to perform the comparison.

Syntax
```
#include <stdlib.h>
void qsort(const void *base, size_t num, size_t
width, int (*compare)(const void *elem1, const void *elem2));
const void *base;        Pointer to beginning of array being sorted
size_t    num;           Number of elements in array
size_t    width;         Size of each element in bytes
int  (*compare)(const void *elem1, const void *elem2);
```
Pointer to a function that compares two elements e l e m 1 and e l e m 2 each of type const void *

Example Use
```
int compare(const void *, const void *);
qsort((void *) envp, (size_t)count, (size_t)sizeof(char *),
compare);
```

See Also
```
bsearch(), size_t
```

\r escape sequence for carriage return

Purpose

Use the \ *r* escape sequence to move the cursor or print head to the beginning of the current line. To move to the beginning of the *next* line, use \ *n* (newline).

Example Use
```
printf("Let's start over\r"); /* cursor goes over L*/
```

See Also
```
printf(), \n; cout, << (insertion operator) for C++ streams)
```

raise()
function

Purpose

Use *raise()* to "raise a signal" that creates an exception condition correspond-ing to the number *signum*. The exception will be handled by invoking a routine that was set up earlier by calling the function *signal*. The *abort()* function uses *raise()* to create the exception *SIGABRT* to initiate actions to be taken when aborting a program. Note that C++ now provides an alterna-tive exception-handling mechanism, although it is not yet supported by all compilers.

Syntax
```
#include <signal.h>
int raise(int signum);
int signum;              Signal number to be raised
```

Example Use
```
raise(SIGABRT);
```

Returns

If successful, *raise()* returns a zero. Otherwise, it returns a non-zero value.

See Also
```
abort(), signal(), SIGABRT; catch(), throw(), try() (for C++
exceptions)
```

rand()
function

Purpose

The *rand()* function generates a pseudo random integer with a value be-tween 0 and the constant RAND_MAX defined in *stdlib.h*. The "seed" or the starting point of the pseudo random integers can be set by calling *srand*.

Syntax
```
#include <stdlib.h>
int rand(void);
```

Example Use
```
random_value = rand();
```

Returns

The *rand()* function returns the pseudo random integer it generates.

See Also
```
srand(), RAND_MAX
```

RAND_MAX predefined value

Purpose

The predefined value *RAND_MAX* is the maximum integral value returned by the *rand* function. It is defined in *stdlib.h*.

See Also
```
rand()
```

rdstate() function

Purpose

Use the *ios* member function *rdstate()* to return the error status of a C++ stream. The stream state flags are returned in a single integer; a return value of 0 means that no error bit has been set and thus the stream is OK. See the entry for *ios* for a description of the error bits and their meanings. The functions *good()*, *eof()*, *fail()*, and *bad()* can be used to examine specific error flags.

Syntax
```
#include <iostream.h>
<stream>.rdstate();
```

Example Use
```
int strflags;
while (cin.rdstate() == 0) {
    // process while no stream errors
    ...
}
```

Returns

The *rdstate()* function returns an integer whose component bits correspond to the stream error flags. You can use the *ios* bit values and logical operators to examine the integer returned by *rdstate()* for particular bit values.

See Also
```
iostream, ios, clear(), fail(), good(), eof(), bad()
```

read() function

Purpose

Use the *ios* member function *read()* to read a specified amount of character data (or character-sized binary data) from a stream.

Syntax
```
#include <iostream.h>
<input_stream>.read(char* data, int num_bytes);
```

Example Use

```
char mystring [81];       // leave room for end of
                          // string character
cin.read(mystring, 80];
```

Note that *read()* doesn't pay any particular regard to white space, CR/LF, or the end of string null character. Everything is read in just as it is found. This means that you can use *read()* to read arbitrary binary data as long as the destination object is a string (array of *char*) with a sufficient number of elements to hold the data. In the above example the string *mystring* is declared to 81 elements, allowing 80 characters for the string plus room for a null character that can be added later to make a standard C++ string. Note that input from *cin* won't stop after the user presses ⎡ENTER⎤: all typed characters will be accepted until 80 characters have been typed or an interrupt character (typically ⎡CTRL⎤-C) is received.

Returns

The *read()* function returns a reference to the input stream used.

See Also

```
istream, ios, cin, >> (extraction operator), get(), getline(),
write()
```

realloc() function

Purpose

Use the *realloc()* function to alter the size of a previously allocated block of memory to the new size given in the argument *newsize*. The address of the block is specified by the pointer *mem_address*. This pointer must be either NULL or a value returned by an earlier call to *malloc()*, *calloc()*, or *realloc()*. If the argument *mem_address* is a NULL, then *realloc()* behaves like *malloc()* and allocates a new block of memory of size *newsize*. The memory block of altered size may not be located at the same address any more, but the contents of the block up to the old size is guaranteed to be unchanged.

Note that C++ provides an alternative (and superior) memory allocation mechanism using the *new* and *delete* operators with class constructors and destructors.

Syntax

```
#include <stdlib.h>
void *realloc(void *mem_address, size_t newsize);
void *mem_address;      Pointer to the block of memory whose size is to be altered
size_t   newsize;       New size of the block in bytes
```

Example Use
```
new_buffer = realloc(old_buffer, old_size+100);
```

Returns

The *realloc()* function returns the address of the block of memory. If *realloc()* fails, the pointer will be unchanged and it will return a NULL.

See Also
```
calloc(), free(), malloc(), NULL, size_t; new, delete (for C++
objects)
```

register keyword

Purpose

Use *register* as a storage classifier for integer data types to inform the compiler that the access to that data object should be as fast as possible. At its discretion, the compiler may use a CPU register to store that variable.

Syntax
```
register <type> <varname>
type                    an integer type (such as char, int, or long)
```

Example Use
```
register int i;
```

See Also
```
auto, extern, static
```

remove() function

Purpose

Use *remove()* to delete a file specified by the name *file_name*.

Syntax
```
#include <stdio.h>
int remove(const char *file_name);
const char *file_name;          Name of file to be deleted
```

Example Use
```
remove("/usr/tmp/tmp01234"); /* Delete temporary file */
```

Returns

If *remove()* successfully deletes the specified file, it returns a zero. Otherwise, the return value is non-zero.

See Also
```
rename()
```

rename()
function

Purpose

Use *rename()* to change the name of a file from *oldname* to *newname*.

Syntax
```
#include <stdio.h>
int rename(const char *oldname, const char *newname);
const char *oldname;        Current file name
const char *newname;        New file name
```

Example Use
```
/* Copy test.exe from /usr/tmp to /usr/bin and give it a new name */
rename("/usr/tmp/test.exe","/usr/bin/grview.exe");
```

Returns

If *rename()* is successful, it returns a zero. In case of an error, it returns a non-zero value.

See Also
```
fopen(), fclose(), remove()
```

resetiosflags()
manipulator

Purpose

Use the *resetiosflags()* manipulator to clear specified *ios* format flags for a C++ stream. The flags corresponding to the bits set in *flag_vals* will be cleared. Typically the flag masks enumerated in the *ios* class are used with the logical or operator (|) to specify the flags to be cleared. Note that *resetiosflags()* takes the same *long* argument as *unsetf()*, which also clears the flags set in the long value. The difference between the two functions is that *resetiosflags()* returns a reference to the stream used, while *unsetf()* returns a *long* value representing the status of the format flags before clearing.

Syntax
```
output_stream << resetiosflags(<long flag_vals>); or
input stream >> resetiosflags(<long flag_vals>);
output_stream,    ostream or istream object
input_stream
long flag_vals    a long int value whose bits correspond to the flags you want to clear
```

Example Use
```
#include <iostream.h>
#include <iomanip.h>  // needed for manipulators with
                      // arguments
cout << resetiosflags(ios::scientific | ios::uppercase);
```

Use of the *or* operator ensures that only the bits representing "scientific notation" and "uppercase base and exponent indicator" are set in the value passed to *resetiosflags()*. These are therefore the flags that will be cleared.

Returns

The *resetiosflags()* manipulator returns a reference to the input or output stream used.

See Also

```
ios, istream, ostream, iomanip.h, setiosflags(), setf(),
unsetf(), flags()
```

return keyword

Purpose

Use *return* to terminate execution of the current function and return control to the caller. Optionally specify a value to be returned to the caller.

Syntax

```
return; or
return <expression>;
```

If the function returns a value, use the statement *return <expression>* to return the value represented by the *<expression>*.

Example Use

```
/* Return the maximum of two integers */
int findmax(int a, int b)
{
    if(a >= b)
        return a;
    else
        return b;
}
```

See Also

```
break, continue, goto
```

scanf() function

Purpose

Use *scanf()* to read characters from the standard input file *stdin* and convert the strings to values of variables according to the format specified in the string *format_string*. For each variable's address included in the argument list to *scanf* there must be a format specification embedded in the *format_string*. The format specification for each variable is of the following form: %[*][Width][Size][Type] where "type" is one of the specifiers for data types listed in the entry for *printf()*.

Normally strings read using the %s format are assumed to be delimited by blank spaces. When you want to read a string delimited by any character other than those in a specific set, you can specify the set of characters within brackets and use this in place of the letter *s* in the format specification. On the other hand, if the first character inside the brackets is a caret (^), the set is assumed to show the characters that terminate the string. Thus, for example, %[^\'"] will read a string delimited by single or double quote characters.

The table below summarizes the purpose of each field in the format specification used by *scanf()*.

Field	Explanation
% (Required)	Indicates the beginning of a format specification. Use %% to read a percentage sign from the input.
* (Optional)	The characters representing the value are read according to the format specification, but the value is not stored. It is not necessary to give an argument corresponding to this format specification.
Width (Optional)	A positive value specifying the maximum number of characters to be read for the value of this variable.
Size (Optional)	A character that modifies the *Type* field that comes next. One of the characters h, l, or L appears in this field to differentiate between short and long integers, and between *float* and *double*. A summary of this field is shown below:

Prefix	When to Use
h	Use when reading integers using *Type* d, i, or n to indicate that the argument is a short integer. Also, use with *Type* o, u, and x to indicate that the variable being read is an unsigned integer.
l	Use when reading integers or unsigned integers with a *Type* field of d, i, or n to specify that the variable to be read is a long integer. Also use with o, u, and x to read values into unsigned long integers and for floating-point variables (when the *Type* field is e, f, or g) to specify a *double* rather than a *float*.
L	Use with e, f, and g to indicate that the variable is a *long double*.
Type (Required)	A letter that indicates the type of variable being read. The following table lists the possible characters and their meanings.

Type Specifier	C++ Data Type	Expected Input
c	Pointer to char	Single character. White space characters (space, tab, newline) will be read in this format.
d	Pointer to int	Decimal integer.
e, f, g	Pointer to float	Signed value in the scientific format—for example, −1.234567e+002 and 9.876543e−002 or in the format "(sign)(digits).(digits)"—for example, −1.234567 and 9.876543.
i	Pointer to int	Decimal, hexadecimal, or octal integer.
n	Pointer to int	This is not a reading format. The argument corresponding to this format is a pointer to an integer. Before returning, the scanf() function stores in this integer the number of characters it has read thus far from the input file or the input file's buffer.
o	Pointer to int	Octal digits without a sign.
p	Pointer to an address	Implementation-defined format for a pointer.
s	Pointer to an array of characters large enough to hold input string plus a terminating null (\0)	Character string.
u	Pointer to unsigned int	Unsigned decimal integer.
x	Pointer to int	Hexadecimal digits.

Syntax

```
#include <stdio.h>
int scanf(const char *format_string, <address>...
const char *format_string;   Character string that describes the format to be used
address...                   variable number of arguments representing addresses of
                             variables whose values are being used
```

Example Use

```
scanf("%d:%d:%d", &hour, &minute, &second);
```

Returns

The *scanf()* function returns the number of input items that were successfully read, converted, and saved in variables. This does not include the items that were read and ignored. A return value equal to the constant EOF (defined in *stdio.h*) means that an end-of-file was encountered during the read operation.

Note that for C++ streams the use of *ios* member functions and the overloaded extraction operator (>>) is preferable to *scanf()* and related ANSI C library functions.

See Also
```
fscanf(), sscanf(); ios, cin, >> (extraction operator for C++)
```

SEEK_CUR predefined value

Purpose

The constant *SEEK_CUR* indicates "relative to current position" when positioning the file pointer with *fseek*. It is defined in *stdio.h*. The equivalent specifier for C++ streams (used with *setg()* and *setp()*) is *ios::cur*.

See Also
```
SEEK_END, SEEK_SET; ios (ios::cur), setg(), setp() (for C++)
```

SEEK_END predefined value

Purpose

The constant *SEEK_END* indicates "relative to end of file" when positioning the file pointer with *fseek*. It is defined in *stdio.h*. The equivalent for C++ streams (used with *setg()* and *setp()*) is *ios::end*.

See Also
```
SEEK_CUR, SEEK_SET; ios (ios::end), setg(), setp() (for C++)
```

seekg()

Purpose

Use the *seekg() istream* member function to reposition the location from which the next data will be read from a C++ file stream. You can position the new location to an absolute location or to a specified number of bytes before or after the beginning, current position, or end of the file.

Syntax
```
#include <iostream.h>
<istream>.seekg(<absolute_position>); or
<istream>.seekg(int num_bytes, position_from);
istream                input stream; object of class fstream or derivative
long absolute_position    typically value returned from tellg()
num_bytes              number of bytes to move read position
position_from          location in file from which to position
```

If you want to set the read position to an absolute location in the file, follow *setg()* with the position as a *long* (*streampos*) value in parentheses. You can save a positiion by calling *tellg()* and then using *setg()* later to return to that position. You can also use the *ios* enumerated values *beg, cur,* and *end* to indicate the beginning, current position, and end of the file, respectively.

You can also specify an offset (the number of bytes to move the position) followed by the location from which to move. (This is again, one of the enumerations *ios::beg, ios::cur,* or *ios:end*).

Example Use
```
istream input_file;
input_file.seekg(0, ios::beg);    // position to very
          // beginning of file
input_file.seekg(5, ios::cur);    // skip next five
          // bytes
input_file.seekg(-20,ios::end); // position to 20
          // bytes before end of file
```

Returns
The *seekg()* function returns a reference to the input stream.

See Also
```
ios, istream, seekp(), tellg(), tellp()
```

seekp() function

Purpose
Use the *seekp() iostream* member function to reposition the location from which the next data will be written to a C++ file stream. You can position the new location to an absolute location or to a specified number of bytes before or after the beginning, current position, or end of the file.

Syntax
```
#include <iostream.h>
<ostream>.seekp(<absolute_position>); or
<ostream>.seekp(int num_bytes, position_from);
ostream                      output stream; an of object of class ostream or derivative
long absolute_position       typically value returned from tellp()
num_bytes                    number of bytes to move write position
position_from                location in file from which to position
```

If you want to set the write position to an absolute location in the file, follow *setp()* with the position as a *long* (*streampos*) value in parentheses. You can save a position by calling *tellg()* or *tellp()* and then use *setp()* later to return to that position. You can also use the *ios* enumerated values *beg, cur,* and *end* to indicate the beginning, current position, and end of the file, respectively.

You can also specify an offset (the number of bytes to move the position) followed by the location from which to move. (This is again, one of the enumerations *ios::beg, ios::cur,* or *ios:end*).

Example Use
```
ostream output_file;
output_file.seekg(0, ios::beg);         // position to very
          // beginning of file--rewrite file
output_file.seekg(-reclen, ios::cur); // rewrite
          // current record if at end
```

Returns
The *seekp()* function returns a reference to the input stream.

See Also
```
ios, istream, seekg(), tellg(), tellp()
```

SEEK_SET predefined value

Purpose
The constant *SEEK_SET* indicates "relative to start of file" when positioning the file pointer with *fseek*. It is defined in *stdio.h*. The equivalent specifier for C++ streams (used with *setg()* and *setp()*) is *ios::beg*.

See Also
```
SEEK_CUR, SEEK_END; ios (ios::beg), setg(), setp() (for C++)
```

setbase() manipulator

Purpose
Use the *setbase()* manipulator to set the base to be used for displaying numeric values. You can set the base to 0, 8, 10, or 16; the default is base 10. Note: alternate manipulators to set the numeric base are *dec* (base 10), *hex* (base 16), and *oct* (base 8).

Syntax
```
#include <iostream.h>
#include <iomanip.h>
<output_stream> << setbase(base);
```

Example Use
```
ostream my_output;
my_output << 24 << setbase(8); displays 30
```

See Also
```
dec, hex, oct
```

setbuf() function

Purpose
Use the *setbuf()* function to assign *buffer*, of size *BUFSIZ*, instead of the system-allocated one for use by *stream* for buffering. Calling *setbuf()* is equivalent to using *setvbuf()* with *_IOFBF* and *BUFSIZ* as the third and the

fourth arguments, respectively. If *buffer* is NULL, the third argument will be *_IONBF*. (For C++ streams set up a *streambuf* for derivative class rather than using *setbuf().*)

Syntax
```
#include <stdio.h>
void setbuf(FILE *stream, char *buffer);
FILE *stream;        Pointer to stream whose buffer is being set
char *buffer;        Pointer to buffer (or NULL if no buffering is to be done)
```

Example Use
```
setbuf(infile, mybuffer);
```

See Also
```
setvbuf(), BUFSIZ, FILE, _IOFBF, _IONBF, NULL; streambuf (C++)
```

setf() function

Purpose
Use the *setf() ios* member function to set an *ios* C++ stream format flag. You can use *setf()* with a mask value (enumerated in *ios)* to set a specified flag without disturbing the others. (This makes *setf()* easier and safer to use than *flags(),* which affects bits throughout the flags value.)

Some flags are arranged as groups of settings. For example, *ios::left, ios::right,* and *ios::internal* control adjustment (justification) of output. When you want to set one flag in a group, use the flag enumerator that you want to set followed by the group (*ios::adjustfield, ios::basefield,* or *ios::floatfield*). In this syntax *setf()* clears all bits in the specified group and then sets the specified flag. See the *ios* entry for descriptions of the flags and flag groups.

Syntax
```
<stream>.setf(mask); or
<stream>.setf(mask, group_specifier);
mask                 a flag mask enumerated in ios
group_specifier      ios::adjustfield, ios::basefield, or ios::floatfield
```

Example Use
```
cout.setf(ios::left, ios::adjustfield);
// sets left justification of output
datastream.setf(ios::showbase);
// sets the showbase flag (not part of a group)
```

Returns
The *setf()* function returns a *long* value containing the *ios* format flag values as they were before the new bit(s) were set.

See Also
```
flags(), unsetf(), setiosflags(), resetiosflags()
```

setfill() manipulator

Purpose
Use the *setfill()* manipulator to set the fill character to be used for padding values displayed from a C++ output stream. (Note that the *ios* member function *fill()* is an alternative for this purpose; *fill()* returns the previous fill character, but the *setfill()* manipulator is more convenient for use when cascading output to a stream.)

Syntax
```
#include <iostream.h>
#include <iomanip.h>
output_stream << setfill(fillchar);
fillchar          character to use for padding
```

Example Use
```
ostream checkdata;
checkdata << setfill('#');
```

Returns
The *setfill()* manipulator returns a reference to the output stream.

See Also
```
fill()
```

setiosflags() manipulator

Purpose
Use the *ios setiosflags()* manipulator to set a stream's format flag bits according to the *long* value specified. (Non-manipulator functions are also available for this purpose: see *flags()* and *setf().*)

Syntax
```
#include <iostream.h>
#include <iomanip.h>
input_stream >> setiosflags(flagvals); or
output_stream << setiosflags(flagvals);
flagvals          a long value containing the flag bits to be set
```

Example Use
```
// set up long flag value with ios enums
long flagvals = (ios::hex | ios::showbase);
// set the hex and showbase flags
cout << setiosflags(flagvals);
```

Returns

The *resetiosflags()* manipulator returns a reference to the stream used.

See Also

```
resetiosflags(), flags(), setf(), unsetf()
```

setjmp() predefined macro

Purpose

Use the *setjmp()* macro to save a stack environment in the *jmp_buf* array named *env* before calling another function. This environment can subsequently be restored by a call to *longjmp()*, achieving the effect of a non-local *goto*. When *longjmp()* is called at a later time with the saved calling environment, it restores all stack-based local variables in the routine to the values they had when *setjmp()* was called and jumps to the return address that *setjmp()* had saved. For all intents and purposes, this will feel like a return, one more time, from the last call to *setjmp()*. Note that this process does not guarantee the proper restoration of register-based and *volatile* variables.

Syntax

```
#include <setjmp.h>
int setjmp(jmp_buf env);
jmp_buf env;      Array data type where the current calling environment is stored
```

Example Use

```
if (setjmp(env) != 0) printf("Returned from longjmp\n");
```

Returns

After saving the stack environment *setjmp()* returns a zero. When *longjmp()* is called with the environment saved by this particular call to *setjmp()*, the effect is the same as returning from *setjmp()* again, this time with the second argument of *longjmp()* as the return value.

See Also

```
longjmp(), jmp_buf
```

setlocale() function

Purpose

Use *setlocale()* to define the locale named in the string *locale_name* for the locale-dependent aspects of your program specified by the argument *category*. The *category* can take one of the values shown in the table in the entry for *localeconv()*.

Syntax

```
#include <locale.h>
char *setlocale(int category, const char *locale_name);
int  category;        Indicates the parts of your program's locale-dependent
                      aspects for which you are defining a locale, one of:
                          LC_ALL, LC_COLLATE, LC_CTYPE,
                          LC_MONETARY, LC_NUMERIC, or LC_TIME
char  *locale_name;   The name of locale that will control the specified category
```

Example Use

```
setlocale(LC_ALL, "C");
```

Returns

If *locale_name* is not NULL and *setlocale()* is successful, it returns the string associated with the specifed category for the new locale. Otherwise, *setlocale()* returns a NULL and the program's locale is not changed.

See Also

```
localeconv(), LC_ALL, LC_COLLATE, LC_CTYPE, LC_MONETARY,
LC_NUMERIC, LC_TIME, NULL
```

setprecision() manipulator

Purpose

Use the *setprecision()* manipulator to specify the number of digits of precision for floating-point numeric values in a stream.

Syntax

```
#include <iostream.h>
#include <iomanip.h>
output_stream << setprecision(digits);
digits              number of digits of precision
```

It is of course not meaningful to set a precision greater than the inherent precision of the data type involved. See the entries for *float* and *double* for details.

Example Use

```
ostream output;
output << setprecision(6); // 6 digit precision
```

Returns

The *setprecision()* manipulator returns a reference to the stream used.

See Also

```
ios (formatting flags), setw()
```

setvbuf() function

Purpose

Use the *setvbuf()* function to assign *buffer* of a size *buf_size* to *stream*. You can also control the type of buffering to be used or turn off buffering for *stream* by specifying appropriate constants for the argument *buf_mode*. If *buf_mode* is _IOFBF, the I/O operations with the stream will be fully buffered. If it is _IOLBF, buffering will be done one line at a time. Setting *buf_mode* to _IONBF causes I/O to be unbuffered. (For C++ a *streambuf* or derivative class would probably be used.)

Syntax

```
#include <stdio.h>
int setvbuf(FILE *stream, char *buffer, int buf_mode,
size_t buf_size);
FILE *stream;           Pointer to stream whose buffer is being set
char *buffer;           Pointer to buffer (or NULL if no buffering requested)
int buf_mode;           Mode of buffering desired
size_t buf_size;        size of buffer in bytes, if any assigned
```

Example Use

```
setvbuf(infile, buffer, _IOFBF, 2048);
```

Returns

If successful, *setvbuf()* returns a 0. In case of bad parameters or other errors, the return value will be non-zero.

See Also

```
setbuf(), FILE, _IOFBF, _IOLBF, _IONBF, NULL, size_t
```

setw() manipualator

Purpose

Use the *ios setw()* manipulator to specify the total field width for output from a C++ stream. Note that the *ios* flags *ios::left, ios::right,* and *ios::internal* determine how values will be padded within the specified field width. If a value is longer than the width specified, the full value will be displayed, overflowing the field.

Syntax

```
#include <iostream.h>
#include <iomanip.h>
output_stream << setw(characters);
characters          integer width in characters
```

Example Use

```
cout << setw(10); // 10 character field
```

Returns

The *setw()* manipulator returns a reference to the stream used.

See Also
```
ios (formatting flags), setprecision()
```

short keyword

Purpose

Use *short* as a size qualifier for *int* and *unsigned int* variables. Note that *short* alone means *signed short int*. A *short* qualifier indicates that the integer data type is at least two bytes in size; on some systems it may be longer.

Syntax
```
short <integer_type> <varname>;
```

Example Use
```
short offset;
unsigned short array_index;
```

See Also
```
char, double, float, int, long, signed, unsigned
```

SHRT_MAX predefined value

Purpose

The predefined value *SHRT_MAX* is the maximum value of a *short int*. It is defined in *limits.h*.

See Also
```
SHRT_MIN
```

SHRT_MIN predefined value

Purpose

The predefined value *SHRT_MIN* is the minimum value of a *short int*. It is defined in *limits.h*.

See Also
```
SHRT_MAX
```

sig_atomic_t predefined data type

Purpose

The *sig_atomic_t* data type allows access as a single entity even in the presence of hardware and software interrupts. It is defined in *signal.h*.

See Also
`SIGINT`

SIG_DFL predefined value

Purpose

The constant *SIG_DFL* indicates default handling of a signal. It is defined in *signal.h*.

See Also
`SIG_ERR, SIG_IGN, SIGABRT, SIGFPE, SIGILL, SIGINT, SIGEGV, SIGTERM`

SIG_ERR predefined value

Purpose

The constant *SIG_ERR* indicates error return from the signal function. It is defined in *signal.h*.

See Also
`SIG_DFL, SIG_IGN, SIGABRT, SIGFPE, SIGILL, SIGINT, SIGEGV, SIGTERM`

SIG_IGN predefined value

Purpose

The constant *SIG_IGN* indicates that a signal should be ignored. It is defined in *signal.h*.

See Also
`SIG_ERR, SIG_DFL, SIGABRT, SIGFPE, SIGILL, SIGINT, SIGEGV, SIGTERM`

SIGABRT predefined value

Purpose

The constant *SIGABRT* indicates that a program aborted. It is defined in *signal.h*.

See Also
`SIG_ERR, SIG_DFL, SIGIGN, SIGFPE, SIGILL, SIGINT, SIGEGV, SIGTERM`

SIGEGV predefined value

Purpose

The constant *SIGEGV* indicates that an invalid storage address was accessed. It is defined in *signal.h*.

See Also
`SIG_ERR, SIG_DFL, SIGIGN, SIGABRT, SIGFPE, SIGILL, SIGINT,`
`SIGTERM`

SIGFPE predefined value

Purpose

The constant *SIGFPE* indicates that a division by zero, an overflow, or another floating-point error has ocurred. It is defined in *signal.h*.

See Also
`SIG_ERR, SIG_DFL, SIGIGN, SIGABRT, SIGILL, SIGINT, SIGEGV,`
`SIGTERM`

SIGILL predefined value

Purpose

The constant *SIGILL* indicates that an illegal instruction has been encountered. It is defined in *signal.h*.

See Also
`SIG_ERR, SIG_DFL, SIGIGN, SIGABRT, SIGFPE, SIGINT, SIGEGV,`
`SIGTERM`

SIGINT predefined value

Purpose

The constant *SIGINT* indicates that the user has attempted to get the attention of (interrupt) the program by pressing a key such as (CTRL)-C. It is defined in *signal.h*.

See Also
`SIG_ERR, SIG_DFL, SIGIGN, SIGABRT, SIGFPE, SIGILL, SIGEGV,`
`SIGTERM`

signal() function

Purpose

Use the *signal()* function to set up the routine *func* as the handler for the exception or signal number *signum*. The handler is expected to accept the signal number as an argument. The signal number *signum* must be one of the constants shown in the table. These constants are defined in the include file *signal.h*. If you want to ignore a signal, use *SIG_IGN* as the second argument to *signal()*. Specifying *SIG_DFL* as the second argument sets up the implementation-defined default handling for the signal.

Signal	Exception Condition
SIGABRT	Abnormal termination of program, for example, by calling the abort function.
SIGFPE	Floating-point error, such as overflow, division by zero, etc.
SIGILL	Illegal instruction in the program.
SIGINT	Generated when user presses a key designed to get the attention of the operating system. For example, pressing (CTRL)-C-C in UNIX or MS-DOS would generate this signal.
SIGSEGV	Illegal memory access.
SIGTERM	Termination request sent to the program.

Note that recent implementations of C++ provide a separate exception-handling mechanism using the keywords *catch, throw,* and *try.*

Syntax
```
#include <signal.h>
void (*signal(int signum, void (*func)(int)))(int);
int signum;          Signal number for which a handler is being set up
void (*func)(int);   Pointer to handler that can accept an integer argument
```

Example Use
```
if(signal(SIGINT, ctrlc_handler) == SIG_ERR)
   {
   perror("signal failed");
   exit(0);
   }
```

Returns
If successful, *signal()* returns the pointer to the previous handler. In case of error, it returns the constant SIG_ERR and sets the global variable *errno* to an implementation-defined error constant.

See Also
```
abort(), raise(), SIG_DFL, SIG_IGN, errno; catch, throw, try (for
C++)
```

signed keyword

Purpose
Use the *signed* qualifier to indicate that data stored in an integral type (*int, char*) is signed. For example, a *signed char* can take values between −127 to +127 whereas an *unsigned char* can hold values from 0 to 255. The *int* and *char* types are *signed* by default.

Example Use
```
int i;  /* signed by default */
signed long int x;  /* signed long integer */
```

See Also
```
char, double, float, int, long, short, unsigned
```

SIGTERM predefined value

Purpose
The constant *SIGTERM* indicates a signal that is sent to a program to terminate it. It is defined in *signal.h*.

See Also
```
SIG_ERR, SIG_DFL, SIGIGN, SIGABRT, SIGFPE, SIGILL, SIGINT,
SIGEGV
```

sin() function

Purpose
Use the *sin()* function to compute the sine of *double* argument x which represents an angle in radians. You can convert an angle from degrees to radians by dividing it by 57.29578.

Syntax
```
#include <math.h>
double sin(double x);
double x;          Angle in radians whose sine is to be computed
```

Example Use
```
y = sin(x);
```

Returns
The *sin()* function returns the sine of x. If the value of x is large in magnitude, the result may be very imprecise.

See Also
```
asin(), cos()
```

sinh() function

Purpose
Use the *sinh()* function to compute the hyperbolic sine of a *double* variable x.

Syntax
```
#include <math.h>
double sinh(double x);
double x;              Variable whose hyperbolic sine is to be computed
```

Example Use
```
a = cosh(b);
```

Returns
Normally, *sinh()* returns the hyperbolic sine of *x*. If the result is too large (a *double* variable can be as large as approximately 10^{308}), a range error will occur.

See Also
```
cosh(), tanh()
```

size_t predefined data type

Purpose
The *size_t* data type is an unsigned integral type that is returned by the *sizeof* operator. It is defined in *stdlib.h*.

See Also
```
sizeof
```

sizeof operator

Purpose
Use the *sizeof* operator to determine the number of bytes that are used to store a particular variable or type of data. When applied to an array (with a reference to element [0]) *sizeof* returns the total size of the array; when applied to a pointer, *sizeof* returns the size of the pointer itself, not the size of the data to which it points. When applied to a C++ reference variable, *sizeof* returns the size of the referenced object. When applied to a class, *sizeof* returns the total size of an object of that class.

Example Use
```
image_size = sizeof(image_array[0]);
```

See Also
```
* (pointer reference operator), & (address-of operator), &
(C++ reference operator), this
```

sprintf() function

Purpose
Use the *sprintf ()* function to format and write the values of specified variables to the string given in *p_string*. See *printf()* for a description of *format_string*. Note that C++ programmers generally use the specialized in-memory string formatting functions in the *strstreambuf* class and its derivatives together with other stream functions.

Syntax

```
#include <stdio.h>
int sprintf(char *p_string, const char *format_string,
<argument ...>;
char *p_string;        pointer to an array of characters where sprintf() sends its
                       formatted output
const char *format_string;  p character string which describes the format to be used
argument ...           A variable number of arguments depending on the number of
                       items being printed
```

Example Use

```
sprintf(buffer, "FY 88 Profit = %.2f\n", profit);
```

Returns

The *sprintf()* function returns the number of characters it has stored in the buffer, not counting the terminating null character ('\0').

See Also

```
fprintf(), printf(), vfprintf(), vprintf(), vsprintf();
```

sqrt() function

Purpose

Use the *sqrt()* function to compute the square root of a non-negative *double* variable *x*.

Syntax

```
#include <math.h>
double sqrt(double x);
double x;              Variable whose square root is to be computed
```

Example Use

```
sqrt_2 = sqrt(2.0); /* sqrt_2 = 1.414 */
```

Returns

The *sqrt()* function returns the square root of *x*. However, if *x* is negative, a domain error occurs.

See Also

```
pow()
```

srand() function

Purpose

Use the *srand()* function to set the "seed" or the starting point of the random number generation algorithm used by the function *rand()*. If *seed* is 1, the random number generator is initialized to its default starting point. This will generate the sequence that is produced when *rand()* is called without any prior calls to *srand()*. Any other value of *seed* sets a random starting point for the pseudo random sequence to be generated by *rand()*. To generate randomly selected random sequences you can use a function that returns the current time from the operating system and use the time value (modified if necessary) for *seed*.

Syntax
```
#include <stdlib.h>
void srand(unsigned seed);
unsigned seed;          Starting point for random number generator
```

Example Use
```
srand(new_seed);
```

See Also
```
rand()
```

sscanf()
function

Purpose
Use *sscanf()* to read characters from *buffer* and convert and store them in C variables according to the formats specified in the string *format_string*. See *scanf()* for a description of the *format_string* argument. Note that C++ programs usually use the overloaded extraction operator (>>) for this purpose.

Syntax
```
#include <stdio.h>
 int sscanf(const char *buffer, const char *format_string,
<argument...>;
const char *buffer;          Pointer to buffer from which characters will be read
                             and converted to values of variables
const char *format_string;      A character string which describes the
                             format to be used
argument...          Variable number of arguments representing addresses of
                     variables whose values are being read
```

Example Use
```
sscanf(buffer, "Name: %s Age: %d", name, &age);
```

Returns
The *sscanf()* function returns the number of fields that were successfully read, converted, and assigned to variables. The count excludes items that were read and ignored. If the string ends before completing the read operation, the return value will be the constant EOF.

See Also
```
fscanf(), scanf(), EOF
```

**static
keyword**

Purpose
Use *static* to localize the declaration of a data item or a function to a program module (file). You can use this to "hide" functions and data from other modules. Static variables have permanent storage; they retain their values throughout the life of the program.

Syntax
```
static <type> <varname>
```

Example Use
In the example below each file has its own copy of the variable *current_index.* Each copy is initialized once, and each retains its last-stored value throughout the execution of the program.

```
/*  FILE1 */
static int current_index = 0;
 main()
{
  ...
  current_index = 1;
  ...
}
 /*  FILE2 */
static int current_index = 0;
void some_function(void)
{
  if ( current_index == 0 ) ...
  ...
  current_index = 2;
  ...
}
```

See Also
```
auto, extern
```

**_ _ STDC_ _
predefined
macro**

Purpose
Use the _ _STDC_ _ predefined macro to check whether the compiler in use complies with the ANSI standard. This macro should supply a decimal constant 1 to indicate conformance.

Example Use
```
IF (_ _STDC_ _)
    printf("ANSI standard compiler.\n");
else
    printf("Not an ANSI standard compiler.\n");
```

See Also
_ _FILE_ _, _ _LINE_ _, _ _DATE_ _, _ _TIME_ _

stderr predefined stream

Purpose
The *stderr* predefined pointer points to the standard error stream. It is defined in *stdio.h*. The equivalent C++ stream is *cerr*.

See Also
stdin, stdout; cerr (C++ standard error stream)

stdin predefined stream

Purpose
The *stdin* predefined pointer points to the standard input stream—by default, the keyboard. It is defined in *stdio.h*. The equivalent C++ stream is *cin*.

See Also
stderr, stdout; cin (C++ standard input stream)

stdout predefined stream

Purpose
The *stdout* predefined pointer points to the standard output stream—by default, the screen. It is defined in *stdio.h*. The equivalent C++ stream is *cout*.

See Also
stderr, stdin; cout (C++ standard output stream)

strcmp()

Purpose
Use the *strcmp()* function to compare the strings *string1* and *string2*.

Syntax
```
#include <string.h>
int strcmp(const char *string1, const char *string2); const
char *string1;          First null-terminated string
const char *string2;    Second null-terminated string
```

Example Use
```
if( strcmp(username, "root") != 0 ) exit(EXIT_FAILURE);
```

Returns
The *strcmp()* function returns an integer greater than, equal to, or less than 0 depending on whether *string1* is greater than, equal to, or less than *string2*.

See Also
```
memcmp(), strcoll(), strncmp(), EXIT_FAILURE, EXIT_SUCCESS
```

strcoll() function

Purpose

Use the *strcoll()* function to compare the strings *string1* and *string2* after interpreting both depending on the character collating sequence selected by the LC_COLLATE category of the current locale.

Syntax
```
#include <string.h>
int strcoll(const char *string1, const char *string2);
const char *string1;      First null-terminated string
const char *string2;      Second null-terminated string
```

Example Use
```
if( strcoll(username, rootname) != 0 ) exit(EXIT_FAILURE);
```

Returns

The *strcoll()* function returns an integer greater than, equal to, or less than 0 depending on whether *string1* is greater than, equal to, or less than *string2* when both are interpreted as appropriate to the current locale.

See Also
```
memcmp(), strncmp(), EXIT_FAILURE, EXIT_SUCCESS,LC_COLLATE
```

strcpy() function

Purpose

Use the *strcpy()* function to copy the null-terminated string *string2* to the string *string1*. The terminating null character ('\0') of the second string is also copied so that *string1* becomes a copy of *string2*.

Syntax
```
#include <string.h>
char *strcpy(char *string1, const char *string2);
char *string1;           Destination string
const char *string2;     String to be copied to the first one
```

Example Use
```
strcpy(command, "resize");
```

Returns

The *strcpy()* function returns a pointer to the copied string which is *string1*.

See Also
```
memcpy(), memmove(), strncpy()
```

strcspn() function

Purpose

Use the *strcspn()* function to compute the length of the maximum initial segment of *string1* that consists entirely of characters not in *string2*. This is the first substring in *string1* that does not "span" the character set *string2*.

Syntax
```
#include <string.h>
size_t strcspn(const char *string1, const char *string2);
const char *string1;        String to be searched
const char *string2;        String describing set of characters to be located
```

Example Use
```
first_q = strcspn(soliloquy, "q"); /*first_q = 6 */
```

Returns

If successful, the *strcspn()* function returns the length of the segment.

See Also
```
strchr(), strpbrk(), strspn(), strrchr(), size_t
```

streambuf class

Purpose

Use the *streambuf* class to handle unformatted operations with streams. The *streambuf* member functions are not generally used directly. Rather, *streambuf* is a base class for deriving two classes: *filebuf* for file-related stream operations and *strstreambuf* for formatting strings in memory. Note that in C++ 2.X most *streambuf* member functions have been made protected and access is now done through the derived classes such as *istream* and *ostream*.

Syntax
```
#include <iostream.h>
```

See Also
```
iostream.h, stream.h, fstream, fstreambase, fstream.h,
istream, ostream, iomanip.h
```

stream.h header filer

Purpose

Use the *stream.h* header file for stream I/O in C++ versions prior to 2.0. Note: Most compilers available today support C++ version 2.0 (or later). With these compilers you should use the *iostream.h* header file instead, since the latter includes expanded and improved stream features.

Syntax
```
#include stream.h        For pre-2.0 C++ streams
```

See Also
```
iostream.h, fstream, fstreambase, fstream.h, istream,
ostream, iomanip.h
```

strerror() function

Purpose

Use the *strerror()* function to obtain the system error message corresponding to the error number given in the argument *errnum*. Note that *strerror* only returns the error message, printing the message is up to you.

Syntax
```
#include <string.h>
char *strerror(int errnum);
int errnum;      Error number
```

Example Use
```
error_message = strerror(errno);
```

Returns

The *strerror()* function returns a pointer to the error message. The text of the message is implementation-dependent.

See Also
```
perror(), errno
```

strftime() function

Purpose

Use the *strftime()* function to format a time in the *tm* structure whose address is in *timeptr* into a string whose address is provided in *str*. At most *maxsize* characters will be placed in the string. The formatting is done according to the formatting codes given in the string *format_string*. As with *sprintf()*, the formatting codes begin with a "%" and are explained in the table. The argument *format_string* is expected to be in multibyte characters. Characters that do not begin with a "%" are copied unchanged to *str*. The LC_TIME category of the program's locale affects the behavior of *strftime*.

Format	Replaced By
%a	current locale's abbreviated name for the weekday
%A	current locale's full name for the weekday
%b	current locale's abbreviated name for the month
%B	current locale's full name for the month
%c	date and time representation appropriate for the locale
%d	day of the month as a decimal number (01-31)
%H	hour in a 24-hour clock as a decimal number (00-23)
%I	hour in a 12-hour clock as a decimal number (01-12)
%j	day of the year as a decimal number (001-366)
%m	month as a decimal number (01-12)
%M	minute as a decimal number (00-59)
%P	current locale's AM/PM indicator
%S	second as a decimal number (00-60)
%U	week of the year as a decimal number (Sunday is taken as the first day of a week) (00-53)
%w	weekday as a decimal number (Sunday is 0, 0-6)
%W	week of the year as a decimal number (Monday is taken as the first day of a week) (00-53)
%x	date representation for current locale
%X	time representation for current locale
%y	year without the century as a decimal number (00-99)
%Y	year with the century as a decimal number
%z	name of time zone (or nothing if time zone is unknown)
%%	a percent sign (%)

Syntax

```
#include <time.h>
size_t strftime(char *str, size_t maxsize, const char
*format_string, const struct tm *timeptr);
char *str;          Pointer to array of characters where result is placed
size_t maxsize;     Maximum number of characters in str
const char *format_string;      Formatting codes for converting the time
                                to a string
```

```
const struct tm *timeptr;        Pointer to structure containing broken-
                                 down time
```

Example Use
```
/* Produce the standard output: Thu Jul 21 19:02:39 1988 */
strftime(s, 80, "%a %b %c\n", &tptr);
```

Returns
The *strtime()* function returns the total number of characters it placed in *str* including the terminating null character. If the number of characters exceed *maxsize*, *strftime()* returns 0 and the contents of the array *str* are indeterminate.

See Also
```
asctime(), ctime(), gmtime(), localtime(), time(),
LC_TIME, size_t, tm
```

strlen() function

Purpose
Use *strlen()* to find the length of *string* in bytes, not counting the terminating null character ('\0').

Syntax
```
#include <string.h>
size_t strlen(const char *string);
const char *string;    Null-terminated string whose length is to be returned
```

Example Use
```
length = strlen(name);
```

Returns
The *strlen()* function returns the number of characters in *string* that precede the terminating null character.

See Also
```
strcspn(), size_t
```

strncat() function

Purpose
Use the *strncat()* function to append the first *n* characters of *string2* to *string1*, and terminate the resulting string with a null character ('\0'). The terminating null of the first string is removed and *string1* becomes the concatenation of the old *string1* and the first *n* characters of *string2*.

Syntax
```
#include <string.h>
```

```
char *strncat(char *string1, const char *string2, size_t n);
char *string1;          Destination string
const char *string2;    String whose first n characters are to be appended to the
                        first one
size_t n;       Number of characters of string2 to be appended to string1
```

Example Use
```
char id[16] = "ID";
strncat(id, name, 10);
/* id is first 10 char of name */
```

Returns
The *strncat()* function returns a pointer to the concatenated string, *string1*.

See Also
```
strcat(), strcpy(), strncpy(), size_t
```

strncmp() function

Purpose
Use the *strncmp()* function to compare at most the first *n* characters of the null-terminated strings *string1* and *string2*.

Syntax
```
#include <string.h>
int strncmp(const char *string1, const char *string2, size_t n);
const char *string1;    First string
const char *string2;    Second string
size_t n;               Number of characters of above strings to be compared
```

Example Use
```
if(strncmp(command, "quit", 4) == 0) quit_program();
```

Returns
The *strncmp()* function returns an integer greater than, equal to, or less than 0 depending on whether the first *n* characters of *string1* are greater than, equal to, or less than *string2*.

See Also
```
memcmp(), strcmp(), strcoll(), size_t
```

strncpy() function

Purpose
Use the *strncpy()* function to copy the first *n* characters of the null-terminated string *string2* to the buffer whose address is given by *string1*. The copy is placed starting at the first character position of *string1*. If *n* is less than the

length of *string2*, no terminating null character ('\0') is appended to *string1*. However, if *n* exceeds the length of *string2*, *string1* is padded with null characters so that it is exactly *n* bytes long. You should avoid situations where the *n* bytes following *string1* overlap *string2*, because the behavior of *strcpy()* with such arguments is not guaranteed to be correct.

Syntax
```
#include <string.h>
char *strncpy(char *string1, const char *string2, size_t n);
char *string1;              Destination string
const char *string2;        String whose first n characters are to be
                            copied to the first one
size_t n;                   Number of characters to be copied
```

Example Use
```
strncpy(fname, "tmp12345678", 8);
/* fname = "tmp12345" */
```

Returns
The *strncpy()* function returns a pointer to *string1*.

See Also
```
memcpy(), memmove(), strcat(), strncat(), strcpy(), size_t
```

strpbrk() function

Purpose
Use the *strpbrk()* function to locate the first occurrence in *string1* of any character in *string2*.

Syntax
```
#include <string.h>
char *strpbrk(const char *string1, const char *string2);
const char *string1;        String to be searched
const char *string2;        String describing set of characters to be located
```

Example Use
```
first_vowel = strpbrk(word, "aeiou");
```

Returns
If successful, the *strpbrk()* function returns a pointer to the first occurrence of any character from *string2* in *string1*. If the search fails, *strpbrk()* returns a NULL.

See Also
```
strchr(), strcspn(), strrchr(), strspn(), NULL
```

strrchr function

Purpose
Use the *strrchr()* function to locate the last occurrence of the character *c* in the null-terminated string *string*. The terminating null character ('\0') is included in the search and the null character can also be the character to be located.

Syntax
```
#include <string.h>
char *strrchr(const char *string, int c);
const char *string;      String to be searched
int c;        Character to be located
```

Example Use
```
char line_cost[] = "10 units at $1.20 ea. = $12.00";
total_cost = strrchr(line_cost, '$');
/* Now total_cost will be the string "$12.00" */
```

Returns
If the character *c* is found, *strrchr()* returns a pointer to the last occurrence of *c* in *string*. If the search fails, *strrchr()* returns a NULL.

See Also
```
strchr(), strcspn(), strpbrk(), strspn(), NULL
```

strspn() functon

Purpose
Use the *strspn()* function to compute the length of the maximum initial segment of *string1* that consists entirely of characters from the string *string2*. This is the first substring in *string1* that "spans" the character set *string2*.

Syntax
```
#include <string.h>
size_t strspn(const char *string1, const char *string2);
const char *string1;     String to be searched
const char *string2;     String describing set of characters
```

Example Use
```
char *input = "280ZX"";
first_nondigit_at = strspn(input, "1234567890");
/* first_nondigit_at will be  3 */
```

Returns
The *strspn()* function returns the length of the segment.

See Also
```
strcspn(), strpbrk(), size_t
```

strstr() function

Purpose

Use the *strstr()* function to locate the first occurrence of string *string2* in *string1*.

Syntax

```
#include <string.h>
char *strstr(const char *string1, const char *string2);
const char *string1;     String to be searched
const char *string2;     String to be located
```

Example Use

```
char input[]= "The account number is ACEG-88-07-11";
acc_no = strstr(input, "ACEG");
/* Now the string acc_no will be ACEG-88-07-11" */
```

Returns

If successful, the *strstr()* function returns a pointer to the first occurrence of *string2* as a substring in *string1*. If the search fails, *strstr()* returns a *NULL*.

See Also

```
strchr(), strcspn(), strpbrk(), NULL
```

strtod() function

Purpose

Use the *strtod()* function to convert *string* to a double precision value. The string is expected to be of the form:

```
[whitespace][sign][digits.digits][exponent_letter][sign][digits]
```

where *whitespace* refers to (optional) blanks and tab characters, *sign* is a '+' or a '-' and the *digits* are decimal digits. The *exponent_letter* can be any one of d, D, e, or E (no matter which exponent letter is used, the exponent always denotes a power of 10). If there is a decimal point without any preceding digit, there must be at least one digit following it. The *strtod()* function will begin the conversion process with the first character of *string* and continue until it finds a character that does not fit the above form. Then it sets *endptr* to point to the leftover string, provided that *endptr* is not equal to NULL.

Syntax

```
double strtod(const char *string, char **endptr);
const char *string;      Pointer to character array from which double
                         precision value will be extracted
char **endptr;           On return points to character in string where conversion
                         stopped
```

Example Use
```
dbl_value = strtod(input_string, &endptr);
```

Returns
The *strtod()* function returns the double precision value as long as it is not too large. If it is too large, there will be an overflow and the return value will be the constant *HUGE_VAL* with the same sign as the number represented in *string*. Also, on overflow, the global variable *errno* is set to the constant *ERANGE*.

See Also
```
atof(), strtol(), strtoul(), ERANGE, HUGE_VAL, NULL, errno
```

strtok() function

Purpose
Use the *strtok()* function to retrieve a "token" or substring from *string1*. The token is marked by delimiting characters given in the second string argument *string2*. All tokens in a particular string *string1* can be extracted through successive calls to *strtok()* as follows. Make the first call to *strtok()* with the string to be "tokenized" as the first argument. Provide as second argument a string composed from the delimiting characters. After that, call *strtok()* with a *NULL* as the first argument and the delimiting characters appropriate for that token in the second string. This will tell *strtok* to continue returning tokens from the old *string1*.

Note that the set of delimiters can change in each call to *strtok*. Also, in the process of separating tokens, *strtok* will modify the string *string1*. It will insert null characters in the place of delimiters to convert tokens to strings.

Syntax
```
#include <string.h>
char *strtok(char *string1, const char *string2);
char *string1;          String from which tokens are returned
const char *string2;    String describing set of characters that delimit tokens
```

Example Use
```
next_token = strtok(input, '\t');
```

Returns
The first call to *strtok()* with the argument *string1* will return a pointer to the first token. Subsequent calls with a NULL as the first argument will return the next token. When there are no more tokens left, *strtok()* returns a NULL.

See Also
```
strcspn(), strpbrk(), strspn(), NULL
```

strtol()
function

Purpose

Use the *strtol()* function to convert *string* to a long integer value. The string is expected to be of the form:

```
[whitespace][sign][0][x or X][digits]
```

where *whitespace* refers to (optional) blanks and tab characters, *sign* is a '+' or a '-' and the *digits* are decimal digits. The string is expected to contain a representation of the long integer using the argument *radix* as the base of the number system. However, if *radix* is given as zero, *strtol()* will use the first character in *string* to determine the radix of the value. The rules are as follows:

First Character	Next Character	Radix Selected
0	0 thru 7	Radix 8 is used, i.e., octal digits expected
0	x or X	Radix 16, i.e., hexadecimal digits expected
1 thru 9	—	Radix 10, decimal digits only expected

Of course, other radices may be explicitly specified via the argument *radix*, The letters 'a' through 'z' (or 'A' through 'Z') are assigned values 10 through 35. For a specified radix, *strtol()* expects only those letters whose assigned values are less than the *radix*.

The *strtol()* function will begin the conversion process with the first character of *string* and continue until it finds a character that meets the above requirements. Then, before returning, *strtol()* sets *endptr* to point to that character, provided it is not a null pointer.

Syntax

```
long strtol(const char *string, char **endptr, int radix);
const char *string;      Pointer to character array from which the long
                         integer value will be extracted
char **endptr;           On return points to character in string where conversion stopped
int radix;               Radix in which the value is expressed in the string (radix must be
                         in the range 2 to 36)
```

Example Use

```
value = strtol(input, &endptr, radix);
```

Returns

The *strtol()* function returns the long integer value except when it will cause an overflow. In case of overflow, *strtol* sets *errno* to ERANGE and returns either LONG_MIN or LONG_MAX depending on whether the value was negative or positive.

See Also
```
atol(), strtoul(), ERANGE, LONG_MIN, LONG_MAX,errno
```

**strtoul()
function**

Purpose
Use the *strtoul()* function to convert a character string to an unsigned long integer. The string is expected to be of the same form as in *strtol*. The conversion also proceeeds in the same manner with *endptr* set to point to the character where conversion stopped, provided that *endptr* is not null.

Syntax
```
#include <stdlib.h>      For function declaration
#include <limits.h>      For the definition of the constants
                         LONG_MIN, LONG_MAX
#include <math.h>        For the definition of ERANGE
```
```
unsigned long strtoul(const char *string, char **endptr, int
radix);
const char  *string;     Pointer to character array from which the unsigned
                         long value will be extracted.
char **endptr;    On return points to character in string where conversion stopped
int  radix;       Radix in which the value is expressed in the string (radix must
                  be in the range 2 to 36)
```

Example Use
```
value = strtoul(input_string, &stop_at, radix);
```

Returns
The *strtoul()* function returns the unsigned long integer value except when it will cause an overflow. In case of overflow, *strtoul()* sets *errno* to *ERANGE* and returns the value *ULONG_MAX*.

See Also
```
atol(), strtol(), ERANGE, LONG_MIN, LONG_MAX, ULONG_MAX,
errno
```

**struct
keyword**

Purpose
Use the *struct* keyword to group related data items of different types together and to give the group a name by which you can refer to it later. Note that in C++ a *struct* has identical syntax to a *class* and can contain member functions as well as data members. The only difference is in default access: by default members of a *struct* have *public* access (are available to any part of the program that is in scope), while the default for a *class* is *private* access (data members accessible only to member functions of the same class).

Syntax

```
/* declare a structure */
struct structure_name
{
      type item_1;
      type item_2;
      ...
      type func1 (type);
      type func2 (type);
      ...
};
/*declare items of that structure type */
structure_name object_name;
```

Note that the more awkward C-style *struct* variable declaration syntax:

```
struct structure_name struct_1, struct_2;
```

is not needed in C++.

Similarly the alternative C-style declaration:

```
struct
{
    <type> <member_name>
    ...
} var_name ... ;
```

is seldom used in C++. In C++ *struct*s are usually used only to hold data that needs to be accessed from many places in the program.

Example Use

```
/* define a structure to be used in a linked list. It contains
several members including one that is a pointer to itself */
struct node
{
    int node_type;
    char node_name[16];
    struct node *next;
};
node *p_node, first_node;
```

See Also

```
union, . (member reference operator), -> (pointer
member reference operator); class (C++)
```

strxfrm() function

Purpose

Use the *strxfrm()* function to transform *string2* to a new form *string1* such that if *strcmp* is applied to two transformed strings the returned result is the same as that returned when *strcoll* is applied to the original strings. No more than *maxchr* characters will be placed in *string1*. If *maxchr* is 0, *string1* can be a *NULL*. In this case, the return value will be the length of the transformed version of *string2*.

Syntax
```
#include <string.h>
size_t strxfrm(char *string1, char *string2, size_t maxchr);
char string1;        String where transformed version of string2 is returned
char *string2;       String to be transformed
size_t    maxchr;    Maximum number of characters to be placed in string1
```

Example Use
```
strxfrm(s_xfrm, s_original);
```

Returns
The *strxfrm()* function returns the length of the transformed string, not counting the terminating null character. If the return value is *maxchr*, the contents of *string1* may be unusable.

See Also
```
strcmp(), strcoll(), NULL, size_t
```

switch keyword

Purpose
Use the *switch* statement to perform a multi-way branch depending on the value of an expression. In such cases the *switch* structure is more readable than a series of nested *if...else if* statements.

Syntax
```
switch (expression)
  {
    case <value> : statement; ...
    ...
    default: statement; ...
};
```

Use *case* labels inside the statement to indicate what to do for each expected value of the expression. Use *break* to separate the code of one *case* label from another. A *default* label marks code to be executed if none of the case labels match the expression.

Example Use
```
/* Execute different routines depending on the value of the
command. Note the use of break statements to keep the execu-
tion from falling through one case label to another */
switch (command)
{
    case 'Q': exit(0);
```

```
        case 'C': connect();
                break;
        case 'S': sendfile();
                break;
        case 'P': newparams();
                break;
        case '?': showparams();
                break;
        case 'H': printf(helplist);
                break;
        default:  printf("Unknown command!\n");
}
```

See Also
```
break, case, default
```

system() function

Purpose
Use *system()* to execute the operating system command contained in *string* from your program. If *string* is *NULL*, *system()* returns a non-zero value only if a command processor (for example, the UNIX shell) is present in the environment.

Syntax
```
#include <stdlib.h>
int system(const char *string);
const char *string;     command to be executed
```

Example Use
```
system("ls");
```

Returns
If *string* is not *NULL*, *system* will return an implementation-defined value.

See Also
```
NULL
```

\t escape sequence for horizontal tab

Purpose
Use the *\t* escape sequence to move the cursor to the next horizontal tab position on the current line. Tab positions are typically found at positions 1, 9, 17, 25, 32, and so on, but this can vary from one system to another.

Example Use
```
/* Print table headers:
Name            Street          City         Zip */
printf("Name\t\tStreet\t\tCity\t\t\tZip");
```

See Also
`printf(), \v`

tan() function

Purpose
Use the *tan()* function to compute the tangent of an angle *x* whose value is expressed in radians. You can convert an angle from degrees to radians by dividing it by 57.29578.

Syntax
```
#include <math.h>
double tan(double x);
double x;        angle in radians whose tangent is to be computed
```

Example Use
```
y = tan(x);
```

Returns
The *tan()* function returns the tangent of *x*. If the value of *x* is large in magnitude, the result may be very imprecise.

See Also
`atan(), atan2(), cos(), sin()`

tanh() function

Purpose
Use the *tanh()* function to compute the hyperbolic tangent of a *double* variable *x*.

Syntax
```
#include <math.h>
double tanh(double x);
double x;        Variable whose hyperbolic tangent is to be computed
```

Example Use
```
a = tanh(b);
```

Returns
The *tanh()* function returns the hyperbolic tangent of *x*.

See Also
`cosh(), sinh()`

tellg() function

Purpose
Use the *tellg() ios* member function to obtain the current read position for a C++ stream. This is the location in the file where the next character will be

read. This function is useful for saving the current read position before working elsewhere in the file.

Syntax
```
#include <iostream.h>
<stream>.tellg();
```

Example Use
```
fstream datafile;
streampos current_pos = datafile.tellg();
```

Returns
The *tellg()* function returns the read position as a value of type *streampos*, which is actually a *typedef long*.

See Also
```
ios, tellp(), setg(), setp()
```

tellp() function

Purpose
Use the *tellp() ios* member function to obtain the current write position for a C++ stream. This is the location in the file where the next character will be written. This function is useful for saving the current write position before reading or writing elsewhere in the file.

Syntax
```
#include <iostream.h>
<stream>.tellp();
```

Example Use
```
fstream datafile;
streampos writepos = datafile.tellp();
```

Returns
The *tellp()* function returns the current write position as a value of type *streampos*. This is actually a *typedef long*.

See Also
```
ios, tellg(), setg(), setp()
```

template keyword

Purpose
Use the 'template' keyword to create sophisticated macro definition statements for functions and classes. Note that this feature is not yet implemented by many C++ compilers, and is not covered in Master C++.

Syntax

```
<type name> fnct_name(. . .) { . . . }    function template
<type name> class_name { . . . }          class template
```

The <type name> is usually a *class* so as to allow any data type. However, the template definition can be more restrictive and specify data types such as *int, double,* or a specific object class.

Example Use

```
template <class TYPE>  TYPE Add(TYPE x, TYPE y)
{
    return(x + y);
}
```

Whenever the *Add()* template function is used, the C++ compiler examines the arguments passed to the function and creates a real function definition replacing the TYPE parameter with the argument types used. For example, using the *Add()* template function as follows:

```
double d = Add(2.0, 3.0);
int i = Add(2, 3);
```

would cause the C++ compiler to create the following function defintions:

```
double Add(double x, double y)
    {
        return(x + y);
    }

    int Add(int x, int y)
    {
        return(x + y);
    }
```

The *template* keyword operates in a similar fashion with class definitions. For example, consider the following vector template class definition:

```
template <class TYPE, int SIZE> struct vector
{
    TYPE elem[SIZE];
    vector<TYPE, SIZE>& operator+=(vector<TYPE,
            SIZE>& x)
    {
        for(unsigned n = 0; n < SIZE; n++)
            elem[n] += x.elem[n];
    }
};
```

The above is a template class for a vector object. The vector can be any dimension and use any data type depending on the TYPE and SIZE parameters used in the declaration. For example, a three dimensional type double vector called d_v3 is declared as follows:

```
vector<double, 3> d_v3;
```

See Also
```
typedef, class, struct, union
```

terminate() function

Purpose
Use the *terminate()* function to abandon exception handling (for example, if the stack has been corrupted or reliable behavior cannot be assured for some other reason). Note that C++ exception handling is a recent addition to the language and may not be supported by all compilers. It is not discussed in Master C++.

When called, *terminate()* calls the last function given as an argument to another special function called *set_terminate()*.

Syntax
```
void terminate();
```

Example Use
```
if !stackchk terminate(); // stack corrupt
```

See Also
```
catch(), throw(), try(), unexpected()
```

this keyword

Purpose
Use the *this* special pointer to refer to the object currently being executed. That is, returning *this* from a class object's member function returns a pointer to the object. Note that *this* is handled automatically by C++; you should not declare it nor examine its address.

Syntax
```
this
```

Example Use
```
return this; // return pointer to this object
```

Returns
The *this* pointer points to the object in which it was used. If you want to return the object itself rather than a pointer to it, use ** this*.

See Also
```
:: (scope resolution operator)
```

throw()
keyword

Purpose

Use the *throw()* function to call the defined exception handler, usually passing an object to it. The data type of the object is matched to one of the *catch* exception handlers defined immediately following the most recently entered *try* block for execution. If a *throw* is executed within a *catch* exception handler, the same object is thrown to the next most recently entered *try* block. If there is no *catch* exception handler matching the thrown object or no *try* block has been entered, then the *unexpected()* function is executed.

When control is passed to the *catch* exception handler or to the *unexpected()* function from a *throw* statement, the destructors for all automatic objects created after entering the *try* block-associated exception handler are called. In addition, all function call return addresses placed after entering the *try* block are removed. The C language equivalent of a *throw* statement is the *longjmp()* library function. Entering a *try* block can be considered the equivalent of calling the *setjump()* function. Note that exception handling is a recent addition to C++ and may not be supported by all compilers. This feature is not discussed in Master C++.

Syntax
```
throw (object);
throw;      only within a 'catch' handler
object      object (such as a message string) to pass to exception handler
```

Example Use
See entry for *catch* for an example.

See Also
```
catch, try, terminate(), unexpected(), longjmp(), setjmp()
```

time()
function

Purpose

Use the *time()* function to get the current date and time (calendar time) encoded as an implementation-dependent value of type *time_t*. If the pointer *timeptr* is not null, the encoded time is copied to the location whose address is in *timeptr*.

Syntax
```
#include <time.h>
time_t time(time_t *timeptr);
time_t *timeptr;          Pointer to variable where result will be returned
```

Example Use
```
time(&bintime);
```

Returns
The *time()* function returns the calendar time encoded in an implementation-dependent manner.

See Also
```
ctime(), gmtime(), localtime(), time_t
```

_ _TIME_ _ predefined macro

Purpose
Use the _ _TIME_ _ predefined macro to display the time the source file is being translated by the preprocessor. The time is inserted as a string with the form "HH:MM:SS".

Example Use
```
printf("at");
printf(_ _TIME_ _);
```

See Also
```
_ _DATE_ _, _ _FILE_ _, _ _LINE_ _, _ _STDC_ _
```

time_t predefined data type

Purpose
The *time_t* data type holds the value returned by the *time()* function. It is defined in *time.h*.

See Also
```
time(), tm
```

tm predefined data type

Purpose
The struct *tm* holds the components of a calendar time. It is defined in *time.h*.

See Also
```
time_t, time()
```

**TMP_MAX
predefined
value**

Purpose
The predefined value *TMP_MAX* is the minimum number of unique names that can be had from *tmpnam*. It is defined in *stdio.h*.

See Also
FILENAME_MAX

**tmpfile()
function**

Purpose
Use the *tmpfile()* function to open a temporary file for binary read/write operations ("wb+" mode). The file will be automatically deleted when your program terminates normally or when you close the file.

Syntax
```
#include <stdio.h>
FILE *tmpfile(void);
```

Example Use
```
p_tfile = tmpfile();
```

Returns
The *tmpfile()* function returns a pointer to the stream associated with the temporary file it opens. In case of error, this pointer will be NULL.

See Also
fclose(), tmpnam(), FILE, NULL

**tmpnam()
function**

Purpose
Use the *tmpnam()* function to generate a temporary file name in the string *file_name* which must have enough room to hold at least *L_tmpnam* (a constant defined in *stdio.h*) characters. You can generate up to *TMP_MAX* (another constant defined in *stdio.h*) unique file names with *tmpnam*.

Syntax
```
#include <stdio.h>
char *tmpnam(char *file_name);
char *file_name;          Pointer to string where file name will be returned
```

Example Use
```
tmpnam(tfilename);
```

Returns
The *tmpnam()* function returns a pointer to the name generated. If the argument to *tmpnam()* is *NULL*, the return pointer will point to an internal static buffer. If the generated name is not unique, it returns a *NULL*.

See Also
```
tmpfile(), L_tmpnam, NULL, TMP_MAX
```

tolower() function

Purpose

Use the *tolower()* function to convert the uppercase letter *c* to lowercase.

Syntax
```
#include <ctype.h>
int tolower(int c);
int c;              Character to be converted
```

Example Use
```
c = tolower('Q'); /* c will become 'q' */
```

Returns

The *tolower()* function returns the lowercase letter corresponding to *c* if there is one. Otherwise, the argument is returned unchanged.

See Also
```
toupper()
```

toupper() function

Purpose

Use the *toupper()* function to convert the lowercase letter *c* to uppercase.

Syntax
```
#include <ctype.h>
int toupper(int c);
int c;              Character to be converted
```

Example Use
```
c = toupper('q'); /* c will become 'Q' */
```

Returns

The *toupper()* function returns the uppercase letter corresponding to *c* if there is one. Otherwise, the argument is returned unchanged.

try keyword

Purpose

Use the *try* keyword to establish an entry point for exceptions thrown using the *throw* keyword. If an exception is thrown, then the desructors for any automatic objects created after entering the *try* block are called and function call return addresses removed from the stack. A *try* block is normally followed by one or more *catch* exception handler definitions. The C language equivalent to a *try* block with multiple exception handlers is as follows:

```
jmp_buf jumper;
int exception;

if(!(exception = setjmp(jumper)))
{  // Entry into the 'try' block
   . . .
}
else
{
   switch(exception)
   {
      case Catch_Def_1:
         . . .
      case Catch_Def_2:
         . . .
      default:
        unexpected();

   }
}
```

Syntax
```
try {
...
}
catch (<type>)
...
```

Example Use
See the entry for *catch* for an example.

See Also
```
catch, throw, unexpected()
```

type()
type cast
operator

Purpose
Use the *type cast operator* to make a value have a specified data type. The desired type is placed in parentheses.

Syntax
```
type (value); or
(type) value /* makes value have type */
```

The first (function-style) syntax is preferred by most C++ programmers.

Example Use
```
int i = 1;
/* convert i to type double */
double(i);    /* C++-style syntax */
(double) i;   /* C-style syntax */
```

typedef keyword

Purpose

Use *typedef* to give a new name to an existing data type. This can improve the readability of your program as well as make declarations simpler to type.

Syntax
```
typedef existing_type new_name;
```

Example Use
```
typedef int (*P_FUNC)();
/* you can now use P_FUNC as a data type that means
"pointer to a function returning an integer" */
```

See Also
```
enum
```

UCHAR_MAX

Purpose

The predefined value *UCHAR_MAX* is the maximum value of an *unsigned char*. It is defined in *limits.h*.

See Also
```
UINT_MAX, USHRT_MAX
```

UINT_MAX predefined value

Purpose

The predefined value *UINT_MAX* is the maximum value of an *unsigned int*. It is defined in *limits.h*.

See Also
```
UCHAR_MAX, USHRT_MAX
```

ULONG_MAX predefined value

Purpose

The predefined value *ULONG_MAX* is the maximum value of an *unsigned long int*. It is defined in *limits.h*.

See Also
```
UINT_MAX, USHRT_MAX
```

#undef preprocessor directive

Purpose

Use the *#undef* preprocessor to remove a symbol or macro definition currently existing in the program.

Syntax
```
#undef symbol
```

Example Use
```
#undef DEBUG /* removes definition of DEBUG */
```

See Also
```
#define, #ifdef, #ifndef, defined
```

unexpected() function

Purpose

The *unexpected()* function is called when no *catch* handler is found in the most recently entered *try* block that matches the exception thrown by the *throw* keyword. The *unexpected()* function in turn calls the function set by the last call to the *set_unexpected()* function. If the *unexpected()* function is executed before any call has been made to *set_unexpected()*, then the *terminate()* function is executed.

The *unexpected()* function is a predefined function pointer which points to the *terminate()* function and is set by the *set_unexpected()* function. It cannot be defined. It is also not normally called directly.

Example Use

See the entry for *catch* for an example of exception handling.

See Also
```
catch, throw(), try, terminate()
```

ungetc() function

Purpose

Use the *ungetc()* function to push the character *c* back onto *stream*. The characters that are pushed back will be returned to subsequent read operations on *stream* in the reverse order of their pushing. You can push any character except the constant *EOF*.

Since *ungetc()* pushes the character into the stream's buffer, any operation that tampers with the buffer or the file's current position (for example, *fseek()*, *fsetpos()*, or *rewind()*), may discard the pushed-back characters.

Note that the equivalent function for C++ streams is the *ios* member function *putback()*.

Syntax
```
#include <stdio.h>
int ungetc(int c, FILE *stream);
int c;            Character to be pushed into the file's buffer
FILE *stream;     Pointer to stream onto which the character is pushed back
```

Example Use
```
ungetc(last_char, infile);
```

Returns
If there are no errors, *ungetc()* returns the character it pushed back. Otherwise, it returns the constant EOF to indicate an error.

See Also
```
fgetc(), fputc(), getc(), getchar(), putc(), putchar(), EOF;
putback() (for C++ streams)
```

union keyword

Purpose
Use *union* to allocate storage for several data items at the same location. This is useful when a program needs to access the same item of data in different ways. The declaration of *union* is identical to that of *struct*, except that in a *union* all data items in the declaration share the same storage location.

In C++ a *union* may have a constructor or destructor as well as other member functions. *unions* cannot be *virtual*, and they can either be derived nor serve as a base class. An object of a *class* that has a constructor or destructor cannot be a member of a *union*. A *union* can have no *static* data members.

Syntax
```
union <union_name>
{
    <type> <member_name>;
    ...
};
```

union_name (sometimes called the union's "tag") can be omitted, in which case variables of the union type must be declared in the same statement as the union definition.

```
union (<type> <member_name>...)
{
// you can initialize members here
// if you don't use a constructor
} var_name ... ;
```

Example Use
```
/* Declare a union that stores a short in the same location as
an array of two characters. Each individual byte of the short
stored in the union x can be accessed by x.bytes[0] and
x.bytes[1]*/
union short_u
{
    short sh_val;
```

```
   char bytes[2];
};
short_u x;
```

See Also
struct, class

unsetf()
function

Purpose

Use the *unsetf()* *ios* member function to clear the specified *ios* formatting flags. *unsetf()* is convenient because it clears only the flag specified in the *ios* enumerated mask without affecting other flags. See the *ios* entry for a description of the flag enumerations.

Syntax
```
unsetf(flagvals);
flagvals          long value with flag bits
```

Example Use
```
cout.unsetf(ios::showbase);
// clear the showbase flag so base and
// exponent letters won't be shown
```

Returns

The *unsetf()* function returns a *long* value containing the flag values prior to unsetting.

See Also
setf(), flags(), setiosflags(0, resetiosflags()

unsigned
keyword

Purpose

Use the *unsigned* qualifier with integer data types (*char, int, short int*, and *long int*) to tell the compiler that the variable will be used to store nonnegative values only. This effectively doubles the maximum value that can be stored in that variable. Another useful feature is that arithmetic involving *unsigned* integers can never overflow because all operations are performed modulo a number that is one greater than the largest value that can be represented by that unsigned type.

Syntax
```
unsigned <integer type> <varname>;
```

Example Use
```
unsigned char data[1000];
unsigned long file_pos;
unsigned i;    /* equivalent to unsigned int i */
```

See Also
```
char, double, float, int, long, short, unsigned
```

USHRT_MAX predefined value

Purpose

The predefined value *USHRT_MAX* is the maximum value of an *unsigned short int*. It is defined in *limits.h*.

See Also
```
UINT_MAX, USHRT_MAX
```

\v escape sequence for vertical tab

Purpose

Use the *\v* escape sequence to move the cursor to the next vertical tab position. This does not work with most video displays or some printers.

Example Use
```
printf("\vf\va\vl\vl\vi\vn\vg");
```

See Also
```
printf, \n, \t
```

va_arg(), va_end(), va_start() predefined macros

Purpose

Use the *va_start()*, *va_arg()*, and *va_end()* macros to access the arguments of a function when it takes a fixed number of required arguments followed by a variable number of optional arguments. The required arguments are in standard style and accessed by parameter name. The optional arguments are accessed using the macros *va_start()*, *va_arg()*, and *va_end()*. See the CBT for a step-by-step description.

Syntax
```
#include <stdarg.h>
<type> va_arg(va_list arg_ptr, <type>);
void va_end(va_list arg_ptr);
void va_start(va_list arg_ptr, prev_param);
```

```
va_list arg_ptr;     Pointer to list of arguments
prev_param           Name of parameter just preceding first optional argument
<type>               Type of argument to be retrieved, for example char*
```

Example Use
```
va_start(argp, firstint);
first_x = firstint;
next_x = va_arg(argp, int);
```

Returns
The *va_arg()* macro returns a pointer to the next argument of a given type. The *va_start()* macro sets a pointer to the beginning of the list of arguments.

See Also
```
vfprintf(), vprintf(), vsprintf()
```

va_list predefined data type

Purpose
The *va_list()* data type hold macros needed by the macros *va_start()*, *va_arg()*, and *va_end()*. These macros are used to allow functions to accept a variable number of parameters. It is defined in *stdarg.h*.

See Also
```
va_arg(), va_start(), va_end()
```

vfprintf() function

Purpose
Use the *vfprintf()* function to write formatted output to an ANSI C-type *stream*, just as as *fprintf()* would, except that *vfprintf()* accepts a pointer to the list of variables (in *arg_pointer*) rather than the variables themselves, allowing a variable number of items to be printed. See *printf()* for a detailed description of the *format_string* argument.

Syntax
```
#include <stdarg.h>
#include <stdio.h>
int vfprintf(FILE *stream, const char *format_string,
va_list arg_pointer);
FILE *stream;              Pointer to stream to which the output goes
const char *format_string;      A character string which describes the
                                format to be used
va_list arg_pointer;      Pointer to a list containing a variable number of
                          arguments that are being printed
```

Example Use
```
vfprintf(stderr, p_format, p_arg);
```

Returns

The *vfprintf()* function returns the number of characters it has printed, excluding the terminating null character ('\0').

See Also

```
printf(), sprintf(), vprintf(), vsprintf(), va_arg(),
va_end(), FILE, stderr
```

virtual keyword

Purpose

Use the keyword *virtual* for a member function in a base class to specify that the function will be able to "pass through" a call to the appropriate derived class at runtime. This will assure that the version of a member function that will be called will be determined by the type of the actual object, not the type of a pointer to that object.

Syntax

```
virtual<type> <member_func_name> () {
... member function definition
}
type                       function return type
member_func_name           name of member function to be declared virtual
```

Example Use

```
class base_class {
...
virtual void membfunc (int& num) {
return scale(num, numeric::scale);
}
```

See Also

```
static, class, derived
```

void keyword

Purpose

Use the data type *void* in a function declaration to indicate the non-existence of a return value or the fact that the function uses no arguments. You can also use *void* * to declare a pointer to any type of data object.

Syntax

```
void func (void);
```

The first *void* if present indicates that *func* does not return a value. The second *void* if present indicates that *func* takes no arguments.

Example Use
```
void a_function(void *buffer);
int get_something(void);
extern void *p_buf;
```

See Also
```
char, int, double, float
```

volatile keyword

Purpose

Use the *volatile* type qualifier to inform the compiler that the variable which follows may be modified by factors outside the control of your program. For example, the contents of a register in the real-time clock in your system will be such a variable. The *volatile* qualifier warns the compiler that actions performed on *volatile* data must not be "optimized out." You can use the qualifier *const* together with *volatile* to qualify objects that must not be changed by your program, yet that may change due to external factors.

Syntax
```
volatile <type> <varname>;
```

Example Use
```
/* The code below shows the declaration of the register in a
real-time clock. It says that our code can not change the
contents (*p_rt_clock), but the contents may change by itself.
We are, however, free to modify the pointer p_rt_clock to
point to another long int */
const volatile long *p_rt_clock = CLOCK_ADDRESS;
```

See Also
```
const
```

vprintf() function

Purpose

Use the *vprintf()* function to peform the same functions as *printf()*, that is, write formatted output to the ANSI C stream *stdout*, when you have only a pointer to the list of variables to be printed (in *arg_pointer*) rather than the variables themselves. This allows a variable number of arguments to be printed. The *format_string* is described under *printf()*.

Syntax
```
#include <stdarg.h>
#include <stdio.h>
int vprintf(const char *format_string, va_list arg_pointer);
```

```
const char *format_string;        A character string which describes the
                                  format to be used
va_list arg_pointer;              Pointer to a list containing a variable number of
                                  arguments that are being printed
```

Example Use
```
vprintf(p_format, p_arg);
```

Returns
The *vprintf()* function returns the number of characters it has printed, excluding the terminating null character ('\0').

See Also
```
fprintf(), printf(), sprintf(), vfprintf(), va_arg(),
va_end(), stdout
```

vsprintf() function

Purpose
Use the *vsprintf()* function to perform the same function as *sprintf()*, i.e., write formatted output to the string *p_string*, except that *vsprintf()* accepts a pointer to a list of variables (in *arg_pointer*) rather than the variables themselves. Thus a variable number of arguments can be formatted. See *printf()* for a description of the *format_string* argument.

Syntax
```
#include <stdarg.h>
#include <stdio.h>
int vsprintf(char *p_string, constchar*format_string,
    va_list arg_pointer);
char *p_string;                   Pointer to an array of characters where vsprintf()
                                  sends its formatted output
const char *format_string;        A character string which describes the
                                  format to be used
va_list arg_pointer;              Pointer to a list containing a variable number of
                                  arguments that are being printed
```

Example Use
```
vsprintf(err_msg, p_format, p_arg);
```

Returns
The *vsprintf()* function returns the number of characters it has printed, excluding the terminating null character ('\0').

See Also
```
fprintf(), printf(), sprintf(), vfprintf(), vprintf(),
va_arg(), va_end()
```

wchar_t predefined

Purpose
The *wchar_t* data type can hold the entire range of values necessary to represent the largest extended character set supported by the compiler. It is defined in *stdlib.h*.

See Also
`char`

wcstombs() function

Purpose
Use the *wcstombs()* function to convert a sequence of codes of *wchar_t* type given in the array *pwcs* into a sequence of multibyte characters and store at most *n* such bytes in the array *mbs*.

Syntax
```
#include <stdlib.h>
size_t wcstombs(char *mbs, const wchar_t *pwcs, size_t n);
const char *mbs;    Pointer to array where multibyte characters will be stored
wchar_t *pwcs;      Pointer to array of wide characters to be converted to
                    multibyte format
size_t n;           Maximum number of multibyte characters to be stored in mbs
```

Example Use
```
wcstombs(mb_array, wc_array, 10*MB_CUR_MAX);
```

Returns
If successful, the *wcstombs()* function returns the number of bytes it stored in *mbs*, not including a terminating null character, if any. If *wcstombs()* encountered a wide character code that does not correspond to a valid multibyte character, it returns –1 cast as *size_t*.

See Also
```
mblen(), mbtowc(), mbstowcs(), wctomb(), MB_CUR_MAX,
size_t, wchar_t
```

wctomb() function

Purpose
Use the *wctomb()* function to convert *wchar*, a character of *wchar_t* type to a multibyte character and store the result in the array *s*. At most *MB_CUR_MAX* characters will be stored in the array *s*.

Syntax
```
#include <stdlib.h>
int wctomb(char *s, wchar_t wchar);
```

```
char *s;    Pointer to start of array where the multibyte equivalent of wchar will be
            returned
wchar_t  wchar;  Wide character to be converted to multibyte format
```

Example Use
```
wctomb(mb_char, wchar);
```

Returns
If *s* is *NULL*, *wctomb()* will return a 0 or a non-zero depending on whether multibyte encodings have state dependencies or not. If *s* is not *NULL*, *wctomb* returns the number of bytes that comprise the multibyte character corresponding to the wide character *wchar*. If *wchar* does not correspond to a valid multibyte character, it returns −1.

See Also
```
mblen(), mbtowc(), mbstowcs(), wcstombs(), MB_CUR_MAX, NULL,
wchar_t
```

while keyword

Purpose
Use the *while* statement to construct a loop that tests a condition and continues to execute the specified statements as long as the condition is true (not 0). Unlike the case of the *do...while* loop, the condition in the *while* statement is checked first, and then the body of the loop is executed if the condition is true.

Syntax
```
while (<condition>)
{
    statement;
    ...
};
```

A *while* loop with only one statement in the body is sometimes written as:

```
while (condition) statement;
```

Example Use
```
/* add up the numbers from 1 through 10 */
sum = 0;
i = 0;
while(i <= 10)
{
    sum += i;
    i++;
}
```

See Also
```
do, for, if, switch
```

width() function

Purpose

Use the *width() ios* member function to set the output width for a C++ stream. (Note that the *setwidth()* manipulator is an alternate method for accomplishing this function.)

The *ios* flags *ios::left, ios::ight,* and *ios::internal* specify how values will be padded and adjusted within the specified width. Note that if a numeric value exceeds the width specified the full number will still be displayed, overflowing the field.

Syntax
```
#include <iostream.h>
<stream>.width(chars); or
<stream>.width();        just returns current width
chars                    integer number of characters
```

Example Use
```
cout.width(10); // set output field width to 10
```

Returns

If called without an argument, the *width()* function returns the current width. If called with an argument, it sets the width to that argument and returns the previous width.

See Also
```
ios, setw(), setprecision()
```

write() function

Purpose

Use the *write() ios* member function to insert the specified number of characters or bytes of binary data into the specified stream.

Syntax
```
#include <iostream.h>
<output_stream>.write(buffer, num_chars);
buffer        array of characters from which to write
num_chars     integer number of characters to write
```

Example Use
```
char message [80];
...
cout.write(message, 40); // write first chars. from
                         // message buffer
```

Remember that *write()* doesn't care about the contents of the characters, so any sort of binary data that fits into the array can also be written.

Returns
The *write()* function returns a reference to the output stream.

See Also
```
ostream, << (insertion operator), get(), getline()
```

ws
manipulator

Purpose
Use the *ws* manipulator to "eat" any white space characters coming from the input stream rather than storing them in the destination object.

Syntax
```
#include <iostream.h>
input_stream >> ws;
```

Example Use
```
cin >> ws >> input;  // put cin in "input" but throw
                     // away spaces, tabs, etc.
```

Returns
The *ws* manipulator returns a reference to the input stream used.

See Also
```
endl, ends
```

APPENDIX A
➤ MASTER C++ COMMAND REFERENCE

This appendix describes the purpose of the commands located at the bottom of the screen in the Option Bar area. Note that not all of these options appear in the Option Bar area at the same time; some are context-sensitive and are displayed only during certain modes. For example, Note and Example appear only in the Option Bar area when a *Note* or *Example* window is available for the screen you are using; Achievement is only shown at menu screens and so on.

OPTION BAR COMMANDS

The following commands can appear in the Option Bar. They are given in the order in which they appear on the screen.

Achievement

Master C++ saves a record of your progress in a special file. Select A to see this record. A highlighted word or small graphic box character will be displayed next to each section as follows:

a) A percentage between 80 and 100 indicates you have successfully completed the lesson and shows your score.

b) BEGUN indicates you have started but not completed the lesson, or that you have failed the lesson.

c) DONE indicates that you have successfully completed a lesson that did not include any questions, hence no percentage is displayed.

d) REPEAT indicates you have restarted a lesson that had been completed with a score of less than 80%.

e) REVIEWED indicates that you have completed the review sections of a chapter but not all preceding lessons.

f) A small box character (■) indicates that the section has not been entered yet.

Forward

Forward is used to move to the next screen in the lesson.

Back

Back moves you back a screen to the previous lesson. If you are at the first screen, Back will take you to the point where you entered the current lesson.

Note

The word Note is displayed flashing on the Option Bar when a special *Note* window is available containing additional information relevant to the current concept. Press **N** to see the *Note* window. Once the *Note* window has been displayed, you can press **R** to remove it and return to the current screen: Note will continue to flash and you can reread the note if you wish. Alternatively, you can press **F** to remove the *Note* window and move forward to the next screen.

Example

The word Example is displayed flashing on the Option Bar when a special *Example* window is available containing related examples for the current screen. Once the *Example* window has been displayed, you can press **R** to remove it and return to the current screen: Example will continue to flash and you can reread the example if you wish. Alternatively, you can press **F** to remove the *Example* window and move forward to the next screen. Some screens may have both a *Note* and an *Example* available.

Glossary

Glossary provides online access to a collection of terms and concepts related to the C++ language. When you access the Glossary you are requested to type in the name of the word you wish to look up. If the word is not available, a list of similar spellings is presented. Once the word is found, a definition is displayed, and you can choose to see a related lesson.

Calc

Calc provides access to Master C++'s built-in calculator.

Write

The Write command provides the name and phone number of The Waite Group.

Help

The Help command provides access to the *Help* window. From this window you can change the color mapping of the screen to monochrome or back to color; or get help on the options that are enabled in the Option Bar. From a menu screen the Help command gives you additional information on menu items. Your name and serial number are also contained in this window.

Refresh

The Refresh option is used to refresh the screen and remove any windows that are enabled (such as *Note*, *Example*, or *Help*).

Obj

The Objective option is used to enable the *Objective* window which identifies the main topics covered in the associated lesson and the time required by an average beginner to complete the lesson.

Done

The Done option is used to exit from a lesson or submenu. After confirmation you will be sent to the previous section you were using in Master C++, usually an originating menu. Note that when you use Done no achievement record is made. Done is normally used when reviewing material or jumping to related material from the Glossary.

Jump

The Jump option is used to move directly to a particular section in a lesson without having to navigate the menu system. This might be useful, if, for example, you are selecting topics of interest from the course map.

You can simply press **J**, and follow it with the number of the lesson found in the map, such as 4.2.1. You can also jump directly to a particular screen in a lesson by adding a comma and the screen number, for example, to go to screen 4 of lesson 4.2.1, type **4.2.1,4**.

Tutor

The Tutor option brings up the online tutor which gives you a lesson in using Master C++.

Quit

The Quit option exits from Master C++ after confirming your intentions. Quit remembers where in Master C++ you quit, so the next time you start Master C++ it will return to that location.

APPENDIX B
➤ FURTHER READING

There are three important areas in which you may want to do further reading on C++. First, there is the C++ language itself—both nuances of object-oriented programming and practical coding techniques. Second, there is the mastery of the features of your chosen C++ compiler and its associated tools and class libraries, Finally, there is useful lore inherited from the established C programming community—especially the use of extensive function libraries such as that specified in ANSI C and enhanced in Borland/Turbo C++, Zortech C++, and others. Here we confine ourselves to mentioning only a few titles that we think might be particularly useful to users of Master C++. While we concentrate on titles from The Waite Group, we acknowledge that there is also a wide variety of excellent books from other publishers, especially ones dealing with the philosophy of object-oriented programming or with particular programming applications.

C++ IN GENERAL

The C Programming Language by Brian W. Kernighan and Dennis W. Ritchie (Prentice-Hall, 1978. Second Edition, 1988) essentially defined the C language for a generation of programmers. In similar fashion Bjarne Stroustrup, main developer of the C++ language has written *The C++ Programming Language* (Addison-Wesley, 1986. Second Edition, 1991). In addition to covering version 2.0 of the language, the second edition adds extensive commentary on OOP philosophy and design issues. Further details on language nuances can be found in *The Annotated C++ Reference Manual* (Addison-Wesley, 1990.)

C++ Primer Plus, by Stephen Prata (Waite Group Press, 1991) is a step by step tutorial that teaches "generic" (AT&T 2.0) C++ and object-oriented programming, from the ground up. While there is some discussion of C++

compilation under both DOS and UNIX, the example programs are not tied to any particular compiler or platform.

C++ COMPILERS AND DEVELOPMENT ENVIRONMENTS

The best-selling C++ compilers today are doubtless the Borland products Borland C++ and Turbo C++. Borland C++ is essentially the "professional" version and includes support for Windows programming, while Turbo C++ is Borland's original C++ compiler, aimed more at students and developers of character-based applications under DOS. Either is fine for learning the C++ language.

Object-Oriented Programming in Turbo C++, by Robert Lafore (Waite Group Press, 1991) has detailed but easy to follow tutorials on both the C++ language and matters specific to Borland's compilers and DOS. The tutorials in Master C++ have been adapted from this book.

The Waite Group's Borland C++ Developer's Bible (Waite Group Press, May 1992) is a detailed reference to use of the Borland compiler, linker, and other tools for developing both DOS and Windows applications. A fractal generation program provides an extensive example.

RESOURCES FROM C

The ANSI C library included in Borland/Turbo C++ is covered extensively in *The Waite Group's Turbo C++ Bible* (Sams, 1990). This book contains both tutorials on aspects of C++ programming and a complete reference entry for each library function. (This book serves as an expansion of the Master C++ printed reference in this book in two ways: the individual entries are longer, with complete program examples, and the numerous special functions that Borland has added to the ANSI library are also covered.)

If you wish to learn the ANSI C language we recommend *Master C*, the predecessor of *Master C++* (Waite Group Press, 1990). The reference manual for *Master C* includes alphabetical entries for all ANSI C library functions.

INDEX

COLOPHON

Production for this book was done using desktop publishing techniques and every phase of the book involved the use of computer technology. Never did production use traditional typesetting, stats, or photos, and virtually everything for this book, from the illustrations to the formatted text, was saved on disk. Only the cover used traditional techniques.

While this book was written on an IBM PC-compatible computer, Apple Macintosh computers were used for desktop publishing. The following method was used to go between machines: A design template for the book was created in Aldus PageMaker for the Macintosh. This template was saved as a Microsoft Word document and then translated into Word for Windows version 1.1. The author wrote into the WinWord files, which used style sheets to apply formatting. The finished documents were saved in an RTF format and transferred directly to a Macintosh on a 3.5" diskette, using Insignia's Access PC. These text files were then opened in Microsoft Word for the Macintosh, which interpreted the RTF formatting.

All book design and page formatting was done in Aldus PageMaker 4.01 on the Macintosh, using the imported Microsoft Word files. Adobe and Emigre fonts were used. Line art work was created in Adobe Illustrator.

PC screen dumps were captured using Pizazz Plus, by Application Techniques, Inc., and saved as grayscale TIFF files. The PC TIFF files were transferred to the Macintosh, again on a 3.5" disk opened under Access PC, and imported into PageMaker. To create the chapter opener pages, the cover painting was photographed in black and white, scanned in grey scale, and saved as a TIFF file. This file was imported into PageMaker.

The cover was created as an airbrush painting and was traditionally separated. Pagemaker 4.01 was used for cover design.

Final page files were sent on a 44 Mb Syquest removable hard drive to AlphaGraphics Electronic Publishing where they were directly imposed to film through a Macintosh IIFx and Linotronic 300 phototypesetting machine. Plates were then made from the film.

The Waite Group's
MASTER C

Computer-Based C Training for the IBM PC

Master C is a revolutionary book/disk package designed to turn your PC into an instructor that teaches you to write powerful C programs.

The Master C disk guides you through all the essential C topics—from data types to pointers and data structures. It teaches you, quizzes you, notices problems, and recommends action. A sophisticated answer judgment technique accepts rough responses and even misspellings.

Master C features windows, an online glossary, a calculator, electronic bookmarks, and it keeps track of student scores for classroom use. Answer collection can be turned on and off. Even screen colors can be changed.

The Master C book provides lessons you can use when you're away from your computer, and it features a reference section that explains the use and syntax of every keyword and function in C. Accumulated answer "blackboards" let you learn C by building the program in a window.

PACKAGE CONTAINS: 360K 5.25" disks, companion book, and registration card.

SYSTEM REQUIREMENTS: An IBM PC or 100%-compatible computer, a 384K system memory, DOS 3.0 or later, a hard disk and 5.25" floppy-disk drive, and a monochrome or color adaptor.

PRICE: $44.95 U.S.A.
See order form on preceding page.

Waite Group Press 100 Shoreline Highway Suite A-285 Mill Valley California (415) 331-0575

WAITE GROUP PRESS

THE WAITE GROUP'S
OBJECT-ORIENTED PROGRAMMING IN TURBO C++
ROBERT LAFORE

Suitable for students, hackers, and enthusiasts, Lafore's practical, real-world lessons teach the basics of object-oriented programming, focusing on C++ as a separate language, distinct from C, and assuming no prior experience with C. Covers Turbo C++, Borland C++, and Borland BGI Graphics. Includes objects, classes, overloading, constructors, inheritance, and virtual functions. End of chapter quizzes and exercises.

ISBN 1-878739-06-9, TRADE PAPER,

776PP., 7 X 9, COMPANION DISK AVAILABLE   **$26.95 US**

THE WAITE GROUP'S
C++ PRIMER PLUS
Teach Yourself Object-Oriented Programming
STEPHEN PRATA

Teaches "generic" AT&T C++ 2.0, and 2.1, in the same style as the author's best-selling *New C Primer Plus* (Winner of the CPA's Best How-To Computer Book Award), over 400,000 copies sold. Gentle, step-by-step lessons teach the basics of OOP including classes, inheritance, information hiding, and polymorphism. No C programming needed. Perfect for UNIX and DOS. "Prata makes a relatively complex subject—professional programming—clear and enjoyable." — Computer Press Association.

ISBN 1-878739-02-6, TRADE PAPER,

744PP., 7 X 9, COMPANION DISK AVAILABLE   **$26.95 US**

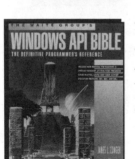

THE WAITE GROUP'S
WINDOWS API BIBLE
The Definitive Programmer's Reference
JAMES L. CONGER

A single, comprehensive, easy-to-use reference with examples for the over-600 Windows Application Programming Interface (API) functions. Like all Waite Group bibles, API functions are organized into categories, preceded by lucid tutorials and feature Windows version compatibility. Contains the latest information on the new Windows version 3.1.

FEBRUARY 1992, ISBN 1-878739-15-8, TRADE PAPER,

1128PP., 7³/₈ X 9 ¹/₄, COMPANION DISK AVAILABLE   **$39.95 US**

THE WAITE GROUP'S
FRACTAL CREATIONS
Explore the Magic of Fractals on Your PC
TIMOTHY WEGNER AND MARK PETERSON

The best-selling book/software package that lets you create over 70 fractals with a press of a key and make them come to life. Fractint, the revolutionary software, lets you zoom in on any part of a fractal image, rotate it, do color-cycle animation, even choose accompanying sound effects and 3-D mode. For programmers, students, and amateur enthusiasts alike. "...A magical ride complete with both the mathematical background necessary to appreciate and understand fractals, and the software, which allows you to display and manipulate them, even in 3-D." *PC Magazine.*

ISBN 1-878739-05-0, TRADE PAPER, 5.25" DISK,

350PP., 7 X 9, POSTER, 3-D GLASSES   **$34.95 US**

INNOVATION NOT IMITATION

FOR FASTER SERVICE, CALL 1-800-368-9369

THE WAITE GROUP'S
TURBO PASCAL HOW-TO
The Definitive Object-Oriented Problem-Solver
GARY SYCK

Everything you need to know to begin writing professional Turbo Pascal programs including hundreds of typical programming problems, creative solutions, comments, warnings, and enhancements in an easy-to-look-up reference format. The how-to solutions are designed to work with the newest object-oriented versions Turbo Pascal 6.0, Turbo Pascal for Windows, and Turbo Vision, as well as previous versions.
ISBN 1-878739-04-2, TRADE PAPER, 500PP., 7 x 9, COMPANION DISK AVAILABLE
$24.95 US

THE WAITE GROUP'S
VISUAL BASIC HOW-TO
ROBERT ARNSON, DANIEL ROSEN, MITCHELL WAITE, AND JONATHAN ZUCK

The task-oriented guide to Microsoft's Visual Basic, a simple, elegant, powerful language for Windows programmers. This book provides valuable answers to the most unusual VB tasks. Each entry contains a question, a description of why the question comes up, and a program solution (including code), along with commentary, warnings, enhancements, and alternative solutions where possible. Many of the solutions use Windows APIs.
ISBN 1-878739-09-3, TRADE PAPER, 3.5" DISK, 500PP., 7 x 9
$34.95 US

THE WAITE GROUP'S
VISUAL BASIC SUPER BIBLE
TAYLOR MAXWELL AND BRYON SCOTT

The complete reference to every command, function, statement, object, method, event, and property in the Visual Basic language detailed in Waite Group high-quality, user-friendly fashion. Each chapter begins with an overview; and each entry includes purpose, syntax, an example, and in-depth descriptions. Enclosed disk contains all example projects, code resources, bit maps, and complete applications developed in the book.
APRIL 1992, ISBN 1-878739-12-3, TRADE PAPER, DISK, 744PP., 7 x 9
$39.95 US

THE WAITE GROUP'S
WORDPERFECT BIBLE
The Definitive Visual Reference
JOSEPH SPEAKS AND ROB WEINSTEIN

A comprehensive easy-to-use reference organized by WordPerfect function.
ISBN 1-878739-01-8, TRADE PAPER, 546PP., 7 x 9 $26.95 US

THE WAITE GROUP'S
MASTER C
Let the PC Teach You C
MITCHELL WAITE, STEPHEN PRATA, AND REX WOOLLARD

A revolutionary computer-based training system that lets you learn C at your own pace.
ISBN 1-878739-00-X, TRADE PAPER, 3 DISKS, 233PP., 7 x 9 $44.95 US

TO ORDER TOLL FREE CALL 1-800-368-9369

TELEPHONE 415-331-0575 • FAX 415-331-1075

SEND ORDER FORM BELOW TO: WAITE GROUP PRESS, 100 SHORELINE HIGHWAY, SUITE A-285, MILL VALLEY, CA 94941

QTY	BOOK	PRICE	TOTAL
____	C++ PRIMER PLUS	$26.95	____
____	FRACTAL CREATIONS ☐ 3.5", ☐ 5.25" DISK	$34.95	____
____	MASTER C ☐ 3.5", ☐ 5.25" DISKS	$44.95	____
____	MASTER C++ ☐ 3.5", ☐ 5.25" DISKS	$39.95	____
____	OOP IN TURBO C++	$26.95	____
____	TURBO PASCAL HOW-TO	$24.95	____
____	VB SUPER BIBLE	$39.95	____
____	VISUAL BASIC HOW-TO	$34.95	____
____	WINDOWS API BIBLE	$39.95	____
____	WORDPERFECT BIBLE	$26.95	____
	CALIF. RESIDENTS ADD 7.25% SALES TAX		____

SHIPPING
UPS ($5 FIRST BOOK/$1 EACH ADD'L)   ____
UPS TWO DAY ($7/$2)   ____
CANADA ($10/$4)   ____
TOTAL ____

SHIP TO
NAME _____
COMPANY _____
ADDRESS _____
CITY, STATE, ZIP _____
PHONE _____

PAYMENT METHOD
☐ CHECK ENCLOSED   ☐ VISA   ☐ MASTERCARD
CARD# _____ EXP. DATE _____
SIGNATURE _____

SATISFACTION GUARANTEED OR YOUR MONEY BACK. NO QUESTIONS ASKED.

NO ONE CAN DO A BETTER JOB RAVING ABOUT OUR MASTER SERIES THAN OUR READERS.
Here are just a few of hundreds of comments we have received:

Please explain the one thing you liked MOST about this product.
VERY HELPFUL PRODUCT!

Please explain the one thing you liked MOST about this product.
the easiest way to work with it the examples and notes

Please explain the one thing you liked MOST about this product.
EXPLANATIONS ARE VERY PRECISE & AT A LEVEL FOR EASY UNDERSTANDING

Any other comments?
Excellent format, thorough, flexible, very effective!

Any other comments?
VERY GOOD, DON'T HAVE DOUBTS NOW AS IF I AM DOING IT RIGHT OR NOT.

Please explain the one thing you liked MOST about this product.
you can take your own pace slow or fast + review or skip as needed

Please give us any additional comments
VERY EASY to USE; VERY GOOD INSTRUCTION

Please explain the one thing you liked MOST about this product.
Really "builds" well, a little at a time, until you find that you're actually learning C!

Any other comments? It's A great PRODUCT even for beginners

Any other comments?
EXCELLENT PRODUCT / VALUE! WELL PLEASED

Please explain the one thing you liked MOST about this product.
Excellent for someone wanting to LEARN programming without going to college

This is the most excellent Tutorial on "C" that I have ever used. Please send brochures on any other such products.

3.5" DISK EXCHANGE OFFER

Most PCs sold today are configured with at least one 5.25" floppy disk drive so most users have access to that disk format. *The Waite Group's Master C++* is packaged with three 5.25" diskettes. Increasingly, new PCs are being configured with an additional 3.5" disk drive. The Waite Group makes available Master C++ on two 3.5" 720K disks for those users who have access only to that disk format.

If you would to exchange your original Master C++ disks for the 3.5" format, fill out the form below and return it to Waite Group Press with your **original set of 5.25" Master C++ disks**. Please include a $5 check or money order for shipping and handling.

Name _____   Phone _____

Company Name _____   Title_____

Street Address (No P.O. Boxes) _____

City _____   State _____   Zip _____

Send to Waite Group Press, Master C++ disk exchange offer, 100 Shoreline Highway, Suite A-285, Mill Valley, CA 94941. Please include your original set of Master C++ disks and the $5 shipping fee.

AS A PUBLISHER AND WRITER WITH OVER 360,000 BOOKS SOLD EACH YEAR, IT CAME AS A GREAT SHOCK TO DISCOVER THAT OUR RAIN FORESTS, HOME FOR HALF OF ALL LIVING THINGS ON EARTH, ARE BEING DESTROYED AT THE RATE OF 50 ACRES PER MINUTE ☙ AT THIS RATE THE RAIN FORESTS WILL COMPLETELY DISAPPEAR IN JUST 50 YEARS ☙ BOOKS HAVE A LARGE INFLUENCE ON THIS RAMPANT DESTRUCTION ☙ FOR EXAMPLE, SINCE IT TAKES 17 TREES TO PRODUCE ONE TON OF PAPER, A FIRST PRINTING OF 30,000 COPIES OF A TYPICAL 480 PAGE BOOK CONSUMES 108,000 POUNDS OF PAPER WHICH WILL REQUIRE 918 TREES ☙ TO HELP OFFSET THIS LOSS, WAITE GROUP PRESS WILL PLANT TWO TREES FOR EVERY TREE FELLED FOR PRODUCTION OF THIS BOOK ☙ THE DONATION WILL BE MADE TO RAINFOREST ACTION NETWORK (THE BASIC FOUNDATION, P.O. BOX 47012, ST. PETERSBURG, FL 33743), WHICH CAN PLANT 1,000 TREES FOR $250.

LICENSE AND WARRANTY

THIS IS A LEGAL AGREEMENT BETWEEN YOU, THE END USER, AND THE WAITE GROUP, INC. ("TWG"). BY OPENING THIS PACKAGE, YOU AGREE TO BE BOUND BY THIS AGREEMENT. IF YOU DO NOT AGREE WITH THE TERMS OF THIS AGREEMENT, PROMPTLY RETURN THE UNOPENED DISK PACKAGE AND THE ACCOMPANYING USER MANUAL FOR A REFUND.

SOFTWARE LICENSE

1. TWG grants you a nonexclusive license to use one copy of the enclosed program on a single computer system (whether a single CPU, part of a licensed network, or a terminal connected to a single CPU). Each user of the program must obtain his or her own copy of the program user manual and book from TWG.

2. TWG or its licensor owns all rights in the program, including all U.S. and foreign copyrights in the program. You may make one copy of the program for backup purposes, or you may transfer a copy of the program to one hard disk drive, using the original for backup. You may make no other copies of the program or its user manual and book. You may not decompile, disassemble, or reverse engineer the program.

3. You may not rent the program or the right to use the program to others, but you may transfer all of your rights in the program and its user manual if you retain no copies of either and if the recipient agrees to the terms of this agreement.

LIMITED WARRANTY

TWG warrants that the program will perform substantially as described in the accompanying user manual and book for a period of ninety days from your receipt of it. This limited warranty does not apply if the program is the object of misuse, accident, or abuse.

TWG's entire liability and your exclusive remedy for breach of this limited warranty will be, at TWG's option, either replacement of the program or a refund of the price paid. You must return a copy of your original receipt along with the program to obtain a refund.

DISCLAIMER OF WARRANTIES, LIMITATION OF LIABILITY

TWG makes no other warranty, express or implied, regarding the program, its user manual, or their merchantability or fitness for a particular purpose. TWG shall not be liable for any indirect, special, incidental, or consequential damages (including lost profits, loss of information, or other economic loss) resulting from the use of or inability to use the program, even if you have advised TWG of the possibility of such damages.

Some states do not allow the exclusion or limitation of implied warranties or liability for incidental or consequential damages, so these exclusions may not apply to you. This limited warranty gives you specific legal rights; you may have others, which vary from state to state.

Master C++ uses a NATAL runtime interpreter supplied under license by Softwords. NATAL is a mark of CPDL licensed to Press-Procepic Limited.

Waite Group Satisfaction Report Card

Please fill out this card if you wish to know of future updates to *The Waite Group's Master C++*, or to receive our catalog.

Company Name: _____

Division: _____ **Mail Stop:** _____

Last Name: _____ **First Name:** _____ **Middle Initial:** _____

Street Address: _____

City: _____ **State:** _____ **Zip:** _____

Daytime telephone: (_____) _____

Date product was acquired: Month _____ **Day** _____ **Year** _____ **Your Occupation:** _____

Overall, how would you rate *The Waite Group's Master C++*?

☐ Excellent ☐ Very Good ☐ Good
☐ Fair ☐ Below Average ☐ Poor

What did you like MOST about this product? _____
_____

What did you like LEAST about this product? _____
_____

Please describe any problems you may have encountered with installing or using Master C++: _____
_____
_____

Please mark an "L" for things you liked and "D" for things you disliked about Master C++. You may provide more details under Additional Comments.

___ Installation ___ Pace of course ___ Ease of use
___ Interface ___ Answer judgment ___ Question length
___ Mastery level at 80% ___ Accompanying book ___ Disk format

What version of C++ are you using? _____

What is your level of computer expertise?

☐ New user ☐ Dabbler ☐ Hacker
☐ Power user ☐ Programmer ☐ Experienced professional

Is there any program or subject you would like to see The Waite Group cover in a similar approach? _____
_____

Please describe your computer hardware:

Computer _____ Hard disk _____
5.25" Disk drives _____ 3.5" Disk drives _____
Video card _____ Monitor _____
Printer _____ Peripherals _____

Where did you buy this book?

☐ Bookstore (name: _____)
☐ Discount store (name: _____)
☐ Computer store (name: _____)
☐ Catalog (name: _____)
☐ Direct from WGP ☐ Other _____

What price did you pay for this book? _____

What influenced your purchase of this book?

☐ Recommendation ☐ Advertisement
☐ Magazine review ☐ Store display
☐ Mailing ☐ Book's format
☐ Reputation of The Waite Group ☐ **Other** _____

How many computer books do you buy each year? _____

How many other Waite Group books do you own? _____

What is your favorite Waite Group book? _____
_____

Additional comments? _____
_____

☐ **Check here for a free Waite Group catalog**

NO POSTAGE
NECESSARY
IF MAILED
I IN THE
UNITED STATES

BUSINESS REPLY MAIL
FIRST CLASS MAIL   PERMIT NO. 9   CORTE MADERA, CA

POSTAGE WILL BE PAID BY ADDRESSEE

Waite Group Press, Inc.
Attention: *Master C++*
200 Tamal Plaza
Corte Madera, CA 94925

FOLD HERE